exotic
marine fishes

by Dr. Herbert R. Axelrod
Dr. Warren E. Burgess
Dr. Cliff W. Emmens

ISBN 0-87666-598-9

t.f.h.

Distributed in the UNITED STATES by T.F.H. Publications, Inc., 211 West Sylvania Avenue, Neptune City, NJ 07753; in CANADA by Rolf C. Hagen Ltd., 3225 Sartelon Street, Montreal 382 Quebec; in ENGLAND by T.F.H. (Great Britain) Ltd., 11 Ormside Way, Holmethorpe Industrial Estate, Redhill, Surrey RH1 2PX; in AUSTRALIA AND THE SOUTH PACIFIC by Pet Imports Pty. Ltd., Box 149 Brookvale 2100 N.S.W., Australia; in SOUTH AFRICA by Multipet (Pty.) Ltd., 30 Turners Avenue, Durban 4001. Published by T.F.H. Publications Inc. Ltd., The British Crown Colony of Hong Kong.

PREFACE TO THE SIXTH EDITION

We at T.F.H constantly strive to produce the most complete, most accurate book on marine fishes in the world. To this end we must continually seek out the latest information on the species included. It is a known fact that as scientists around the world investigate the fishes and report on their findings, changes are made. We have tried to keep up with this scientific progress to bring you the most up-to-date information possible; you will notice in this edition that several names have changed to reflect the newest information available, on those species. In addition, some of the hitherto unidentified or undescribed species have been given names as a result of the research into the group or because the proper description of the species was finally published.

We are also constantly searching for better and better photos of the fishes presented here. In the past, to be able to bring you certain species, the best available photo was used. In many cases, although the photo accurately depicted the species in full color, it was not able to present the fish at its best. You will see that in this new edition many new photos are included to replace those that, although they have served their purpose well, could be improved. In addition, we have updated many of the instructional photos in the tank management sections to keep pace with recent product developments in the field.

The result is a better book, one that you can refer to time and time again with confidence.

Dr. Herbert R. Axelrod
Dr. Warren E. Burgess
Neptune, New Jersey
September, 1982

Preface and Acknowledgments

In 1952 I took my first color photograph of a marine fish, and that might be the starting point of this present volume dedicated to EXOTIC MARINE FISHES. Ever since that time I have been diligently collecting, buying and borrowing colorful marine fishes to photograph "for my last big book." Now that it's done and published I have a feeling of having lost a great friend . . . like there isn't much left.

Actually this is a companion volume to EXOTIC TROPICAL FISHES, which deals with freshwater aquarium fishes. It has the same basic format and can be obtained in both the looseleaf edition or the hardcover edition. Those who have the looseleaf edition of EXOTIC MARINE FISHES can keep it up to date with the supplements which will be published irregularly as new, popular species are imported. These supplements are published in booklet form and if you register your copy of EXOTIC MARINE FISHES with the publisher you will be notified as these supplements become available.

The title of this book really took quite a bit of thinking through. The title had to indicate that the book was primarily for hobbyists who skin-dive or keep fish for aquarium purposes. It had to be extensive enough without being all-inclusive. Several titles were rejected because they were too specific. *Reef Fishes* or *Coral Fishes* meant I had to include *every* coral fish or *every* reef fish to the exclusion of others. Since no one really knows what an *exotic* fish is, I felt this was the safest of all titles. *"Exotic"* to me means a fish which I thought was interesting enough to be collected alive and kept in an aquarium. This eliminates most herring, anchovies, sharks, rays, skates, eels (except morays) and tunas, but I'm sure there will be some folks who can find some "exotic" specimens in all of these groups.

So, really, this is merely a group of marine aquarium fishes for which I was able to get acceptable color photographs and fair identifications. I wish I could say I had all the chaetodons or all the anemone fishes. I do not. But I hope that as the years go by, I will be able to illustrate in color every known species of most of the more popular groups of fishes.

So many people helped me in the preparation of this book that it would be impossible to name all, so to those whom I have forgotten, please forgive me. Bill Vorderwinkler really helped me get the book started in the late 1950's. Poor Bill had a stroke and is bedridden, but he would have been my co-author had he more luck with his health. Cliff

Emmens, who is probably the world's leading home aquarist, wrote the whole section on aquarium management. Cliff is Chairman of the Veterinary Physiology Department at the University of Sydney in Australia. He has written many books on aquarium management and is well known in the scientific community for his contributions in other fields. Gerald Allen helped me immeasurably, not only by writing the descriptions of almost 250 fishes, but in checking the identifications of almost every fish in this book and in our files. He worked very intensively at the Smithsonian Institution and at the California Academy checking specimens and the literature to make this book as accurate as possible. Gerald is one of Jack Randall's students. He is currently revising the genus *Amphiprion,* and the anemone fishes which appear in this book have all been carefully checked by Allen. You'll find that the identifications of this group of fishes hardly corresponds to other books in print, including the books I have written previously.

More credit must go to Jack Randall than to any other single person. Without Jack's constant assistance, without his traveling thousands (maybe hundreds of thousands) of miles all over the Pacific to collect and photograph fishes for me, this book would still be years away from completion. Jack should have been my co-author, for certainly he made major contributions to the book, but he didn't want to be responsible for the identifications of many fishes which he knew were incorrect, but which couldn't be more correctly identified without years of effort . . . effort which he couldn't undertake at this time.

Last, but far from least, I must thank the staff at the U.S.N.M., especially Dr. Leonard P. Schultz, who is always a constant source of inspiration to me. Victor Springer helped with "exotic" blennies.

I hope the professionals in the field, like Earl Kennedy of the Philippines, and Rodney Jonklaas of Ceylon, will continue sending me photographs of the more rare beauties that they find as they dive to collect aquarium specimens for sale. I welcome anyone who can send me photographs good enough for reproduction (transparencies are best) of any fishes which are not represented in this book, along with the preserved specimen and whatever information they have collected on the fish.

And my final thanks to Neal Pronek and Fredric M. Schwartz, who helped in the final stages, along with Seymour Weiss (the world's leading authority on Dandie Dinmonts), when we actually read the galleys and designed the book.

Dr. Herbert R. Axelrod
Taipei, Taiwan
June 25, 1969

6.00

Contents

I

Starting a tropical marine tank

1. INTRODUCTION

Marine aquarium keeping, like aquarium keeping in general, was in vogue in the Victorian era. However, the home aquarium did not advance beyond a rather primitive stage, which was adequate for keeping many fresh water fishes, but not for the successful long term maintenance of most inhabitants of the sea.

There was only a weak interest in keeping marine aquaria during the greater part of the present century. An upsurge of interest has occurred during the last decade, in part because more suitable equipment is available, in part because fishes are more easily transported across the world, and also because a number of so-called marine mixes were put on the market which can be dissolved in ordinary tap water or distilled water to give a good imitation of sea water. The first wave of activity in the late 1950's was not maintained for a variety of reasons. Some at least of the marine mixes were not particularly successful, tanks were in general too small, and some of the filtration methods advocated were not very successful either. As most marine fishes were then very expensive to purchase, particularly those from tropical reefs, hobbyists who spent a lot of money on equipment and fishes rapidly lost interest when their pets died within a few days or weeks.

We are now in the midst of a second and more recent upsurge of interest in the keeping of marine fishes, particularly tropical marines. People are beginning to learn how to keep them more successfully, how to control their diseases, and although the fishes themselves are still quite expensive they are more readily available in a healthy state. This in turn reflects the great increase in skin diving and the collection of suitable specimens without injury, the increasing knowledge on the part of exporters of how to keep fishes healthy before sending them overseas, and how to pack and ship them so they arrive in good condition at the other end. The speed of modern air transport adds to the ease with which these aims are achieved.

There are, unfortunately, still quite a number of advocates of small tanks in which a rather overcrowded collection of fishes is kept in perilous balance by constant aeration and filtration, any breakdown in which is followed by their death within a few hours. While it is possible for an expert to maintain such a collection in a small tank almost indefinitely, it should certainly not be attempted by a beginner, nor are there usually any very good reasons for attempting it at all. Such advice as to *"start in a small way,"* so that you are not too disappointed by the death of fishes after having spent a lot of money on expensive equipment is, in fact, quite misguided. The main expense of the equipment is really the high powered filtration and aeration set-up required to maintain a small tank successfully.

It is therefore wise to start the marine hobby with as large a tank as you can afford, and to keep it under-populated rather than the reverse.

Besides offering a much greater latitude for artistic aquascaping, larger tanks are safer for use by beginners as they tend to minimize the problems arising from sources of pollution. Photo by Dr. Herbert R. Axelrod.

Should the minimum filtration and aeration equipment needed in such circumstances fail, the inhabitants will not die shortly afterwards, but can be expected to live on quite happily until repairs are effected. There are many other reasons for having a large tank, such as the display which becomes possible, the swimming area available to the inhabitants and their tendency to fight if not given reasonable hiding places and space in which to support themselves. The water in a large tank changes less rapidly, particularly if it is not overcrowded, and will support a moderate number of inhabitants almost indefinitely as long as some elementary precautions are taken. Large tanks do not change rapidly in temperature, so that if the heating equipment fails you are not faced with the necessity for rapid emergency action, or with returning home from work to find the fishes chilled and dead or dying. The minimum tank size to achieve these conditions is about 30 gallons, but something between 50 and 100 gallons is decidedly better.

It has yet to be demonstrated that any artificial sea water is preferable to properly collected and properly treated natural sea water, but there is little doubt that artificial sea water can be superior to poor quality marine water collected from a dirty harbor or polluted estuary. The good quality mixes now available are certainly adequate for the maintenance of marine life, even including invertebrates which are on the whole touchier than the fishes. It is therefore preferable to use a good artificial salt water than to use poor quality natural sea water, or sea water whose quality is unknown.

2. COLLECTION AND USE OF SALT WATER

If natural sea water is available and can be collected in clean conditions it is still to be preferred. There is no need to collect miles off shore as sometimes advocated; any clean looking area even within a harbor is likely to be useable as long as it is not suffering from undue dilution from fresh water. This can be checked by using a hydrometer as described below. However, there are dangers associated with using naturally collected marine water without first treating it to get rid of most or all of the micro-organisms it contains. Sometimes it will contain quite a large amount of visible plankton (the larval forms of various marine life) which it is usually desirable to eliminate as well. The simplest although not the most rapid way of achieving this is storage in the dark. Newly collected water, whether collected by yourself or supplied by a dealer, should be stored in total darkness in large plastic or glass containers for at least two weeks before use. During this time the plankton will die and settle to the bottom and there will be an increase in bacterial count which reaches a peak anywhere from three to ten days after the beginning of storage. Most of the bacteria will in turn disappear and settle out of the water, which before use should look crystal clear and if examined under a microscope should be almost free of living organisms. At the bottom there will be a brown sediment which can be left behind if the water is carefully siphoned off from the container.

The more rapid method is filtration through a coarse and then a very fine filter capable of removing all but the smallest forms of life. Adequate bacterial filtration, however, requires extensive equipment and is rather slow. Another rapid method is to heat the water to at least 140°F., which will kill almost everything in it, and a day or two for settling will achieve the same result as dark storage. Heating large volumes of salt water is not, however, a very easy operation, particularly since it must not be contaminated by contact with metals or virtually anything but inert plastic or glass. Hanging several glass immersion heaters into the storage container is about the most practical way of tackling the job.

3. ARTIFICIAL SEA WATER

As discussed above, there are a number of marine mixes available which provide artificial salt water for use when the natural water is not obtainable, or even by choice when it is. Some of these are adequate to support fishes but will not support all forms of marine life. Others will support invertebrates as well as vertebrates and are recommended for permanent use in any type of salt water tank. There are various published formulae for relatively simple or complex substitutes for natural sea water, most of which are rather complicated to make up because the ingredients cannot just be thrown in together, as precipitates will form. Instead the mixes usually have to be made up in stages, adding sets of ingredients separately. The artificial mixes available commercially can usually however be dissolved straight into tap water or distilled water.

The composition of sea water at a density of 1.025 is approximately as follows, in grams per liter:

Na	11.23	Cl	20.20
Mg	1.35	SO_4	2.82
Ca	0.427	HCO_3	0.149
K	0.404	Br	0.069
Sr	0.014	Boric Acid	0.028
O_2 (gas)	0.010	F	0.0014

All other material is present at less than 0.0005 gm/liter, but includes almost all known elements in trace amounts.

The above ions (chemical elements dissolved in water) can be added to natural fresh water or distilled water in various combinations of salts. Thus, in the Berlin Aquarium the following formula is used, given in the amounts required to make up approximately 100 gallons at 1.025.

NaCl	10.3 kg
$MgSO_4 \cdot 7H_2O$	2.59 kg
$MgCl_2 \cdot 6H_2O$	1.98 kg
$CaCl_2$	0.432 kg
KCl	0.234 kg
$NaHCO_3$	0.090 kg
KI	0.36 gm
NaBr	0.36 gm

Note that strontium (Sr), fluorine (F) and boron are not included.

The Cleveland modification of a formula used in the Frankfurt Aquarium, although complicated, is claimed to support invertebrates successfully, while many artificial marine mixes do not. It is given here in an amount to make up 100 gallons at 1.025 specific gravity:

Part I

NaCl	10.5 kg	Dissolve in warm
$MgSO_4 \cdot 7H_2O$	2.62 kg	water and keep
$MgCl_2 \cdot 6H_2O$	2.04 kg	fairly concentrated.
KCl	0.274 kg	Then add Part II
$NaHCO_3$	0.079 kg	and bring to specific
$SrCl_2 \cdot 6H_2O$	7.5 gm	gravity 1.025—
$MnSO_4 \cdot H_2O$	1.5 gm	this should be
$Na_2HPO_4 \cdot 7H_2O$	1.25 gm	around 100 gallons.
LiCl	0.375 gm	
$Na_2MoO_4 \cdot 2H_2O$	0.375 gm	

Part II

$CaCl_2$	0.52 kg	Dissolve in hot water and add to Part I.

Part III

KBr	270.0 gm	Dissolve in 2 liters
Ca gluconate	6.25 ,,	of distilled water and
KI	0.90 ,,	add 80 ml to Parts I plus II after bringing to 1.025

Part IV

$Al(SO_4)_3$	4.5 gm	Dissolve in 2 liters
$CuSO_4 \cdot 5H_2O$	4.3 ,,	of distilled water and
RbCl	1.5 ,,	add 80 ml to Parts I
$ZnSO_4 \cdot 7H_2O$	0.96 ,,	and II as above
$CoSO_4$	0.50 ,,	

Marine hobbyists living inland are almost completely dependent upon artificial saltwater mixes for their tank water, while even those at the sea shore seem to prefer the artificial mixes over collecting their own because of their excellent quality. Photo by Vincent Serbin.

The trace elements in Part IV can be supplied in smaller quantities if made up by a professional chemist, thus one tenth or one twentieth of each quantity given above could be dissolved in 200 ml or 100 ml of distilled water respectively.

It is sometimes stated that artificial salt water and natural salt water should not be mixed. It is also sometimes stated that artificial salt water should always have a certain amount of natural sea water added to it, so the reader can take his choice. There does not seem to be any objection to mixing different types of natural and artificial sea water unless the whole object of the exercise is to use a completely artificial medium and avoid any chance of contamination from natural sources.

4. TREATMENT OF THE TANK AND DECORATIONS

Sand, rocks, corals, shells and other natural material for the marine tank may be collected or purchased according to opportunity or taste. It is best to use only such rocks and sand as can be obtained from the sea itself as these will have been pretreated naturally and are least likely to be a source of trouble. However, they should not be placed directly into

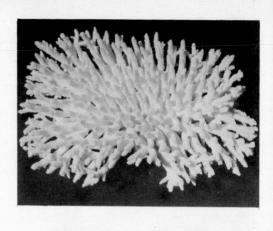

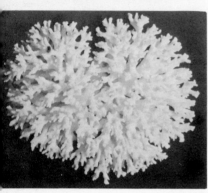

Corals in all their many shapes and textures are the most universally employed and probably the most attractive and useful decorations for the marine aquarium; various pieces can be combined to achieve handsome effects, and many fishes feel more secure if coral is provided as a refuge. Photos by Dr. Herbert R. Axelrod.

This piece of brain coral, so named because of the resemblance between the convolutions of the calcareous secretions made by the creatures that once inhabited it and those of the human brain, has been completely cleaned and sterilized and made ready for use in a tank.

the marine tank without thorough cleaning and preferably a spell of a few days immersion in fresh water, which will rid them of unwanted parasites and most other sources of potential trouble. Coral which will almost certainly be obtained from commercial sources, must be checked extremely carefully. Even though you may be assured that it has been completely cured, it should be placed in fresh water and left there for a week or two to make quite sure that there is nothing noxious remaining. The coral once contained minute polyps, the remains of which may still be inside. If all is well, the coral in the fresh water will remain odorless and of good appearance and may then be transferred to the marine tank. If all is not well, it will not remain odorless and it will usually start to show grey areas and often masses of fungal or other material growing over its surface which will be obtaining nutrient from the decaying remains within it. When this occurs it is best, if the time can be spared, to leave it in the open in fresh water to finish its process of decay. It can then be bleached in the sun and returned for a further period to fresh water to check that all is indeed well and eventually placed in the marine tank.

If you are in a hurry the coral may be boiled in fresh water for several hours and then dried off and if necessary bleached with a suitable domestic bleach, washed very thoroughly in several rinses of further fresh water and then again left in fresh water for a further week or so to make sure that everything has been removed. There is unfortunately no more rapid way of being sure of coral except to obtain some which has been used in another marine aquarium without trouble. This should be washed or boiled in fresh water to make sure that it is not conveying disease and then placed in the new tank.

Sea shells must be treated with similar care. Clam shells and other open shells which can be fairly readily cleaned should not present too much difficulty. Shells of the larger spiral mollusks are best pierced at the finer end so that they may be flushed through completely and cleaned out as far as possible prior to being given the fresh water treatment to test for their suitability. Rocks need only a general cleaning up unless you are going to try the experiment of keeping so-called live rocks, i.e. rocks which are to be placed in the aquarium still coated with algae, barnacles and other sessile invertebrate forms which naturally cover them. We shall discuss below the circumstances in which this may be tried out. Sand is fairly readily cleaned by placing several handfuls at a time into a bucket and hosing thoroughly with frequent swirlings until the water runs off crystal clear. This process will usually rid it of undesirable parasites at the same time, but it would not be unwise to boil it the first time it is to be used to make sure. The type and quality of sand to be used in a marine tank depends on the particular set-up. If the sand is to be used as part of an undergravel filter it should be fairly coarse and incapable of passing through the slots in the filter bed. If it is to be used without such a device it is better to select a finer grade so that unwanted pieces of debris and food do not settle down into the sand, but sit on its surface. Again natural sea sand which will usually be silicious is the most suitable, but ground up shell or shell grit, or ground up coral or natural coral sand, make excellent substitutes in the tropical marine tank.

The reader is probably aware that it is difficult to maintain marine plants in the usual tank. There are a few varieties, which differ from one part of the world to another, which can be successfully cultivated but most will be eaten by the fishes and so will not flourish for long in a populated tank. Instead of attempting to keep the larger forms of marine plants, most of which are algae, the hobbyist may substitute some of the quite acceptable and decorative plastic varieties which are now available, or he may spurn these and make a very successful decoration of coral, rocks, etc. on their own. In a suitably maintained tank these will eventually become encrusted with smaller forms of algae which will be brown if the light is not very intense but green if it is strong enough. Brown algae do not look particularly attractive but a nicely greened series of rocks and corals can be very pleasant in the tank. If the amount of encrusting algae becomes

Caulerpa is one of the very few marine plants suitable for inclusion in the salt-water aquarium; in general, it is best to avoid the introduction of free-standing living plants, because their death and subsequent decomposition can rapidly foul the tank. Photo by R. P. L. Straughan.

19.00

Sea shells make fine natural decorations for the marine aquarium, provided that all remnants of the living tissue they contained has been removed from them. The shells of bivalve mollusks are generally more suitable than those of univalves, since they present less hidden surface in which organic material can be trapped. Photo by Doris Whitney.

too excessive it is usually readily removed by taking some or all of the coral or rocks from the tank and flushing under a hose. They may then be returned directly to the tank with a moderate amount of algae for further growth left on them.

Sometimes the sterilizing process just discussed has been so successful that no good start is made with algae growth until the tank is purposefully inoculated with a few scrapings of suitable green algae taken from another tank. This inoculation is often a sensible procedure in any case, so as to give a quick start with the type of algae one wishes to see flourishing.

Apart from the carefully treated materials discussed above, nothing should be introduced into the salt water tank which is not completely inert to the water. This means that all aeration, filtration, heating and other equipment which comes in contact with the water must be guaranteed safe from corrosion or attack of any kind. Glass and certain modern resins, such as fiber glass, and various epoxy resins fall into this class; so also do high grade plastics of various types. Cheaper plastics and anything smelling of camphor should never be risked and material in any way suspect must be carefully tested before introduction into the salt water tank. Some plastics even soften and dissolve and then poison the inhabitants. No metal of any kind should be allowed to come into contact with salt water. It is sometimes stated that iron or lead in small amounts is safe but this is not true of lead, and although true of iron, the discoloration which is consequent on the rusting of iron in water renders it undesirable. Even the rust resistant grades of stainless steel are liable to a degree of attack and should not be purposely immersed in salt water, although it is preferable to use stainless steel framed tanks. The degree to which the frame of such tanks is affected is minimal and can be controlled to a large extent by a suitable coating of resin or plastic inside and outside the top rim.

The biggest problem with the normal type of glass aquarium is aquarium cement or putty, which may be toxic. Some manufacturers guarantee their tanks for use with salt water and a tank from a reputable source of this kind can be used with confidence. All other tanks should be carefully treated before use so that no contact remains possible between the water and the cement. This can be achieved by running small quantities of a suitable resin along all of the glass joints and around the inside top of the frame. However, no tank should be chosen for such treatment unless the glass is in the first instance very closely fitting so that almost no exposure of cement takes place.

If a stainless steel framed tank is to be used as a marine aquarium and it is not of recent manufacture guaranteed against corrosion, treatment with resins as outlined above will normally be sufficient, since old aquarium cement does not usually poison the water very readily and so small areas accidentally left exposed to the salt water should not seriously contaminate the tank. The gradual change-over of salt water usually practiced by the hobbyist will be sufficient to prevent a build-up of toxic materials.

Tanks without stainless steel frames may be constructed of glass and concrete, even of glass and wood, of glass alone, or of plastic. Sufficiently large plastic tanks are very expensive and difficult to manufacture because of the flexibility of any but very thick slabs of material. They are also liable to scratch and are therefore not in general advisable. It is only fairly· recently that the technology to manufacture large all-glass tanks has been perfected, but these, although still somewhat expensive, are available in sizes up to 100 gallons or even more. Such tanks need greater care in handling and positioning than the somewhat more robust framed tank, but they look extremely elegant when filled with decorative rocks and corals and crystal clear marine water. The materials used for sealing glass to glass or plastic to plastic are usually non-toxic and there is then no source of contamination from the materials of the tank itself. Cement tanks usually have only a front glass section and are easy to manufacture. They are popular in places such as Ceylon and Singapore, but rarely seen elsewhere. They seem to be quite impervious to salt water and in view of their cheapness and the large size in which they may readily be manufactured there seems to be a great deal in their favor. Smaller sizes can have the glass cemented directly into the front of the tank but differences in coefficient of expansion make it necessary for large tanks to have the glass set into the cement frame with an aquarium cement as with a stainless steel framed tank.

5. TANK SIZE AND SHAPE

The proportions of a marine tank, as with a fresh water tank, must satisfy a combination of biological preference and aesthetic appearance. A broad shallow tank is best as it gives the greatest area for the exchange of gases at the surface of the water, but such a tank is not very nice to look at. The usual tank is therefore something near to a double cube in dimensions such as $36'' \times 18'' \times 18''$, a tank which would hold about 50 gallons. This gives a reasonable surface area for gas exchange and is deep enough to look quite elegant and to allow the construction of attractive rock or coral scenery. It also allows the considerable depth of sand desirable if an undergravel filter is to be used. A tank of this size would be quite good to start with and should be manufactured of not less than quarter inch plate glass with a reinforced glass base. The tank and its contents will weigh some 400 to 500 lbs and will require a good solid stand and a steady floor beneath it. Larger tanks may pose a problem in older homes where floors are liable to be somewhat more rickety than in modern dwellings, and care should be taken over siting the tank and deciding how large it may be without special reinforcement of the flooring. The gallon capacity of a tank may be calculated by the following formula:

$$\frac{\text{length} \times \text{breadth} \times \text{height}}{231} = \text{American gallons}$$

The inside dimensions of the tank should be used, allowing for a $1''$ air space on top and for whatever depth of sand is to be employed.

Since a gallon of water weighs $8\frac{1}{4}$ lbs and the likely weight of the rocks, etc., in the tank can readily be ascertained, the total weight of the complete set-up can be estimated accurately enough for all practical purposes.

6. LIGHTING

The marine tank is best placed where little direct sunlight reaches it. Indeed, there are many marine aquarists who feel happier when their tank receives little but artificial light. This is because they will not usually be attempting to maintain the growth of large marine algae, although they may be interested in the maintenance of a certain amount of encrusting algae on rocks and coral, or on the back and side glass. Such growth is much more easily controlled when relatively little daylight falls on the tank but there are, of course, methods of shading the tank so that it receives adequate but not too much direct sunlight. The nature of the artificial illumination of the tank is in part a matter of taste and in part depends on the extent to which algal growth is to be encouraged. A natural warm sunlight effect is still best obtained with incandescent lighting, using either strip lighting or ordinary bulbs. In a small tank such lighting can be troublesome because it tends to overheat the contents, but in any tank larger than 30″ in length, this is not a problem. A whiter light is given by the general run of fluorescent tubes, even the so called warm white is decidedly whiter than the light given by incandescent bulbs. However it is possible to use mixtures of incandescent and fluorescent lighting to give practically any effect one wishes and this is accompanied by the advantage of the generation of little heat. Fluorescent lighting, however, does not generally promote the growth of algae to the extent of incandescent lighting, unless special tubes such as the Gro-lux or the Miracle Plant tubes are used. These tend to give a rather redder light than is preferred by many hobbyists and make the reds and blues in the fishes more gaudy.

If incandescent bulbs are used, as a rough guide, about 2 watts per gallon will give adequate illumination and promote adequate algal growth. As far as illumination is concerned, this wattage can be divided by three or four for fluorescent lighting but not necessarily for the promotion of the growth of algae. The light will normally be enclosed in a hood which is preferably made of stainless steel with a good internal reflecting surface. Even if stainless steel is used the lights must be protected from salt water splash and from condensation by having a sheet of glass cover all or practically all of the top of the tank, leaving only space for the inlet of heater cables, etc., and with a removable strip for feeding. This top cover need not be of as thick a glass as the sides of the tank but should preferably have internal strips of glass so spaced and glued that the cover fits tightly into the top of the tank and little movement is possible. This achieves two objects; first it prevents the cover glass from slipping about and being accidentally chipped or broken, second it helps to direct splash from within the tank back into the tank without excessive seepage of salt water around the edges of the top glass. The lights with their hood should rest at least half an inch above this glass or relatively intense local heating may crack it. With fluorescent lighting this is of less importance.

Different effects can be obtained according to whether the light over the tank is placed towards the front or back. Placing it towards the front causes light to be reflected from the sides of the fishes and of the decorations and causes the back of the tank to tend to disappear into a hazier background and in general gives a pleasant effect. This so-called front lighting does however tend to cause excessive growth of algae on the front glass which therefore has to be cleaned off more frequently. If the light is placed towards the back of the tank the appearance of mysterious depths disappears and the fish tend to be less well illuminated unless they themselves are swimming at the back, but the growth of algae on the front glass is less and the growth of algae on the rocks and coral which will normally be towards the back will be encouraged. The simple solution is when you are not looking at the tank to place the hood towards the back, but when you wish to show it off to your friends or enjoy it yourself, to slide the lights towards the front.

7. HEATING

Heating in the marine tank follows the same general principles as in fresh water aquaria with the exception that nothing metallic should come into contact with the water. For this reason external thermostats applied to the outside of the glass are often preferred since at least one of the elements controlling heating in the tank is by that method removed from within it. However all-glass heaters or heater thermostat combinations are perfectly acceptable but must be carefully inspected from time to time since the rubber and even plastic seals which are inevitably in the tank are more susceptible to deterioration in salt water. Leakage of fresh water into a standard type heater often leads to little trouble until it

Heaters should have no metal parts that would come in contact with the salt water (including the spray from an airstone). They should also be checked periodically for leakage. Shown is a submergible heater.

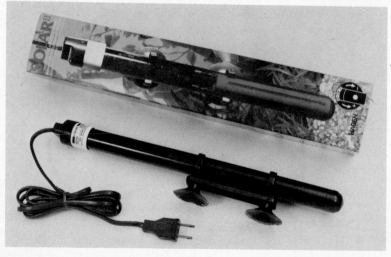

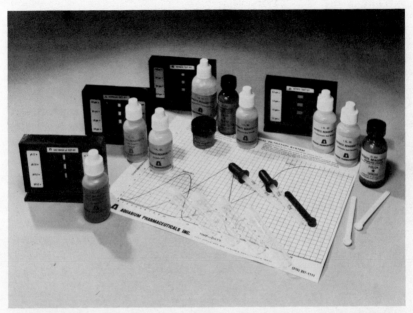

A wide variety of test kits are available to the marine aquarist. They are necessary for the proper monitoring of the chemical conditions in your tank. Photo by Vincent Serbin.

becomes excessive, since the water is evaporated by the element and disappears through the cable to the outside air. Leakage of salt water, however, leaves behind deposits of salt and any actual contact of the salt or the salt water with the heater element is liable to be followed by spectacular effects since it is a good conductor of electricity.

As with all heated aquarium set-ups it is best to place the heater in an inconspicuous position towards the rear base of the tank where it will cause a rising current of heated water to circulate throughout the tank. However the position of the heater in a marine tank which will usually be filtered or aerated or both is less critical since the water will circulate effectively and carry heat around the tank. There are several reasons why it is best to use a heater of somewhere near the lowest reasonable capacity. In a normal indoor situation a 40 gallon tank is adequately served by a 100–150 watt heater. Larger tanks because of their slower heat loss can have relatively fewer watts per gallon. If the thermostat sticks and the heater remains continuously on, this will not be followed by a catastrophic rise in water temperature. Since the heater is of rather low capacity it will also remain on for longer periods at a time than would a higher rating heater. This means that it will not switch on and off so frequently and thus will not wear the points of the thermostat out so rapidly.

If one's collection of marine fishes is particularly expensive or precious it is wise to provide the tank with two heaters so that the capacity of both added together is only a little more than sufficient to maintain the desired temperature. If one of these fails the other one will prevent the temperature of the water from dropping too severely, and any undue rise and any undue fall due to equipment failure is avoided as far as is easily possible.

There seems to have been relatively little use in marine tanks of base heating either by an insulated cable buried in the sand at the bottom of the tank or by similar equipment applied externally to the base of the tank. Both of these would seem to commend themselves for salt water use because of their relative safety and lack of contact with the salt water. Perhaps we shall see them employed more in the future.

The water in which tropical marine fishes live varies between about 70° and 85°F.; sometimes in isolated stretches of water or tide pools this is much exceeded. The lower limit is approximately that at which coral seems to flourish, although sometimes outcrops of coral are found even in waters which fall to the mid 60°s during the winter season. Most of the coral fishes, which form the bulk of the attractive marine specimens available to us, come from waters which are towards the top of the range quoted and although they will be reasonably happy in any temperature above 75°F. it is wiser to keep them nearer to 80°F. Others even of the same species which happen to come from cooler regions can of course be kept at more like 70°F. Thus in a room in temperate regions which is centrally heated or air conditioned at a temperature of say 70°F. only a slight boost need be given to the tropical marine tank. In an unheated room which may well fall very severely in winter nights a much more robust heating system must be employed so that a temperature differential of as much as perhaps 40°F. can be coped with. This is not quite so bad as it may sound because few living-rooms in which such tanks are likely to be kept will not be heated in the daytime, and a tank of reasonable size will not fall drastically in temperature even if the outside temperature drops considerably. Thus a heater capable of maintaining on the average a 25°F. differential should be sufficient even with rooms which are unheated at night. They will fall a few degrees but not to a dangerous extent. However a careful check should at first be kept on the behavior of the tank because an excessive day to night fluctuation of say, more than about 5°F., can be a source of trouble. Most marine fishes are not accustomed to large sudden temperature changes although they can stand periodic seasonal changes. Only those accustomed to living in tidal pools where quite sudden fluctuations may occur with the incoming tide are likely to survive such rough treatment.

26.00

8. OTHER EQUIPMENT

In addition to the heating equipment, all tanks should have a thermometer permanently in position. It is best in the marine tank to use an alcohol plastic thermometer so that if an inquisitive fish bites the end off and releases the fluid into the water the small amount of alcohol will be of no consequence whereas an equivalent amount of mercury might cause trouble. This thermometer should be fixed in a convenient position where the temperature of the tank can be read at a moment's notice. It should be routinely inspected when feeding the fishes each day so that any variation from the required temperature is noted in time. In this regard it is worth while mentioning that the type of external thermostat which has an indicator light is well worthwhile installing since one can tell at a glance whether the thermostat is in the *on* or *off* position. Note, however, that when the indicator light is on, showing that the thermostat terminals are closed, it does not necessarily mean that a current is passing and if the heater is burnt out this is exactly what will happen. The use of the indicator light is mainly that if it continues to show up, this means that an inspection is necessary because heater failure may have occurred. A glance at the thermometer will show whether the thermostat is on and the heater functioning normally, or whether it is on with a burnt out heater.

Another necessary piece of equipment needed in conjunction with a marine tank is a hydrometer, by which one measures the density of the salt water. The hydrometer is a glass bulb with a long stem attached to it on which graduations denote the density of the water in relation to pure fresh water. The denser the water the higher the hydrometer floats. Normal marine water has a density of around 1.025 (fresh water equals 1.000), but it varies in different parts of the world and according to temperature from about 1.020 to 1.030. In salt lakes much higher densities may be encountered. There are various opinions about the density at which an aquarium is best maintained, as it does not necessarily follow that this is 1.025. Many fishes are quite happy at a somewhat lower density than average, down even to about 1.017 and some can actually be gradually acclimatized to fresh water. The majority of marine fishes are happy at about 1.020, in other words at the lower limit of natural sea water, and it seems that they are less subject to parasitism at this density than at higher ones. The lower density also tends to slow down their rate of movement and metabolism and this may be an advantage. Some of the chaetodons (butterfly fishes) lose color at too low a water density and it usually pays to hold it between 1.025 and 1.030 when such fishes are kept.

The water from every tank should be tested occasionally for its current density by floating the hydrometer in it or by running off a sample into a suitable vessel and testing it there. The hydrometer is usually calibrated

The specific gravity of the tank water should be checked periodically with a hydrometer and adjustments made if it is not within the proper range. Photo by Vincent Serbin.

for 60°F. and if the water is tested at 70°F., 0.001, or if at 80°F., 0.002 should be added to the actual reading as a correction for the value at 60°F. When salt water evaporates the salt is left behind, and if the evaporation is made good by the addition of more salt water, the salt concentration will gradually build up and become too high. It is therefore the normal practice to replace evaporation by the addition of tap water which only very gradually increases the overall salt content. However, a certain amount of salt is lost by splashing, on nets and by the removal of other objects from the aquarium, and so the occasional addition of more salt by adding salt water is necessary. Corrections can be made by the gradual addition of suitable amounts of fresh water or salt water as the case may be. A daily increase or decrease of 0.002 is about right, until the desired density is achieved.

9. AERATION AND FILTRATION

Aeration and filtration in the marine tank may be synonymous or may be independently achieved by the use of separate filters and air stones. However the process of filtration by almost any method normally used also aerates the water to a greater or lesser extent, and separate aeration may only be needed with filters of a special type or if the total population of the tank is rather high. With an underpopulated tank and particularly with rather small tanks it is quite satisfactory to have a bottom corner filter of the type used in fresh water tanks, in which a small air stone causes a current of bubbles and water to rise through a central tube pulling the water down into the equipment and through the filtering section. This combines direct aeration and filtration within the same piece of equipment. The air stone should function quite briskly and the nature of the filtering medium will be varied according to requirements which are discussed later on.

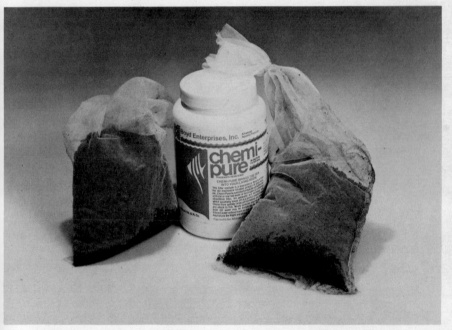

Synthetic resins can serve as a chemical absorbtion filter, ion generator and exchange unit to keep pH at a constant level.

More commonly, a separate air stone or stones, and outside or inside filters, i.e., filters which are hung on the outside or inside of the aquarium will be used, and the filters will be operated by one or another of the usual types of air lift. Modern filters using adequately designed air lifts are capable of turning over many gallons per hour of aquarium water and of keeping marine tanks up to 50 or 100 gallons in capacity in quite good

For the filtration of extremely small particles, a filter using diatomaceous earth is recommended. Photo by Vincent Serbin.

shape. As far as adequate filtration and aeration of the water are concerned this combination of filter and air stone is quite reliable in any but heavily populated aquaria, but it does lack one desirable feature in the majority of marine tanks, i.e. brisk water movement. The sea is very rarely quiescent and fishes flourish better if the water in which they live is agitated to a greater extent than is common in fresh water aquaria. For this purpose as well as for even more adequate and brisk filtration of the water one form or another of power filter is frequently employed. A power filter pumps water and usually moves more gallons per hour (up to 200) than an air lift- operated filter but it may not necessarily do so. What it will do is to swish the water back vigorously into the aquarium so that after aeration a current formation within the tank may be arranged. Any really heavily populated tank should be fitted with a power filter, both because of the high degree of filtration needed and because of this water moving action.

There are quite a number of power- filters commercially available, some of which employ specially designed filter capsules which have to be purchased with them and replaced at intervals, whereas with others one is free to choose the filter medium one wishes. Any filter with a relatively

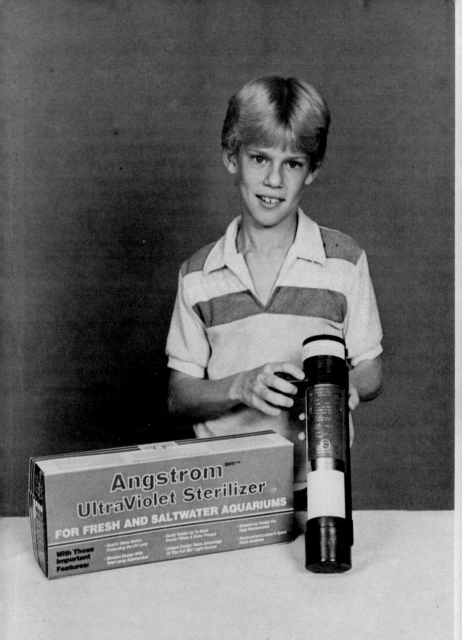

Ultraviolet sterilizers are being used more and more by marine aquarists to help reduce the number of harmful organisms in their tanks. Photo by Vincent Serbin.

31.00

carefully washed with marine water before use. It is never worthwhile risking the suitability of a particular batch and this may vary from sample to sample in a quite unpredictable manner. The normal method of preparation of activated charcoal, which involves heating to about 300°F., should guarantee the absence of any simple toxic compounds since these would be evaporated or broken down. The deposit remaining is probably associated with metallic contamination but this does not appear to have been unequivocably demonstrated. The fact remains that a batch of activated charcoal may kill aquarium inhabitants within a few days if not carefully washed beforehand. The charcoal should be placed in a simple filter through which at least several gallons of water per pound of charcoal is recirculated for several days and then replaced for a short period by a second batch of salt water. A good test of the suitability of the charcoal after it has been washed is to use a sample from the second batch of water which has been used to wash it, for hatching brine shrimp eggs. These should hatch in a normal manner and the young newly hatched shrimp should survive for a day or two without trouble. When this test is passed the charcoal may be used in the aquarium.

If a rather coarse grade of charcoal is employed it may well be necessary to use quite a large quantity of it, in fact an awkwardly large quantity for most purposes. It is commonly recommended that such an amount as 1 pound per five or ten gallons of aquarium water should be placed in a filter and at the same time it is also commonly recommended that it should not be put in all at once, or it may adversely affect the fishes. Hence a rather cumbersome undertaking of gradually adding increasing amounts of charcoal or of gradually bringing a filter loaded with such charcoal into operation is advised. However, if a very fine so-called gas absorption grade of activated charcoal is used, the granules of which are of pin head size or slightly larger, it is the author's experience that quite small quantities are sufficient. A 50 to 100 gallon tank can be maintained with sparkling white water for several months at least with no more than a quarter pound of this grade of charcoal. Such a fine grade of charcoal is in any case more effective in removing any unwanted material and gases from the tank. It can take up to about 50% of its own weight of materials from the water and will remove a great variety of unwanted dissolved material including to a limited degree various heavy metals, although it can be a source of metallic poisoning if initially loaded with them. It is possible to reactivate such charcoal by washing in fresh water or better still by washing in fresh water and then heating in an oven to about 300°F., but the amount used per time and the relatively low frequency with which renewal is required is such that it is hardly worth it. The charcoal should be placed in between layers of synthetic wool because of the small grain size. Readers may be surprised that the use of glass wool is still advocated despite frequent warnings in the literature of its danger in the aquarium. In actual fact the only danger of glass wool for which adequate testimony exists is to the aquarist, in that some varieties are liable to pierce his fingers or to give off a cloud of fine spicules which if not particularly dangerous can be irritant. Allegations that there is a severe danger to fishes from spicules being ingested or embedded in the gills seem to be pure fantasy.

A filter consisting of a layer of 1″ to 2″ of synthetic wool followed by 1″ of gas grade activated charcoal and then a retaining layer of glass wool again is all that is normally needed in the marine tank. If however the tank does not contain a reasonable amount of coral, shells or coral sand or shell grit it could help, and certainly could do no harm, to add a layer of such material up to an inch in thickness to the filter bed. The water in the aquarium should at some stage come into constant contact with lime-containing material of one kind or another in order to help maintain its pH. This should not fall below a reading of about 8.0; natural sea water is about 8.3.

Other various materials advocated for addition to the marine fiilter are of dubious value and may even do harm. There was a considerable vogue for the use of ion exchange resins of one kind or another which have a clear function in the maintenance of soft water in the fresh water tank but the function of which is largely obscure when they are used in a salt water tank. Sea water, natural or artificial, is heavily charged with magnesium and calcium ions which would immediately flood the ion exchange resin of the type normally used, and therefore its role in the filter would seem to be very questionable. It would however remove heavy metals and could perform a useful function in supplementing the activity of the charcoal. Sometimes this would be unwanted as when low concentrations of copper are purposely added to the tank to cure certain diseases and if resin is in use, the filter would have to be turned off during copper treatment. In the author's own tanks the removal of copper after it has done its work is the only role that has been found useful for ion exchange resins. Even this is usually unnecessary because the copper gradually disappears from the water as it is absorbed by coral or into detritus.

Various other materials which may well have a place in the filters of fresh water tanks are not relevant to a salt tank. This includes any kind of water softener, which cannot usefully affect marine water, any normal kind of pH adjusting media which would tend to bring the pH to neutral instead of the alkaline level needed in the marine tank, and the large majority of the disease cures of a chemical nature designed to minimize or prevent disease in the fresh water tank. Disease in the marine tank mentioned in a later section needs other methods of control.

10. STERILIZATION

An adjunct to both fresh water and marine tanks, which seems to be more particularly useful in the latter, however, is some method or the other of sterilization or near sterilization of the water as it circulates. The oldest and most obvious way of achieving this is to pass the circulating water at some stage over ultra-violet lamps of sufficient output to kill nearly all of the bacteria or other organisms in the water. This can be most efficiently arranged in conjunction with the filtration system and in any case must be arranged so that the ultra-violet output does not penetrate the tank itself. A very simple method of attaining the desired objective is to clip a sterilizing ultra-violet lamp into the filter so that the water passes around it before descending through the filter bed. At any one moment all of the water in the filter chamber will be receiving ultra-violet irradiation of an intensity which varies according to its distance from the light source. Contrary to statements sometimes made, ultra-violet light penetrates either salt or fresh water for many feet before it is finally all absorbed. It does not seriously matter if much more radiation is given than is necessary and a six watt ultra-violet source in the average filter serving a tank of say 25 to 100 gallons will be all that is necessary. If the walls of the filter are transparent to ultra-violet light it must be shielded so that neither the fishes nor the onlooker gets irradiated. Since filters are often made of sufficiently thick plastic material it is fortunate that this absorbs ultra-violet light and there is then no danger. There are commercially made sterilizers working on this principle which can be lowered into the tank and attached to bottom filters or to the outflow of almost any type of filter and these contain an ultra-violet source shielded by opaque plastic.

There is the danger in using the simple set-up just suggested in that one of the useful functions of a filter may be to an extent at least nullified because bacteria which it contains will be partly killed off by the ultra-violet light. However, this will only be true of bacteria directly exposed on the surface of the filtering medium and down inside it they will be protected from the lethal effects and so the overall disturbances to their function of the filter may not be severe enough to matter.

As is so often the case, in this particular field there does not seem to be enough real scientific evidence of the value of ultra-violet treatment of the water in the home aquarium. There is however plenty of evidence from modern biological laboratories that sterilization of water used for such purposes as experimental oyster cultivation benefits the inhabitants and that disease and its spread can be controlled. It is therefore reasonable to suppose that the equipment does good in the normal salt water tank and from the experiences of a number of writers on the subject this belief receives considerable support. It is generally felt that even if disease is introduced into a tank its effects tend to be minimized with an ultra-violet lamp in operation, that the spread from one fish to another does not readily occur since re-infection is kept down to a minimum as the water circulates time after time through the filter and the causative organisms are killed off. Not all types of infection can be expected to be affected by treatment of the circulating water, since some are passed on by contaminated fecal matter remaining in the tank, and others are due to organisms which are sufficiently large and motile to swim from one fish to another without getting swept through the filter. The control of disease by ultra-violet irradiation is therefore particularly effective with bacterial and protozoan diseases.

The efficiency of the ultra-violet lamp gradually decreases with use, declining to about half of the original output after a few hundred hours and thereafter declining more gradually to a very low figure. However a lamp of the capacity recommended is more than necessary and it continues to be of use for six months or a year, after which the output will be so much reduced that the lamp should be replaced.

A more recent and in some ways more controversial method of sterilization is by using ozone. Various forms of small ozone generators are now available for use with the marine aquarium. If the output of ozone is kept minimal and well controlled it is feasible to release it via the so called "ozonator" directly into the aquarium water. But it is usually recommended as with ultra-violet irradiation that treatment be given somewhere in the circulation system rather than directly into the tank. There are various more or less complicated set-ups for doing this, the essence of which is that a trickle of ozone is released into the water after it has left the tank and as it goes into the filter, or perhaps preferably after it has left the filter and before it once more re-enters the tank, or in an entirely separate vessel independent of the filter system.

Ozone is a molecule containing three atoms of oxygen instead of the usual two and is a very powerful oxidizing agent. It acts therefore as does hydrogen peroxide, as a powerful bleach and also is a poison to fishes if they get too much of it. This is why care must be taken in its use so that the fishes in the tank are not directly exposed to heavy general or local concentrations of the gas. There would seem to be little doubt that discreetly used, ozone-producing equipment can be as effective as ultra-violet irradiation but there are undoubtedly greater potential risks associated with it in that there is always some danger of over-dosage and adverse effects on the inhabitants of the tank. It has also not been as conclusively demonstrated that ozone does in fact sterilize effectively as has been the case with ultra-violet irradiation, and it does not appear to have been used nearly so extensively in laboratories where such phenomena can be scientifically measured. This does not mean however that the aquarist should not welcome the possibility of experimenting with the method as only accumulation of experience will eventually lead to proper assessment and use of the method.

The method of sterilizing and at the same time of heating, particularly in the large marine tank, is to heat the circulating water at some point outside the tank. In order to maintain adequate temperatures in the tropical marine tank this would necessitate the raising of the temperature of a small volume of water at a time as it passes over the heat sources to such a degree as would sterilize or severely reduce the bacterial content of the water. A few arrangements of this type appear to have been tried out, but the method is more talked about than used at present. There are obvious dangers and great care should be taken in any experimentation with such a system that there are adequate safe-guards against too hot a stream of water entering the tank and against break down which could leave the tank unheated. Ozone also converts ammonia and nitrites to harmless compounds, and it is asserted that adequate treatment with it prevents the new tank syndrome from developing. As it may also prevent the necessary bacterial development to establish a biological filter, it is a very moot question whether ozone should be used in the newly set up tank unless it is to be maintained permanently as a "sterile" system. As a back-up measure when an established tank is overloaded, as with a new lot of added fishes, it can be a life-saver.

11. SUB-SAND FILTERS

If a sub-sand or undergravel filter is not employed in the marine tank it is necessary to keep the depth of the sand or gravel to not more than a quarter to half an inch. Otherwise, areas of development of anaerobic bacteria will occur which will blacken the sand and eventually give rise to foul-smelling and potentially toxic products which may be released into the aquarium either by gradual dissemination or more drastically by some disturbance of the sand. The use of the sub-sand filter removes all worries of this kind as long as care is taken to see it is functioning adequately. The sub-sand filter consists of a raised platform with a series of fine slots so arranged that the whole of the area served by any particular filter element pulls water down through the sand and then underneath the raised platform into the air lift which raises the water back into the tank either directly, or if required, through a further filter mechanism or an ultra-violet sterilizer. Thus, a general stream of water percolates through the area concerned, which in a marine tank should be the whole of the tank bottom. If the sand is of the right grain size almost none of it will pass through the slots and clog up the under side of the filter. If it is too fine it will pass through the slots and the filter will cease to function

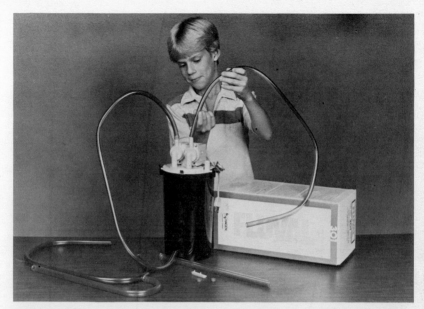

It is up to the aquarist's individual preferences whether he leans toward a canister filter (above) or an undergravel filter (below). Both work. Photos by Vincent Serbin.

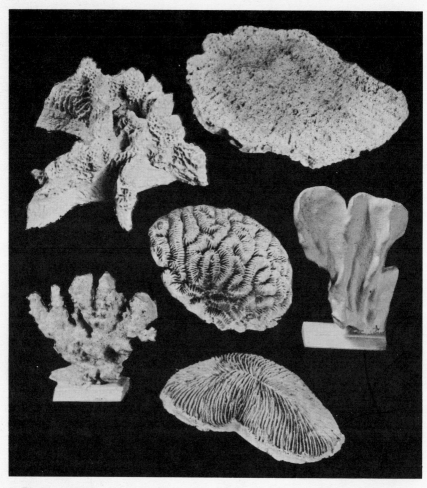

Plastic imitation coral, which costs only a small fraction of the price of real coral and needs no curing or sterilization, is one of the most useful products available to marine aquarists. The artificial coral comes in a number of different colors.

40.00

properly. If the sand is too coarse too much unwanted material such as particles of uneaten food and mulm will be sucked down into the bed of the sand and perhaps also be returned via the air lift to the water. Both of these are undesirable and it is therefore important to choose the right consistency for the filter being used. This is usually an average grain size of about $\frac{1}{32}$ of an inch.

Eventually the sub-sand filter will clog, however carefully the sand has been selected. Depending on the density of tank inhabitants and frequency of feeding, this may occur within a few months or not until about a year has elapsed. The average would perhaps be six months. Even prior to this the surface layers of the sand are liable to clog up but the slowing down of filtration that this causes can be relieved by scraping the surface occasionally with a stick. Sooner or later however the filter will cease to function properly and a general cleaning will be necessary. The preferred method of overhaul has already been indicated above. Never remove all of the gravel, leave enough to regenerate a fully active biological filter in a very short time, keeping a careful eye on the inhabitants to see that all is well. Back up with carbon or ozone treatment if it looks necessary.

Some aquarists elaborate on the simple arrangement just outlined by having layers of different types of sand or gravel above the filter so that a coarse layer of sand is perhaps overlaid with a finer layer, the idea being to achieve better filtration through the fine layer of sand without a significant amount of it passing through the slots of the filter to the floor of the tank. This arrangement usually breaks down in the end either as a result of natural sedimentation within the sand layers or because of disturbance created by fishes or other tank inhabitants and the object fails to be achieved for any length of time. It is also possible to place a fine layer of activated charcoal beneath the surface sand but this again is liable to disturbance and the emergence of the charcoal at the surface of the bottom of the tank.

12. AQUASCAPING OF TANKS

All of the various equipment, coral, rocks, and sand should be arranged in a marine tank so as to look as nice as possible. We are bound to differ considerably in our views of the best-looking tank but most of us can do a good deal better than many of the tanks one sees. It is not very enterprising to have a flat layer of sand with or without a bottom filter with a few isolated clumps of rock or coral dumped along the middle of the tank for the fishes to swim around. Yet this is exactly what is shown even in photographs of aquaria in magazines with such captions as "a beautiful aquarium set-up." The marine tank looks best, just as does the fresh water tank, with some kind of more purposeful landscaping and arrangement of the material in it.

A wide variety of special purpose fluorescent bulbs are available for your aquarium light. Some are used to promote algae, others to highlight certain colors in the fishes, and still others to imitate natural sunlight. Photo by Vincent Serbin.

The gaudy coloration and striking appearance of the majority of tropical marine aquarium fishes is such that they themselves contribute more to the overall decoration of the tank in which they live than does the fresh water tropical fish in its own tank. In a typical fresh water tank it is really the plants and the rocks that first catch one's eye and give an impression of beauty, but in the marine tank a much larger contribution is made by the fishes. These are not therefore to be overwhelmed by their surroundings. It is often best to give them a dark background which will contrast with the whiteness or light coloration of corals and shells, so that many a striking marine aquarium has the back and perhaps the sides painted black or deep blue. This can be done with any ordinary paint on the outside of the glass. Against this dark background at the back of the tank there may be heaped up rocks and corals in an arrangement which is both pleasing to the eye, which gives shelter to the fishes and which will eventually become encrusted with sufficient algae to give a natural and pleasing overall appearance. A careful selection of plastic plants and plastic coral of a type which can now be obtained closely resembling in appearance some of the natural plants may be added to the rocks or coral and with care the appearance will be enhanced and not spoiled. These plastic plants will in turn become in part encrusted with other minute life, particularly algae which will lend to their natural appearance. Depending on the size of the tank the foreground may contain little but sand, gravel or shells. If there is room it may contain a few built up prominences of further rock or coral so that the front to back depth of a large tank may be utilized to give some kind of perspective within the tank. Do not forget however that this depth in an aquarium is always reduced to the viewer by the higher refractive index of the water which, when a tank is viewed from the outside, tends to reduce the apparent depth considerably.

All of these arrangements are to be made after having placed the sub-sand filters in position if they are to be used, and having placed any other internal filters, heaters, thermostats and aerators in position towards the back of the tank so that these may be hidden behind decorations, but in such a way that their functioning is not impaired. Heaters in particular must have a free flow of water around them, must not be buried or be in danger of becoming buried in sand at the bottom of the tank, nor should they be in contact with the back glass or they may crack it. It is wise to place each heater in a little bed of rock or coral so that it will not shift after its position has been determined. Aerators or corner filters giving aeration can be so overlain with rock or coral that all that is visible is the stream of bubbles emerging from them. The aquarium thermometer must remain visible so that it can be read, but the greater part of all other equipment should be hidden.

Obviously this type of tank decoration has its dangers. Fishes may choose to lurk and die in the most awkward parts of the back of a large tank and cause a lot of trouble. Nevertheless the overall potential beauty of such an arrangement makes it worthwhile to run the risk of having occasionally to destroy a corner of it in order to cope with such eventualities. It is also surprising the extent to which even a large dead fish will be devoured by his mates eventually giving little or no trouble. The only drawback of such a means of disposal is that he may have died of something that is best kept to himself and not transmitted to his tankmates by becoming a meal for them.

We have already discussed the treatment of material that is to be placed in the aquarium and it is sufficient to remind the reader at this stage that every object entering the marine aquarium must have been carefully cleaned, sterilized and guaranteed so far as is reasonably possible of being incapable of contaminating the tank. If there is any doubt about any object it should be omitted from the tank until the doubt has been resolved.

It should also be noted that we have so far been discussing the so-called sterile type of marine aquarium which we do in fact advocate as a start for the normal aquarist. Into this type of aquarium the only living thing that should be purposely introduced apart from food is the fishes and perhaps an inoculation of green algae. Certainly at first, and probably forever, it is a mistake to introduce any invertebrates such as living coral, anemones, crabs, shrimps, shell fish, or indeed any other living creature of any kind into the tank. It has been asserted that the fishes in a sterile tank do not color up as well as those in a more natural set-up in which various other living creatures are introduced. This is very questionable. It is certainly true that in a brightly illuminated sterile tank the light-colored rocks, coral and gleaming sand so reflect the light that the overall effect is very bright and the fishes pale off. Once such a tank is allowed to become coated with brown and green algae, preferably pre-determining the latter by inoculation, and the intensity of illumination is arranged so as nicely to balance this to keep the algae alive and generally growing and not to give a glaring brightness in the tank, then it will be found that the fishes are as brightly colored and as happy looking as they are in any other kind of arrangement.

II

The tank in action

1. TANK STERILITY

A sterile tank is much easier to maintain than one containing living creatures other than fishes, if it is to contain fishes. It is quite possible to have tanks set up for the display of invertebrates and these in their turn can be maintained by techniques which we shall discuss later, but the techniques which will maintain such a tank are not those that will usually benefit the fishes most. It is most difficult of all to maintain satisfactorily a completely mixed tank in which there are living corals, crustacea, shell fish, and fishes for example, and there are several reasons for this. First the fishes will attack various other inhabitants even more readily and vigorously than they will attack each other. This will usually lead to dead and decaying material within the tank because with such a lot of potential food the fishes will not finish up what is available to them and will kill more than is needed for their own nourishment. Thus the tank will tend to become housed with dead and dying invertebrates, rapidly followed by dead and dying fishes. The author (C.E.) is perfectly aware of such articles as those of Mr. Lee Chin Eng who has published, and on whose behalf others have published, some very beautiful looking tank arrangements in which masses of living coral and encrusted rocks and various other invertebrates appear to be flourishing quite happily with fishes. It is to be noted however that there are never many fishes visible in the photographs of such tanks and it is probably this fact which contributes to their relative success. Just how long such tanks remain things of beauty is not too clear but it would seem that a few small fishes in a large tank full of other living creatures can be tolerated, and that the damage they do is insufficient to cause overall failure. Such a tank therefore is primarily an invertebrate tank into which a few fishes have been successfully introduced. Its maintenance and its problems may be quite different from the tank primarily intended as a display of marine fish, to be populated with a reasonable number of them and in which the maintenance of other living creatures will normally present a very different problem.

45.00

The living coral polyps are extended in this photograph of one of Lee Chin Eng's marine tanks; unfortunately, tanks housing living coral cannot contain the same concentration of fish life that other tanks can successfully maintain. Photo by Lee Chin Eng.

While it is also possible that in as far as fishes are concerned, in a very underpopulated tank there may be a minimal danger of the fishes developing infection, this again would not be true of a tank in which there is a heavier population of fishes. One of the big problems of learning to keep marine tanks successfully for any length of time has been the problem of fish diseases. While these are far too poorly recognized and understood we do nevertheless have some treatments which are effective in keeping some of the most prevalent aquarium diseases within check. It is most unfortunate however that in our present state of relative ignorance of the subject the best overall remedy for the control of disease in marine fishes is the introduction of minute amounts of copper into the tank. Copper treatment will be discussed in detail and the topic is introduced here only in order to point out that whereas small concentrations of copper which will kill fish parasites can be introduced into the aquarium without severe danger to the fishes, these concentrations are lethal to the average invertebrate.

Therefore if the fishes in a tank require treatment for disease, copper cannot be used in the presence of invertebrates, and thus one of the most potent remedies is removed from the aquarist's hands. Either he must catch his fishes out and treat them in a separate vessel or he must attempt a cure by some other means. Neither of these alternatives is very satisfactory because cures by substitutes other than copper are not as likely to succeed and because if the fishes are removed and cured elsewhere the problem of the infected tank still remains and reinfection would most probably result when the fishes are returned to the tank.

It is unfortunate that the use of antibiotics in the marine tank is not as successful as in the fresh water tank and that for reasons which remain obscure the usefulness of even the broad spectrum antibiotics is quite limited.

We have thus the severe dilemma that in our present state of knowledge, mixed tanks containing fishes, coral and other invertebrates, with few exceptions, cannot be expected to continue to flourish for a long time. Instead until a good deal of further experience is gained it is best to confine one's ambition to a tank of decorative but dead corals and rocks and living fishes, or to living and decorative invertebrate specimens in the absence of all but at the most one or two small fishes. If these become diseased, net them out and treat them separately or throw them away rather than attempt to treat them in the invertebrate tank.

All rules have exceptions and the exception to the above rule is the purposeful introduction of living material which serves as food for the fishes. Certain fish may eat only living materials and must be fed on other live fishes at first anyway, or on corals or coral-like materials.

Some chaetodons never seem to learn to eat prepared foods and many require something closely resembling their normal surrounding of corals into which they pick for their food. Thus if the material is available to the aquarist fortunate enough to be so situated he may purposely choose to place some pieces of living coral in the tank from time to time or to place in it some "live rocks" encrusted with living shell fish, barnacles, corallines, etc., upon which the fish will also feed. These can be rinsed in fresh water before introduction into the tank to minimize the chance of infection and must be watched to see that they do not die off and pollute the aquarium. Naturally they will normally be placed where they can easily be seen and removed when no longer required.

In a similar manner, other marine live food such as small shrimps and crustacea may be introduced as food for fishes with the expectation that they will be consumed virtually on the spot and not remain as a source of danger. This is again a practice which will only be available to the aquarist who can obtain such material, but the inland aquarist may also introduce living fresh water creatures as food, covering practically the whole gamut of live foods given to fresh water fishes. This again forms an exception to the rule of not introducing other living material than fishes and these creatures are once more introduced with the expectation that they will be consumed in a few minutes, for they will not live very long in salt water in any case.

Clearly, such introductions must be made with care and with careful observation of the results that follow. They can, however, make all the difference between long-lived healthy fishes and ones which gradually decline. We shall see later how the increasing volume of preserved, deep frozen, freeze dried, tinned or dried fish foods of suitable quality now available on the market may be used successfully as substitutes for much of the above procedures.

2. PERIODIC CHECKS

We have already discussed some of the periodic checks that should be made to ensure the constancy in density and pH in the aquarium and that fishes do better at a somewhat lesser salinity than is natural. If there are plenty of corals present in the aquarium and if it is not grossly overcrowded there will not usually be any drastic change in pH. When it occurs it may be corrected by the careful addition of sodium carbonate (Na_2CO_3), not sodium bicarbonate ($NaHCO_3$) as is often advised. However the need to correct pH in this fashion should not arise and should be regarded as a danger signal that the contents of the aquarium need careful investigation. When the pH is corrected keep a careful check on it, look for a drift of the pH towards an acid direction, which may again occur, and try to correct it. The usual cause might be overcrowding, insufficient aeration and filtration, overfeeding and resulting pollution of the tank, or the presence of dead or dying material of some description or another.

When the tank is first set up it should be left for a day or two to make sure that everything is working properly, that the tank temperature is correct and that a suitable aeration and filtration speed has been established. There is no point, however, in waiting for a particularly long period in a newly established tank intended for marine fishes as there is with the newly set up fresh water tank for the establishment of plant life. Instead the fishes may be introduced after a day or two and this itself needs some discussion.

It is unfortunate that the newly set-up marine tank is also most vulnerable, and when in the hands of a novice it is doubly so. If you are starting to keep marine fishes and have experience with fresh water fishes it isn't so bad, but if you are starting fish keeping with marines you have a problem. It bears repeating that the safest way to start is with a large under-populated tank that won't change its condition very quickly, drop in pH, in temperature, or suddenly go foul. A small tank with a full load of fishes is the very last thing to begin with in marine fishkeeping. Failure of a pump, a heater or a thermostat, unsuspected poisoning or over-feeding, and many other potential upsets can all prove fatal in a few hours.

As the fishes grow, and algal growth occurs and the tank settles down, as the filter system gets truly operational and water conditions stable, you may start to breathe more freely. If no disease has appeared within a month, it probably won't unless new specimens are added or something upsets the fishes' resistance. You will have become accustomed to feeding and cleaning routines and to the peculiarities of your fish collection. Check that they are breathing and behaving naturally each time you look at them. Look for trouble, for signs of disease, for any fish not behaving normally. Smell the tank and check its clarity, look at the thermometer to check the temperature, notice if the filter and aerator systems are working properly. A day's neglect can cause severe trouble; two days can be fatal. When trouble occurs in a tropical marine tank it happens *fast*; in a small one it happens *very fast*.

If all is going well, leave it alone. Don't change any of the water un-necessarily, don't disturb the rocks and coral and don't do any needless cleaning or filter changing. Part of the enjoyment of keeping fishes is the gadgetry and doing things for them, but it's easy to overdo things and to upset a tank which would be fine if left alone. Take care not to over-feed, just for the pleasure of watching the fishes eat. Learn how much to feed and how frequently and stick to a routine.

The serious aquarist will often keep a diary of each tank. This should record water changes, filter changes, entry and death of individual fishes, periodic pH, temperature and specific gravity readings. When a filter is changed, record why it was necessary—clogged up, water getting yellow, etc. If a fish dies, record why you think it did so, or that you just don't know. Gradually, the diary will tell you things you would be unlikely to realize without keeping it.

3. NEW ARRIVALS

Fishes newly purchased or newly arrived from overseas need particularly careful handling as they are often severely disturbed. They may have been shocked, chilled, bruised or otherwise ill-treated, although every pre-cuation is normally taken to avoid this. First, they should not suddenly be taken from a dark container into a brightly lit tank. This may shock them so severely that death will ensue. Second, they should not be trans-ferred from one type of water to another unless these are known to resemble each other very closely. A check should be made of the tempera-ture and salinity of the water in which the fishes arrive, or which has been supplied by the dealer, and this must be compared with conditions in the tank. Any adjustment must be gradual. A temperature change of more than about 2°F. downwards or 4°F. upwards should be avoided. If the fishes are in a reasonably sized transport container the best thing to do is to leave them in it, lowering an air stone so they do not suffocate, and to add successive quantities of aquarium water until the water in the container approaches that in the aquarium in its properties. Perhaps it may be necessary to bale some of the mixture out and to go on adding further aquarium water, and the process may need to take the best part of a day.

If the two waters resemble one another fairly closely to begin with it may only take half an hour. One must use one's judgment. During this period the fishes should be kept in a dim light and the degree of illumination gently increased. Finally, when all is ready the container or plastic bag in which the change over has been manipulated should, if possible, be floated in the aquarium water and the fishes gently tipped into the aquarium, after a further equilibration period of about half an hour. Measures like those above should take care of total pH and salinity differences of up to 0.5 and 0.005 respectively but if by some mischance there is a greater difference than this between the transport water and the aquarium water it would be best to try some makeshift arrangement in which the new fishes can be housed for a day or two while the more extreme change is managed. Fortunately, there should not often be the occasion to do this.

It is possible to put new fishes into a tank together and hope for a reasonably peaceful community even if they are quite a mixed batch. Marine fishes are naturally pugnacious and a certain amount of bickering and fin tearing must be expected both between individuals of the same species and between different species. Many of the pomacentrids are particularly pugnacious, so are medium and large specimens of various trigger fishes. Others such as the lion fish should normally be kept on their own as they may sting or eat their tank mates if the latter are small enough to be swallowed. When fishes are placed together as strangers into a new tank they are all unaccustomed to their surroundings. They have no established territories or peck order of any kind within the tank, therefore perhaps are somewhat scared of one another and so a degree of peace reigns. As they settle down bickering between them will usually remain at a bearable level, but any fish that appears to be too dominating should be removed for the comfort of the others, even if he is your choicest specimen. In a very crowded tank, which should in any case be avoided, the fishes seem to remain in a state of constant mix up and do not seemingly try to establish ownership of any part of the tank. Thus in a dealer's tank they may be reasonably happy for the week or two that he may keep them, even though they are crowded together.

When the fishes are placed in a more permanent home, in which they should be given a good deal more room, they tend to establish territories, to regard particular areas and nooks and crannies as belonging to indi-

Balistoides viridescens and the other triggerfishes are among the most territory-minded of all marine aquarium inhabitants, and they have the equipment to defend their chosen areas. Photo by Klaus Paysan.

viduals and to drive away others who try to take possession or even approach their own area too closely. Not all fishes do this but the coral reef fishes are particularly inclined to do it. This is because in nature they establish similar territories on the reef. When the fishes are all placed in the tank together they will come to some reasonable arrangement and each will have his particular territory or will perhaps decide to do without one. Usually peace will be maintained or at least belligerence will be kept at a reasonable minimum.

If a new fish is introduced into a tank, even though he may be large and quite fearsome and well able to look after himself in normal circumstances, the behavior of the existing inhabitants must be watched very carefully because they may tear his fins and injure him severely within a few minutes or give him such a hard time of it that he dies shortly afterwards. This is particularly liable to occur if the new fish is of a species already in the tank or of a closely related species. It may occur however, irrespective of species. If the new fish is small and timid it is very likely to be the finish of him straight away. There is thus considerable difficulty in adding to an established tank of fishes; the longer they have been established, the more difficult it is liable to be. This presents quite a serious problem because fishes do of course die and replacements are desirable and yet they are often most difficult to make. The best solution seems to be to wait until several additions are needed in the tank, then to take the opportunity of a partial or general cleaning out so to disturb the existing inhabitants. When even without actually removing them from the tank the familiar scenery has been changed around and territories have been disturbed, new fishes can be introduced much more safely than otherwise would be the case. In extreme instances it would be desirable to net all the fishes out of the tank, to rearrange the scenery, then to put the old and the new ones back together when there is a good likelihood of a minimum amount of fighting and danger.

Fortunately, belligerency caused by new introductions dies down after a few days, but these days are a very critical period during which most newly introduced fishes may be killed unless precautions of the type just described have been taken. It is possible with caution to introduce a batch of new fishes without disturbing the tank, which is much better than introducing single fishes individually because the pugnacity is spread out amongst several new arrivals and they may sustain only a certain amount of bearable damage. If they are fortunate, they find some nook or cranny where they can hide away for a day or two from whence they may emerge as accepted new tank inhabitants, from then on to be left in relative peace.

It seems quite surprising how well the existing fishes recognize each other and discriminate against the new one who may be almost indistinguishable to our own eyes. The situation has resemblance to a story of the early days of the London Zoo where, owing to shortage of space it was necessary to introduce some new perch into a tank already inhabited by a large voracious pike. Knowing what the effect on the new fishes would be if precautions were not taken, the keeper placed a dividing glass between the pike and the new inhabitants, and he proceeded to dash himself against the glass in an attempt to devour the others until finally he learned that his efforts were of no avail. The keeper then made the bold experiment of removing the partition and found that the pike made no attempt to eat the smaller fishes even though he now mingled freely with them. However, he still had to be fed and this was accomplished by throwing in other fishes which he devoured immediately although they might closely resemble the ones he had learnt to leave alone. Perhaps we should learn a lesson here that it is possible to introduce new fish by placing a dividing glass in the tank which may be removed after a period of time. In actual fact this is not usually practicable because it interferes with the set-up too much and prevents proper circulation and temperature control in the home aquarium.

4. REMOVING FISHES

When it is necessary to remove a fish from a tank this may present severe problems. It is difficult to manipulate nets when the tank is full of rocks and coral; the latter in particular snags nets and provides excellent hiding places for the fishes you are trying to remove. Sometimes it is possible to lure the fish to the top of the water by feeding it after first having removed the top light and cover, but this very action often alerts the fishes who crouch away at the bottom of the tank and refuse to come forward. In the end it is the author's experience that it pays to make up one's mind to strip the tank down, to catch out the fish which need to be caught and then to rebuild the scenery. This may take an hour in a large tank but it is in the end less damaging to both the fish and one's patience than any other way of attempting their removal.

It is sometimes possible to catch a fish from a dark tank with a flashlight and a net. This can be done if his night time resting place is an open part of the tank such as a top back corner in which some fishes do in fact tend to spend the night. Unfortunately, most of them are not so obliging and will hide away in the most inaccessible parts of the tank at night time so that the problem is as bad as ever.

5. FISH CAPACITY OF TANK

The fish capacity of a marine tank is severely limited, but must be considered in two contexts. First, what is the safe capacity of a large tank which can be expected not to suffer losses from suffocation or pollution even though a filter cuts out or the air supply is off for half a day? This is the ideal capacity to consider, but one which may not satisfy the aquarist who wants to keep as many fishes as possible on display. Second, how many fishes can reasonably be maintained, even in a small tank, as long as everything keeps working?

The first question, the safe number in a large tank, is about thirty 2″ to 3″ fishes per 100 gallons, or about 3½ gallons per medium-sized fish. Not many more smaller fishes can be maintained, because the marine tank must allow for removal of excess food and fish waste to a greater extent than the fresh water tank. If the fishes exceed 3″ in size, drastic cuts must be made in number, so that no more than about ten 4″ to 5″ fishes could be maintained safely in the same 100 gallons. A simple filter using only synthetic wool, a little activated charcoal, and one aeration stone could service such a tank.

Dascyllus aruanus, a pomacentrid, is one of the hardier species and can take crowded conditions fairly well. Photo by Gerhard Marcuse.

Gnathanodon speciosus and other members of the family Carangidae are fast-moving open water fishes that need a lot of room and will not do well if crowded. Photo by Gerhard Marcuse.

The second question is answered by doubling or even tripling the estimates just given, allowing only 1 to 2 gallons per medium-sized fish, but relying on heavy filtration and aeration, with an undergravel filter and/or a large power-pump operated outside filter with all the trimmings. Thus, a 20 gallon tank can hold 10 to 20 medium-sized fishes if you are prepared to lose them when a breakdown occurs, or if disease starts up, when it is much more difficult to control in an overcrowded tank. Further, you must not expect the fishes to grow much, or to settle down to any kind of territorial existence as in nature, and to exhibit really normal behavior.

Apart from the considerations above, the nature of the fishes also influences fish capacity. The estimates are for a mixed community but must be lowered for active, delicate types such as chaetodons, file fishes and many angels. On the other hand, scorpion fishes, clowns of many types, most of the demoiselles and gobies can be crowded more successfully, although they do better when in a community of their own type than in a completely mixed community.

6. GENERAL MAINTENANCE

When an aquarium is first set up there is perhaps the greatest danger of things going wrong than at almost any other time during its existence unless it is really thoroughly neglected. The new tank has not achieved any kind of balance. In a marine tank it is not usually wise to introduce very much in the way of growing plants because they almost always die and pollute the water. Nevertheless, a certain amount of plant growth in the form of algae will occur. We have seen that if the lighting is adequate green algae will be dominant and will form an attractive addition to the furnishings of the tank. They do more than this, however, in that they grow on nutriment obtained from the contents of the tank, primarily the water, and therefore absorb a certain amount of waste material. Since the algae in turn is usually eaten by the fishes to a lesser or greater extent, a cycle is set up by which the proportion of material which would otherwise contaminate the tank resides in tissues of the growing algae. There is an additional effect which is perhaps not of very great importance, that adequately lighted algae produces oxygen and absorbs carbon dioxide and thus helps to keep the water aerated.

It is, therefore, a mistake to discourage actively the growth of algae in a tank just as it is a mistake to allow too much of an overgrowth so that everything is covered with an unwanted layer of green. A balance must be obtained in which the fishes will help because so many of these will nibble on the algae and help to keep it down. It is quite easy to remove some pieces of rock or coral and to wash them under a jet of water and to clean away most of the algae in a minute or two, leaving behind a certain portion to regenerate.

Algae adhering to the glass back and sides of the tank are usually best left alone but the front will need a periodic clean either with the fingers or with a non-scratching pad of plastic or chamois leather or some such material. It should be noted that the addition of certain medications to the aquarium water, particularly of copper, will tend to kill algae if given in excess. Fortunately the amount of copper usually needed to cure those fish diseases which it affects is not so badly toxic to most forms of algae that they will die off completely, although they may receive a set-back. If however more than the standard dosage is added or if the standard dosage is added fairly frequently, which may unfortunately be necessary for the control of some diseases, this will tend to kill practically all algae in the tank, particularly the green algae and to spoil the whole arrangement. It should also be noted that a heavy dose of copper which may kill practically all of the algae in the tank in one go must at all costs be avoided because of potential pollution. The filtering system may not be capable of taking care of the sudden flood of dead or dying plant material.

It is possible with care to introduce successfully small amounts of frond or hair-like algae and to get them growing successfully in a strongly lighted tank. Unfortunately the fishes are very liable to nibble them down and spoil the effect but clown fish and some others do not do this if they are otherwise well fed. It would seem reasonable to assume that red and brown colored seaweeds from the rather dimmer parts of the ocean some feet or fathoms down in the water might be more suitable for the marine aquarium than the green algae which requires a strong light to flourish. Strangely, however, this is not so. Attempts to keep some of the very attractive and colorful algae found in rock pools and in deeper locations on the reef are rarely successful and usually amount to rapid pollution of the water. Naturally any such algae which occasionally starts to form of its own accord in the aquarium should be cherished with all care because it will be a rare attraction.

7. THE BIOLOGICAL FILTER

Some aquarists have tried the maintenance of a type of biological sewage farm which includes a section away from the main aquarium which is brightly illuminated and in which algal growth is encouraged. It is possible to maintain various types of algae in such intensive illumination and to benefit from the purification of the water which they help to maintain. It is an interesting experiment but somewhat doubtful whether the trouble is worthwhile. The capacity of activated charcoal to absorb material of much the same type used by the algae is such that there may be no real need for such a biological setup.

The biological filter has been especially advocated by Mr. Stork, of Suva, Fiji. A lush growth of green algae must be maintained in a vessel isolated from the aquarium, but in circulation with it. Ideally, this vessel

The brown alga known as Sargassum weed will maintain itself in a tank for a short time but, like other algae that don't originate as growths within the tank itself, usually quickly dies off. This clump of Sargassum weed contains a specimen of *Histrio* that is almost perfectly camouflaged.
Photo by New York Zoological Society.

is sunlit, and shallow, so that a large water surface is available and algal growth is maximal. The algae may be allowed to grow spontaneously, or suitable sprouts of a green hairlike algae may be introduced to speed up the process. If it is not feasible to have an exterior, sunlit auxiliary tank, bright artificial illumination can substitute for it.

The details of construction are as follows. A bed of sand covers the outlet pipe from the algae-containing vessel, which can be a regular aquarium fitted with a sub-sand filter, or a cruder affair such as a plastic bath with a pipe pierced with holes, placed under the sand. In the latter case, a coarser gravel bed is advocated, overlain with a sand-bed separated from it by a layer of fine nylon cloth. A pump sucks water from the outlet pipe back into the aquarium from which water is siphoned to the filter.

It is asserted that, when in full operation, such a biological filter can absorb a remarkable amount of waste, and that sparkling clear water can be maintained even in the presence of decaying coral and sponges. In

57.00

the case of a filter operating under natural sunlight, the pH fell at night but was restored to normal each day, as the algae got to work, absorbing waste material. Finicky methods of feeding were abandoned, and the fishes flourished, even though overcrowded. It is clear that experimentation along these lines may repay the serious aquarist.

From the above it will be seen that growth of algae in the marine tank is both attractive in the view of most aquarium keepers and certainly performs a useful series of functions. However some aquarists prefer clean and gleamingly white corals and will therefore clean out the algae as soon as it has started to form. It is, in general, a mistake to make such a preference because not only will the fishes fail to benefit from the presence of the algae but they will also tend to look pale and washed out with such gleaming bright surroundings. The average marine tropical only looks its best when the decoration is not too brilliant. There are two reasons for this. First, its color is more intense when it is not subjected to too bright light; second, such color that it does possess looks better when viewed against a variegated and on the whole a different background rather than pure white coral. It should be noted that in nature the gleaming white of the coral skeleton is for much of the time hidden by the polyps which emerge from it and which are often quite brightly colored. The overall formation of a coral reef or rock pool is much better imitated by algae encrusted rocks and corals than by the gleaming white set-up preferred by some aquarists.

8. MAINTENANCE OF SUB-SAND FILTERS

The great desirability of leaving undergravel filters operating for as long as possible has already been discussed, but if the construction of a unit is such that it gets irrevocably clogged, with perhaps masses of polluted material under the filter, the situation must be relieved. Apart from their biological function, such filters have many virtues. A good depth of sand may be used in the tank and is necessary for the adequate functioning of such a filter. In this sand various marine creatures including some fishes may burrow, and in the tank containing an undergravel filter it is practicable to have some invertebrates which are sand burrowers and which would otherwise not stay alive. Some of the fishes such as the parrot wrasses dive down into the sand both in nature and in the aquarium and when not provided with suitable depth of sand they have to learn that they cannot do this. Sometimes they languish and die because of the injuries they inflict upon themselves in attempting to burrow down through a thin layer of sand. The sub-sand filter is also very efficient during its useful period. It is not absolutely necessary to have any other type of filtration if it is employed, although a gradual yellowing of the water is liable to occur unless an additional small activated charcoal filter cartridge is

Apart from its effect on the appearance of the tank, the amount of light entering a marine aquarium also has a great effect on the fishes' color patterns and behavior. The group of *Pseudochaetodon nigrirostris* shown above in their natural daytime color pattern would exhibit quite different markings under varying lighting conditions. Photo by Edmund Hobson.

employed. It is also unnecessary to employ separate aeration unless the tank is heavily stocked, as a degree of aeration is provided by the bubbles arising from the filter itself.

Modern sub-sand filters employ airstones lowered into a wide uplift tube rather than gadgetry operating under the sand or gravel, and so air-lift troubles rarely occur with them. Older types, which you may be unlucky enough to have installed, cannot be adequately serviced from above, and need much digging around to get working again if an air-line or jet gets clogged. This too, apart from pollution below the filter bed, may cause the need for a thorough clean-up. There is a routine for doing this which should be carefully followed.

First, turn off all equipment and remove thermometers, aerators, inside filters, heaters and other auxiliaries so as to give a clear field of action.

Also remove all rocks and coral leaving a bare tank with its sand and filter at the bottom and the fishes. It goes without saying that care must be taken during this part of the operation so that the fishes are not unduly frightened or damaged. It will now be easy to net out the fishes, which should be placed in a temporary home containing water siphoned from the main aquarium and temporarily aerated with an air stone and if necessary kept warm with the thermostat and heater removed from the main tank. If the aquarium is say 40 gallons in capacity, then the fishes will be quite happy in a temporary home containing only five gallons of water for the hour or two during which they will stay there but they will need aeration. A large plastic container is perhaps the most suitable to use for the temporary accommodation of the fishes because in their agitation they are liable to damage themselves. A large covered plastic garbage can or large plastic bag such as is used for commercial shipments forms a much better temporary home than a tank or enamelware.

Returning to the main tank, the sand over the sub-sand filter should then be siphoned off with a large bore siphon, which can normally be done without the removal of more than half of the water in the tank. It will then be possible to lift the sub-sand filter bodily from the tank to clean it, and to siphon off any remaining debris at the bottom of the tank still leaving some marine water behind. The latter point is emphasized because it is unwise to allow the tank water level to fall below about half-way; the larger the tank the wiser it is to take this precaution since really large tanks are liable to spring leaks if the water pressure to which the tank has been subjected for so long a period is suddenly lowered too far. It pays therefore to return some of the water that has already been siphoned out in order to maintain about the half-way level.

With this operation in progress the opportunity will naturally be taken to clean up rocks and equipment to such a degree as is desirable. This is also the time to introduce any new fishes as described earlier. In addition, and depending upon the rate at which a turnover of water has been maintained in the marine tank it may be the time to replace some, but never all, of the water with new water. General experience shows that the addition of not more than half of new marine water is perhaps desirable at this stage. It is very likely that the water in the tank is now quite cloudy but that does not matter because of the high efficiency of the sub-sand filter once it is set up again. The sand which has been siphoned off should now be very gently washed, so as not to remove its coating of bacteria so essential to the functioning of the filter. Wash in marine water, not fresh water, and don't worry about flushing everything clean. If desired, a portion of the sand can be thoroughly washed or replaced with new material for making a clean-looking surface layer, but only a portion. If for any reason—such as replacing old sand with a more suitable coral sand or gravel—a total change to new material is made, treat as for a new
60.00

tank, and house the fishes elsewhere for the settling in period. If new sand is used, just as in the original setting up of the tank, it should be thoroughly washed by the aquarist himself because even so called "washed sand" bought commercially is never clean. The filter may now be replaced in the tank, the new or washed sand carefully put in position above it—all of which can be done with a tank half full of salt water quite easily. In fact it is easier to do it with the water in than to do it with a completely dry tank. The rocks and coral and other equipment may then be replaced in preferably some new arrangement to that which occurred before, so that if the fishes are being augmented there will be a reduced tendency to fight.

Finally, the water should be filled up so that it comes just under the rim of the top frame and the fishes can be re-introduced. If the aquarium water has been partly changed then the same care should be taken over the re-introduction of the fishes as is taken when a new shipment of fishes is received. Check the final specific gravity and pH of the newly set up tank against that of the water in which the fishes have been temporarily kept, to make sure that too drastic a modification has not occurred, then put the fishes back in their tank with any new ones that have been added. The water will still be cloudy but this does not matter and it is better to put the fishes back into a rather cloudy tank than to hold them too long in temporary storage. However if this worries the aquarist and his temporary holding arrangements are adequate he can keep the fishes out for half a day or a day until the tank is clear again and then re-introduce his fishes. With anything but the smallest tanks, be prepared to devote a whole morning or the whole of an afternoon to the task as just described. A small tank, smaller than that advocated in this volume, can be dealt with in an hour or so; a really large tank will take you all day long.

9. MAINTENANCE WITH OTHER FILTERS

In a tank which does not employ sub-sand filtration, such occasional cleaning may never be necessary. The larger the tank, the more onerous a complete clean out becomes, and with a really large tank holding more than say 100 gallons, it can be such a nuisance that many aquarists would prefer other methods of control to the sub-sand filter, were it not for its outstanding merits. Some modern sub-sand filters are even sealed into the base of the tank, such is their alleged reliability, but the author remains skeptical! Any other type of filter can be cleaned without disturbing the body of the tank. This cleaning may be required more frequently than with the sub-sand filter but since it is much easier there is no difficulty. Even a rather complicated filter with layers or compartments containing different materials such as synthetic wool, activated charcoal and perhaps coral chips can be cleaned out and in operation again within 15 to 30 minutes.

If the tank has a good circulation of water and if the water flowing into the filter is taken by a suitable arrangement of siphons from the bottom of the tank as well as from other regions, the tank will not collect a serious amount of debris even over long periods of time. If, however, the more usual type of commercial filter is used by which tank water is collected only from one or two points of the tank, then pockets of unsiphoned debris may well occur in various areas, particularly under and around rocks and coral. These are harmless at first but as they gradually accumulate they may be a source of contamination and will need occasional cleaning up. This involves far less a disturbance once more than cleaning out a sub-sand filter. All that is necessary is to siphon as far as possible from around the back corners and from underneath rocks and corals, so that when these are moved a minimum amount will be left to swirl up into the water, then to remove the main tank decorations and siphon away the rest of the material as far as is possible from the bottom of the tank. The amount of sand in a tank without a sub-sand filter will be small and this is easily washed and replaced or replaced with new sand. Much of the equipment in the tank may be left behind when this is done, the fishes do not have to be removed and the whole process is easier and quicker.

We have already had some discussion about the frequency of cleaning of ordinary filters, and unless something is obviously happening which is not beneficial to the inhabitants the best advice is to leave such filters in operation until they are getting clogged up. Do not just automatically renew the material in ordinary outside or inside filters because you feel that it must be time for it to be replaced, but wait for it to perform the very useful function of aiding in the bacterial removal of unwanted tank pollutants, which it will tend to do most efficiently as it clogs. With an ordinary filter the necessity for a change will become very obvious because the water will cease to pass through the filter quickly enough for the filter to function properly and so the return of the water to the tank will be kept down. With the quite useful bottom corner type of filter, the clogging of the filter can be detected by the fact that bubbles are obviously not pulling through very much water with them, resulting according to the particular type of filter in use in an almost uninterrupted air stream rising from the center stem, or in the type where fine bubble aeration is used, the bubbles will be seen to be rising up from an almost static accumulation of water instead of pulling the water up with them.

10. FEEDING THE FISHES
Marine fishes are voracious, and although they may sometimes be choosy about their food and may even starve in the aquarium, this is because something drastic is wrong with their surroundings, or because they are not being fed correctly. Many factors contribute to the readiness

Species such as this *Plagiotremus rhinorhynchos* which eats almost nothing but scales which it rips off its tankmates, have specialized feeding habits that are impossible to duplicate in the aquarium. Such fishes are very poorly suited to maintenance by hobbyists. Photo by Dr. Wolfgang Wickler.

of marines to accept a particular food. When they are first caught, depending on species, age and previous history, they may refuse anything not closely resembling their previous diet. If they are kept with one or two educated fishes who have already learned to take food from their owner, they may soon learn to accept a variety of foods which they certainly never encountered in the wild. If not, they may have to be coaxed quite a lot before they will feed readily on material that is foreign to them.

The hardest to feed are those fishes which normally take only live food, such as the lion fish and the angler fishes. Some species will learn quite rapidly to accept at first dead fish and then any lump of edible material, but normally only meaty material, not vegetable. In the angler fishes this may mean the loss of the interesting habit of angling with the bait—a modified ray which in some species carries a wriggling worm-like excrescence at its tip. However, if the aquarist cannot keep up a supply of live food, this may be a necessary sacrifice. Other species are more difficult, and may refuse dead food consistently and will die unless live prey can be offered. This does not have to be marine; guppies or gambusia have saved the life of many a precious specimen!

Crustaceans such as the grass shrimp (top) and brine shrimp (nauplii, below) are natural foods for many salt-water fishes and may be fed in either live, frozen or freeze-dried form. Photos: grass shrimp by Dr. Herbert R. Axelrod, brine shrimp by Dr. C. Emmens.

64.00

The angelfish species like *Chaetodontoplus mesoleucus*, shown here grazing on algae-encrusted coral, are among the more picky eaters; unfortunately, some of the most beautiful of the butterfly fishes never become accustomed to the foods hobbyists are able to provide. Photo by Klaus Paysan.

Other difficult fishes are many species of butterfly fish (chaetodons and allied species). These have the habit of picking around living coral or rocks, from which they peck morsels of polyp or other material. They often find it hard to take food which is not of this nature, and living coral usually isn't easy to supply to them. However, tubifex worms or live brine shrimp (newly hatched or otherwise) are often a suitable early substitute, or even chopped clam or shrimp dropped over a dead coral, which they will often be investigating as a food source. Many chaetodons learn eventually to take food from the bottom of the tank, or even to rise into the water and take it from the top, or as it is falling through the tank. Finally, they will be eating almost anything, but the really finicky ones will never learn to do this.

Luckily, most marine fishes do not present such difficulties. They will usually eat live, frozen, canned or freeze dried foods initially and then learn to eat dry food as well. The presence of one or two old timers always helps, but their absence only means a little longer period of education. In the case of all fishes but the strict live food eaters, the presence of algae-covered rocks or coral or algae on the back and sides of the tank also offers food, which will be picked at frequently, and even cleaned right off if sufficient other food is not offered.

Special foods are available not only for marine fishes but for marine invertebrates as well.

66.00

We turn now to appropriate types of food for normal feeding. Many fishes are omnivores—eating both animal and vegetable material and needing both, while others are predominantly vegetable feeders, such as the surgeons. Even though the latter will accept a meat or fish diet, they gradually decline if not offered vegetable food as well. A mixed diet should therefore be offered to a typical community tank of marines. The author's favorite staple food is deep-frozen or freeze-dried prawn, shrimp, crab, clam, brine shrimp or tubifex, or canned fish roe or crustaceans. All such food should be rinsed before giving it to the fishes, to wash away unwanted juices and fine debris which tends to cloud and pollute the water. The vegetable part is supplied primarily by frozen green lettuce, chopped to a suitable size for the particular customers in the tank. It is a curious fact that few fishes will eat fresh chopped lettuce and few will refuse the same material after it has been frozen and thawed out again. It then resembles the soft green algae on which many fish feed in nature, so perhaps that is why it is acceptable. Other frozen vegetables—peas, beans, spinach, for example—when chopped to suitable size, rinsed thoroughly in a fine net or piece of cloth or strainer are also readily accepted.

Special treats are the usual live foods fed to fresh water tropicals, which if not given in excess will live long enough in the salt tank to be eaten before they die and pollute the water. Mosquito larvae survive longest, and may be fed in mild excess, but beware of the fishes that kill more than they eat and thus cause trouble. Daphnia, tubifex, white worms and other small worms die quite rapidly and must be eaten or removed within a few minutes. Although it may be advisable to feed tubifex to tempt such fishes as chaetodons to feed, it seems best not to use it live as a staple food. Freeze-dried tubifex is better, and seems to be refused by fewer fishes than any other food. Freeze-dried mosquito larvae or daphnia are also accepted with great relish and are probably as good as the living creatures.

Another special treat is 'live' rocks or coral, which when available are much picked over and relished, but beware of accustoming fishes to such diets when there is any danger of a failure of supply, as it may be hard to get them back to normal feeding. Carefully selected fronds or snippets of green algae and even other soft algae are also appreciated, but aquarium fishes do not eat the tougher brown varieties, which also do not flourish in the tank and may pollute it.

Dry foods suitable to the marine tank are identical with those offered to fresh water specimens. Protein-rich flake preparations are much appreciated, but shredded dried shrimp, baby cereals, oatmeal and indeed most prepared fish foods are taken quite readily by most tropical marines— usually after a short period of acclimatization. It is doubtful whether dry foods should ever predominate in the diet, but they can certainly form a significant part of it and even be used exclusively for short periods when necessary. Some tough species can live for a long time on dry food, but most of them gradually decline in health and trouble starts. *Note that this does not necessarily include freeze-dried foods, which appear to be suitable as staple foods.*

Newly hatched brine shrimp are often a great help as a "starter" for small marine fishes, but are not usually necessary for a long period. However, they are a very good stand-by even for quite large fishes when no other live food is available. Remember that quite large quantities are needed in any but the smallest tank. If you normally feed the equivalent of a teaspoonful of food to your tank, then two teaspoons of eggs, when hatched, will give you something like its equivalent. This is quite a hatch—requiring several $\frac{1}{2}$ to 1 gallon pans or jars, according to how you hatch the shrimp.

Frequency of feeding depends on species and sizes of fishes concerned. Generally speaking, small or young fishes require frequent feeding, while the larger specimens can get along with one feed a day, or even every other day. Small chaetodons must have almost a continuous supply of food to flourish. This can be supplied as 'live' rock or coral, algae growing in the tank, tiny mosquito larvae, or newly hatched brine shrimp. However, the continuous presence of brine shrimp requires special filtering arrangements—either a sub-sand filter alone or a filter which can be turned right down or off while they swarm in the water. A bottom filter or corner filter can often be operated as long as top lighting is supplied, and as long as no very great stirring of the water occurs. Then the young brine shrimp stay mostly at the top of the water and are not trapped by the filter in significant numbers.

Other small fishes—up to say 1″ in length—need to be fed, unless continuously as above, several times a day or *at least* twice daily. Larger fishes of the omnivorous types do best with twice daily feeding, but can stand a single feed per day without serious detriment as long as they all get enough. Be very careful, with either frequent or infrequent feeding, that the bullies and quick ones don't regularly grab most of the food, leaving others to starve gradually.

Carnivorous fishes like the lion fish need feeding when they are hungry. This will only be every few days if they are given heavy meals. If they are lightly fed they will eat several times a day, but in general they should be kept on rather short rations or they grow rapidly and soon outgrow their tank—dwarf species excepted. Too heavy a meal is sometimes followed by rejection, which may foul the tank, particularly if partially digested food is voided into the tank in the absence of the aquarist. Even the best filtering system cannot keep pace with gross pollution of this type.

For feeding purposes, marine fish can be classified in two major groupings; the nibblers (such as the butterflyfishes and some others) and the swallowers (such as the grouper, *Epinephalus* sp., shown here). The size of a fish's mouth generally gives a good clue as to which type of feeder it is. Photo by Hilmar Hansen.

The same rules apply in the marine tank as in the fresh water tank. Feed only enough food to be eaten almost immediately—and this *includes* all live food except of marine origin or mosquito larvae. Then clean up all the remainder as much as possible; the smaller the tank and the more sterile the setup, the greater is the necessity for strict attention to this rule. Do not rely on filters to take care of particles of uneaten food, as these simply decay in the filter and may pollute the water just as if they were left at the bottom of the tank. If a filter traps an appreciable amount of uneaten food, clean it out. Only in a tank with natural filters such as mussels, scavengers such as small crabs or growing algae can any appreciable amount of uneaten food be dealt with, and then not much. Crabs in particular create more debris than they consume if there is an excess of uneaten food or if they are allowed to pick over live rock or coral. Large lumps of food which could have been removed are converted into fine particles which scatter all over the tank or pollute the filter.

69.00

11. DISEASE AND PARASITES

Any aquarist familiar with the keeping of fresh water tropical fishes will know that detailed information about their diseases is still mostly lacking. Nevertheless, quite a number of external and a few internal diseases of these fishes have been described and treatments for some of them are available. Our knowledge of the diseases of marine fishes is at an even more primitive stage than with the fresh water fishes and it is not really possible to write a very informative section on this topic. There has been a certain amount of research, although quite inadequate and sporadic, on the diseases of fishes in the ocean but very little is known about the diseases that particularly affect coral reef and other favorite marine aquarium fishes.

This situation is likely to change as more people keep marine fishes, and as disease control in oceanaria, hatcheries and other public aquaria becomes more and more important. The study of fish disease in aquaria will make an important contribution to our knowledge of disease processes in the wild since it is usually only possible to trace the natural history of a disease on individuals in captivity. It is unfortunate that many of the methods of handling the diseases of fresh water fishes are not applicable in the marine tank. The old fashioned but still widely used salt treatment for fungus and some other diseases in fresh water fishes is clearly inappropriate to marine fishes.

Many of the chemicals used in fresh water tanks are unsuitable or ineffective in the marine tank and this is particularly true of the antibiotics. Effective doses of penicillin seem to be particularly liable to cause blindness in clown fish and other coral fishes, while quite high doses of some of the wide spectrum antibiotics such as aureomycin and chloromycetin are not very effective in the marine tank. They also tend to cause severe clouding of the water and in some cases to undergo spectacular color changes not seen in the fresh water tank. The following is therefore a very sketchy report on some of the most common diseases affecting marine fishes in the aquarium and of remedies which have proved successful in at least some circumstances. Differences between aquarists' tanks and general methods of keeping their fishes can have a very profound effect on the efficiency of any particular remedy. It should therefore not be regarded as surprising that a treatment highly recommended by one aquarist fails in the hands of another one. The first may be using subsand filtration and the second may be using activated charcoal, which perhaps removes the particular remedy from circulation almost immediately if he leaves the filter on.

12. WHITE SPOT DISEASE

This is the marine equivalent of the white spot of fresh water fishes—

Ichthyophthirius multifiliis, but is said in the marine tank to be due to the ciliate parasite *Cryptocaryon irritans*. It is found in the wild but apparently exists there as a very light infection. In the aquarium it can build up at tremendous speed to become a lethal disease. It usually starts as a result of stress or chilling, as the causative organism is frequently present, but giving no trouble until it is given the opportunity to cause an outbreak in weakened specimens. The first signs of the disease are the fishes scratching themselves on the rocks or coral or even on the sand, dashing around the aquarium and exhibiting general restlessness. If the fishes are then examined carefully, small white spots may be detected, usually on the fins or tail but sometimes on the body. They are usually smaller in size than those which cause the fresh water disease and in advanced stages of the disease they will cover the whole body. When this stage is reached there may be no hope of curing the tank without the loss of at least some of the specimens.

White spot settles first in the gills of the fish, where it is naturally filtered out from the aquarium water as respiration occurs. There it causes inflamation and difficulties in breathing and will eventually suffocate the victim. This is why the disease is usually accompanied by rapid respiration in addition to the symptoms already described. By the time the infection has developed enough for the parasites to start settling externally, where they are visible on areas like the fins, there is really quite a heavy infection, so that no time should be lost when the presence of the disease is suspected. The full cycle of the parasite has not been discovered but it again appears to resemble that of fresh water white spot in that the mature parasite drops from the host and encysts at the bottom of the aquarium. It then divides into large numbers of motile infective organisms which swim up into the water and re-infect the fishes.

It will be apparent from this description that the disease is highly contagious and it can readily be transferred from one aquarium to another. Once it is known or suspected to be present every care must be taken not to infect other tanks. All equipment including hands must be thoroughly sterilized or washed before being used in any other but the infected tank. The disease can of course be transferred to an aquarium on new specimens, which may not be showing it overtly but because they have been weakened in transport may readily develop it. Sometimes it comes from the tank itself and flourishes on the new specimens because they have been weakened, but whichever way round it happens it is clear that the introduction of new specimens is a particularly dangerous period when white spot may occur and it should therefore be looked out for very carefully. Even quarantine procedures may not guarantee the absence of an outbreak when the new specimens are introduced, since the infection may really be from the tank and not introduced with the new fishes.

The most successful treatment of marine white spot is with copper. As has already been seen, copper is highly toxic to fishes themselves and to plant life in the aquarium, but it is fortunately even more toxic to some of their parasites. Its primary action on the fish is to cause the formation of copious mucus which helps to rid it of existing parasites although not those embedded firmly in the integument of the fish, and it helps to prevent further parasites from settling onto the fish. Its secondary action is directly on the free-swimming stages of the parasite itself, in that it kills them if present in sufficient concentration. When used in an ordinary home aquarium copper may be added as copper sulphate, which should be made up at a strength of 1% (10 mg/liter) of the ordinary blue crystals in distilled water, *not* tap water, as a stock solution to be added to the tank. One ml. (approx. 1/5th of a teaspoon) should be added for every gallon of tank water, but this dose is best divided into two successive treatments to be given two days apart. Naturally if a rapid and effective cure appears to have taken place before the second half of the treatment is due, it is best not to add it but to keep a careful eye on the tank for a recurrence of the disease. The use of a 1% solution of copper sulphate in ordinary water gives a final concentration of metallic copper ions of 0.4 parts per million, which is a safe dose for fishes but lethal to *Cryptocaryon irritans*. Many fishes can take twice the dose but not all can do so, and so care should be taken not to overdo it by adding more copper if by bad luck the cure is incomplete. More copper may be added after two or three weeks since much of that present will have been absorbed on to coral and detritis and will have left the aquarium water.

When the copper sulphate solution is first added to the aquarium, a slight cloudiness appears which disappears again within a few minutes. This indicates that the material has precipitated from the solution but soon re-dissolves as it circulates around the tank. However, some aquarists are worried by this and there is also a worry in the minds of people managing large aquaria where there is a circulation of new salt water in the tanks. In such cases copper citrate may be substituted for copper sulphate, as it is more soluble and it may be fed into the commercial aquarium as a constant drip at a rate calibrated to keep the necessary concentration of copper in the water. If too much copper has been added the fishes slow down and may even begin to turn on their sides. If left in this condition they will die. Fortunately the copper may be removed by filtering the aquarium water through an ion exchange resin such as Zeocarb 225, which will quite rapidly lower the concentration of copper. Less acute but more chronic copper poisoning may cause popeye, especially in clown fish, which will go down again after some of the copper is removed.

Another recommended treatment which may be used in the presence of marine invertebrates is sodium sulphathiazole, or even plain sulphathiazole. Either should be added to the aquarium at a dose of 1 level teaspoon of the powder for each five gallons of aquarium water, but dissolve the drug in a glass of fresh water before adding it to the aquarium. It is stated that this treatment is increased in effect by simultaneously raising the water temperature to 85 or 90°F., in which case the aeration should best be increased as well. Very mild cases of the disease may be cured by heat or by the drug alone but you have to be lucky for this to occur. It seems doubtful whether the sulphathiazole treatment is in general as reliable as copper treatment, but it has the advantage of low toxicity and little danger of doing damage.

13. VELVET DISEASE

This again parallels a fresh water disease going by the same name, and is in fact caused by a closely related organism. The marine parasite is *Amyloodinium ocellatum* (Brown). The fresh water parasite is *Oodinium limneticum* and sometimes other species of *Oodinium*. It is a dinoflagellate which also affects the gills and later the external surface of the victim. As with marine white spot, it causes damage to gill filaments and respiration, however, in heavy infections it also spreads over the body, first appearing on the fins and tail and later almost everywhere. Velvet disease differs from white spot in that it is more superficial and smaller than the latter. When it is visible on the outer surface of the fish they seem to have been dusted over with a white powder which may sometimes be seen to be moving, since the causative organism is not embedded so deeply into the skin of the fish as is white spot. The corresponding fresh water infection is typically yellow in appearance, not white.

The oodinium organism has a rather similar life history to white spot, settling to the bottom of the tank after maturing on the fish and giving rise to several hundred free-swimming dinospores, which are again rapidly infective in the marine tank and must be treated as quickly as possible. There seems to be little doubt that other species of dinoflagellate also infect fishes, and have not yet been identified, but treatment of them seems to be the same for all namely, copper. Exactly the same treatment should be given as for white spot but it does not seem as likely that the alternative treatment, sulphathiazole sodium and heat will cure the disease. If therefore you are uncertain whether the infecting organism is white spot or velvet it is by far the safest to treat with copper straight away since it will have a good chance of curing both diseases. Velvet is, if anything, more rapidly fatal than white spot. An error in diagnosis followed by sulphathiazole treatment can lead to the loss of a tankful of fishes.

14. NON-SPECIFIC ITCHES

Quite a number of bacterial or other infections can cause fish to behave as they do when infested with white spot or velvet disease, and a number of these are frequently helped by copper treatment. However, the scratching behavior, although not usually the appearance of white spots or other external parasitism, can be due to toxic conditions in the tank which copper treatment would only intensify. If therefore no causative organism can be seen on the fish and yet it is definitely scratching itself frequently, treatment with copper should be withheld and general thought be given to the hygiene of the tank itself. If there is any cloudiness, bad smell or other signs of pollution in the tank, filtration and aeration should be increased and a general clean up given as far as is possible. If there is any reason to suspect toxicity due to metallic poisoning or to other gross contamination of the water, which would of course be made much worse by the addition of copper, new activated charcoal and an ion exchange resin should be added so as to help clear up the toxicity should it be present, and a partial change of water should be given if it is possible.

Careful observation should follow over the next day or two to see if conditions do in fact improve, and see if the fishes settle down again and above all to watch carefully for the appearance of any more definite signs of disease, which should initiate active chemical treatment. If spots indicating white spot or velvet or some related disease start to show up and the distressed behavior of the fishes continues, it is then best to add copper as outlined above rather than risk further neglect of the disease.

15. BACTERIAL INFECTIONS

Various bacterial infections causing skin ulcerations (so-called *body rot*) and fin and tail infections (so-called *fin* and *tail rot*) sometimes occur in the marine tank. If these are not treated, progressive erosion of the fin and tail or increased ulceration of the skin is liable to occur and to cause unsightliness and mortality among the fishes. Various different bacteria have been found from time to time by investigators encountering these problems and in this condition the best treatment appears to be sulphathiazole as outlined above, or chloromycetin. Chloromycetin at a strength of 50–100 mg per gallon will often assist in clearing up such bacterial infections. However, if the fishes readily gulp down any food to which between 0.1 and 1% of chloromycetin powder can be added, so that most of the drug is ingested, this is often a much cheaper and better form of treatment. Keep it up for a week, and with any luck the antibiotic will have cured the condition. Don't worry about overdosage, the fishes can stand it.

Some aquarists risk a rather heroic treatment of fishes with body rot or fin rot, which involves netting them out and dabbing the infected areas with common antiseptic such as hydrogen peroxide or argyrol. It seems unlikely that this kind of treatment will help and much more likely that the difficulties of catching the fish and treating them will cause more harm than good and also be likely to cause the spread of the infection to other tank inhabitants. If the fish is caught out for treatment, it would seem best to keep it away from its fellows until it has either died or is cured.

16. LYMPHOCYSTIS

This consists of quite large spots somewhat resembling pimples or boils which occur on the skin of the fish and often have a grayish appearance. It is best to leave this infection alone and to treat for general cleanliness and to install ultra-violet sterilization or perhaps an ozonizer if such equipment is not already in use. Some authorities recommend surgery for this condition but it does not appear to be outstandingly successful. For the same reason as mentioned above it is unwise to remove infected fishes from a tank and to attempt procedures on them unless this is absolutely unavoidable.

17. ICHTHYOPHONUS

This is a fungal parasite which infects both fresh water and salt water fishes and appears to be passed on in food or by the eating of feces from other fishes. It may be recognizable as a bloated condition of the body, somewhat like the well known dropsy in fresh water fishes, or it may break the surface of the fish in the form of spots or ulcerations. Essentially, however, the parasite is internal and is very difficult to treat. It is stated that 250 mg of streptomycin plus 250 mg of penicillin per gallon can effect a cure. If this is true some of the wide spectrum antibiotics might also be successful.

18. EXOPHTHALMOS (POPEYE)

This condition has already been referred to when discussing copper treatment of fishes; an excess of copper may bring about popeye, particularly in clowns. It is also alleged that excessive aeration with air bubbles which are too fine can cause popeye, because the bubbles get into the blood stream and block the capillaries in the more delicate parts of the body such as in the back of the eye. This seems to be a pure fantasy and there would appear to be no foundation whatsoever for this assertion. The fact remains that the cause of popeye, unless it be copper, is usually unknown and probably varies from one example to another. It often affects one eye or one individual fish in the whole tank and sometimes subsides of its own accord. Those inclined to heroic treatment have given us accounts of piercing the back of the eye and releasing the pressure of gas or blood or whatever may be present, but this once more would seem to be an inadvisable procedure.

Sometimes either through popeye or through predation or damage a fish will loose an eye completely. This is surprisingly sometimes followed by regeneration of the eye, which may grow back to a perfectly functioning organ.

19. SAPROLEGNIA OR FUNGUS

This is a rather rare infection in the marine tank but sometimes follows damage caused by dashing into rocks or coral or by fighting. When it occurs it is rather difficult to treat and its incidence forms one of the rather rare occasions when it is in fact preferable to pick the fish out of the tank for treatment if possible. Treatment is with quite a strong solution of zinc-free malachite green or rather less preferably brilliant green. These dyes are dissolved in marine water at a strength of one in 15,000 and the fish placed in them for a 30 second period. The fungus is strongly colored by the dye and the fish may be returned to its tank, when, if a cure results, the fungus will drop off and not re-occur.

20. ARGULUS

Argulus, the sea louse, is a crustacean parasite occasionally seen on coral fishes but very frequently found on sea horses. The parasite is quite large, about a quarter inch in length and can be picked from its victim with a pair of forceps. It does not cling strongly to the sea horse which does not suffer any severe damage on its removal.

21. SHOCK

When discussing the introduction of fishes to an aquarium considerable time was given to the precautions which must be taken to avoid shock, and to avoid damage from attacks by other fishes. If these precautions are not taken and too sudden a change in salinity or even too sudden a change in pH occurs, the fish may dash wildly around the aquarium, turn upside down within a few minutes and die, or it may retire and cower in a corner of the tank and die there. Once this occurs the only hope of saving the fish is to return it rapidly to the transit water in which it arrived. There it may recover and should then be introduced more carefully into the new surroundings. Most often, however, once shock has set in there is no saving the affected fish.

22. POISONING IN TANKS

Precautions have been stressed to prevent the occurrence of poisoning, particularly of metallic poisoning in the tank. It is rather important to recognize the symptoms which may arise from such poisoning and not to mistake them for disease. If fishes look distressed, if they stop feeding or they are obviously suffering from poor balance, and no definite sign of disease can be detected, poisoning must always be suspected. If the poisoning is severe the fishes will usually start showing blotchy discoloration of their scales and skin, looking rather as if they had been rubbed

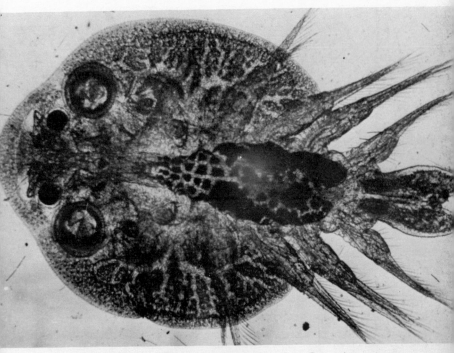

Ventral side of female fish louse, *Argulus*. Photo by Knaack.

against a rough surface so that part of the pigment had been eroded. This appearance has to be seen to be easily recognized.

The cure for poisoning is the removal of the cause. If possible, take the fishes out of the tank and place them with all transfer precautions into new surroundings with new or safe marine water and hope that they will recover. Then treat the tank in which they have been kept so as to remove the cause of the poisoning and if possible to clean up the water along the lines already indicated. At least partial renewal of the water would always be advisable. Look carefully for any source of the suspected poisoning, such as exposed metal surfaces, cracks in protective coatings, bacterial contamination of sand or decaying dead material, including fish, hidden away in the tank. Look carefully over every part of the tank and suspect all materials present such as filters and heaters of being potential sources of contamination. On the other hand don't worry about a minute amount of exposed metal surface which could not reasonably have been the cause of the trouble, and do not imagine that by covering such a spot up you will be likely to have cured the cause of the condition.

Trunk fishes like this *Lactoria cornuta* are best maintained in separate aquaria by themselves, since they occasionally release poisonous substances that can kill everything in a tank. Photo by Gerhard Marcuse.

It must always be stressed that very great care should be taken to eliminate the probability of disease before going to the trouble mentioned above. It is only if no conceivable disease can be causing the trouble that one should neglect to treat for it, at the same time looking for potential other trouble sources. It should be mentioned here that fishes sometimes poison each other. Some of the trunk fishes are good examples which, if disturbed, actually release sufficient toxic material into a tank to kill all the inhabitants including even themselves. If a trunk fish or puffer fish is present always suspect him of being a potential source of trouble. The author would prefer never to include such a specimen in a tank of mixed fish for that very reason.

Another quite frequent source of poisoning in the modern household is external to the tank itself in the form of fly sprays, new paint or even very heavy tobacco smoke. The aerator should never draw air from within a room where such contamination may occur. If fly spray is used there is no severe danger if the fish tanks in the same room are properly covered, but if the aerator is pulling air from the room into the tanks this may convey sufficient spray to cause death of the fishes. In such circumstances it is best to place the aerator in some other locality, such as beneath the house or on an outside verandah so that there is less likelihood of polluted air being used. If the house is then treated for white ants or some other infestation do not forget that your air pump down in the basement may then be an extreme source of danger, because this is the area where the treatment will probably be given.

Either in the form of smoke or shreds of tobacco, nicotine is highly toxic to fishes. It is therefore essential to see that one's hands are clean without even traces of tobacco under the fingernails when handling any part of the fish tank, and it is inadvisable to smoke while doing so. If you entertain in a room where the tanks are kept, not only must this source of contamination be guarded against, but also the unfortunate habit of thoughtless guests who drop unwanted material into the fish tanks even including martinis or cigarette butts.

Although the uninitiated often take them to be flowers, or at least vegetable in nature, anemones in reality are motile animals, among the most interesting of all invertebrates normally kept in salt-water aquaria. The anemones encamped upon the crab's shell slow the crustacean down but otherwise do no harm; in fact, a number of crab species benefit from their association with anemones that attach themselves to the crabs. Photo by Gunter Senfft.

III

Tank inhabitants

1. INVERTEBRATES

Reference has been made to the fact that a very attractive aquarium can be furnished with invertebrates even though it may be difficult to keep them together with fishes. Some care must be taken about mixing the different kinds of invertebrates since many of them feed on others. Perhaps the commonest invertebrate tank is one containing anemones of various kinds together with some crabs or shrimp and a few shell fish. Even many of the cold water anemones are quite spectacular, although few grow to as large a size as some of the tropical ones. An attraction is that many desirable specimens can be collected from cold water coast lines and do not need a heated tank in which to flourish. In fact, many of the cold water specimens present the opposite problem to their tropical counterparts, in that care must be taken in that the tank does not become overheated in summer months. It is possible to buy refrigerated tanks but a large tank in a reasonably cool situation will not need refrigeration and in an extreme it can be cooled a few degrees by placing ice cubes into plastic bags and floating them on the surface of the tank. Just as a large tank does not cool too rapidly so it will not heat up too rapidly either.

2. ANEMONES

Some anemones are plankton feeders but the majority catch large prey and sting it with the poisonous cells which are embedded in their tentacles, the nematocysts. When collecting them one must be careful not to damage the base of the anemone unduly as it is often quite difficult to pull off the rock on which it will usually be found. Fortunately the majority of anemones feed on fairly large prey and will also accept pieces of meat or fresh shrimp and do not necessarily have to catch living prey. They will either pass relatively small pieces of material down to their mouth and there ingest it, or they will fold over and actively push larger material into their mouth by active movements of the tentacles. They do not need feeding very often; once or twice weekly is sufficient, and care should be

Large, highly predacious crabs should not be kept with anemones, but many small crabs, some of which are very colorful, do no harm and can even be helpful through their scavenging activities. Photo by Gerhard Marcuse.

An opened anemone may look harmless and beautiful, but the waving tentacles carry stinging cells that spell certain death for many small creatures of the oceans. Photo by Gerhard Marcuse.

taken not to overfeed. Unwanted residues or unacceptable food will be regurgitated in the form of slimy pellets which can be removed from the aquarium with a dip tube. Other anemones feed on plankton and may be fed with newly hatched brine shrimp or by swirling a small amount of finely chopped up shrimp or similar material over their surface. The latter is a rather messy procedure which should be avoided unless absolutely necessary. Small crabs or hermit crabs kept in an anemone tank will not worry the inhabitants unduly and are useful scavengers of material neglected or rejected by the anemones.

Many anemones are live bearers and eject their young from the body cavity. These are miniatures of their parents and are at first attached to the body of the parent by a fine thread, which is eventually broken and the offspring scatter around the tank. The young can be fed on newly hatched brine shrimp or on very small pieces of dead food similar to that fed to their parents. They will fall prey to other tank inhabitants unless they are shielded from predation.

The large tropical anemones such as *Stoichactus* varieties are the hosts of a number of fishes and invertebrates, notably of different varieties of clown fish or anemone fish. These are the only types of fish that it is safe to keep in a tank containing large anemones and they make the anemone their home and actively chase away others not accepted in the community. The large specimens will often house several clown fish and there does not seem to be a necessary association of any particular species with any particular anemone. The clown fish towel themselves on the tentacles of the anemone, from which they are said to receive some degree of protection from parasitism or disease. They will even suck the tentacles into their mouths without obvious harm. Tests have apparently shown that their protection against damage by the anemone is a copious slime on the skin which may be removed by detergents, whereupon the clown fish is stung and killed by the anemone as are most other species of fish. It is doubtful what benefit the anemone derives from the fish. Some assert that the droppings of the fish are food for the anemone, others that the fish lure different species of fish to become the prey of the anemone, but this latter assertion seems very unlikely since the clown fishes are typically seen to be very active in defending their possession of the anemone and drive other fishes away. It has even been asserted that some of the clown fishes feed their anemone by taking pieces of food and purposefully dropping it on the tentacles. Whatever benefit the anemone may derive from the fishes, there is little doubt of that which the fishes derive from the anemone themselves, simple protection. However other than clown fish, various species of *Dascyllus* are also seen in nature to frequent giant anemones, from whose attack they appear to be immune. The sting of a giant anemone is quite perceptible to the human hand, although it is not exactly painful it can be felt as a prickling and stinging sensation.

A tank of giant anemones and clown fishes is a very attractive sight, but one which few of us are able to maintain successfully for any length of time. The fish cannot be treated by the most successful remedies if they fall sick, which they unfortunately do despite the presence of the anemone, and the anemone is liable to die and to foul the tank before its death has been detected. Despite this many feel it to be worth a try and get great enjoyment from the spectacle as long as it lasts.

3. LIVING CORAL

The keeping of living coral is another ambition of the advanced aquarist and it is not as difficult as many try to make out. The most successful type of coral for this purpose seems to be that containing single or very large polyps rather than the commoner types which are constituted with a multibranch system of connecting small polyps. Thus, specimens of so-called mushroom coral, each of which consists of a single polyp inhabiting a plate of coral up to several inches in diameter, can be removed from the sea bed without damage, and form the best type to try to keep initially. Some of the attractive branch corals such as the staghorn are

Momentarily safe from its enemies, this clown fish nestles comfortably within the tentacles of its host anemone. Photo by Klaus Paysan.

85.00

much harder to manage because they must almost certainly be broken off and death of the connecting system may commence at the point of breakage. Many corals fluoresce in ultra-violet light, and this can be used to set up a beautiful looking display such as is seen in the aquarium in Noumea. It is an interesting demonstration that, contrary to popular belief, ultra-violet light can penetrate many feet of water, because the corals deep in large tanks fluoresce when the light is turned on.

This profusion of different types of coral (photographed in shallow waters off the Maldive Islands) provided refuge and food for many small fishes and invertebrates. Photo by Scheer.

All corals, even those with large polyps, feed upon very small organisms. Some at least can be successfully fed with newly hatched brine shrimp, others with a dusting of fine dry food. Material like newly hatched brine shrimp should be preferred as it does not foul the water when unconsumed. It should be remembered that when any substantial amount of living coral flourishes it will be extracting lime from the sea water in order to build its skeleton, and for this reason alone coral requires frequent partial changes of water. It also seems to appreciate frequent fresh water apart from this and so the invertebrate tank containing corals should only be undertaken if a reasonable rate of change is possible. Some corals come out at night, but others, like some anemones, have symbiotic algae in their tissue; these algae help feed the coral and need intense lighting to flourish.

Many small fishes such as this cardinal fish, *Apogon fasciatus*, are heavily dependent upon coral growths to provide refuge from their enemies; maintained in aquaria, species like this are unhappy unless provided with coral or something similar in which to hide. Photo by Klaus Paysan.

This close-up of a gorgonian coral shows the polyps partially extended. Unlike the hard corals, gorgonians are daytime feeders. Photo by Robert P. L. Straughan.

87.00

Although corals do have a stinging action this is not usually particularly intense and fishes are not worried by them. However, it is a mistake to introduce fish with living coral because they will pick at it and not only spoil the scenery but also start to kill it. Even other invertebrates such as crabs and prawns feed on coral so that a coral tank should contain only such other creatures as are going to be harmless to the main exhibit. These are the algae-eating shellfish and any quite tiny crabs, worms, etc., unlikely to do significant harm. They can also be kept very elegantly with sea horses which will not worry them and which if of a small variety will feed on the brine shrimp or other plankton as will the corals themselves. Good aeration should be maintained as the coral flourishes where the sea is particularly well oxygenated.

4. WORMS

There are two types of marine worms of especial interest to the aquarist, those which inhabit tubes made of sand or shells and therefore remain in the same position, and those which live under rocks or in sand which to some extent they help to keep clean.

Sabella, a common tube worm, is quite beautiful, emerging from its tube when undisturbed as a large fan looking more like a flower than an

Tube worms, often mistaken for small anemones, are interesting invertebrate additions to the marine tank, although they cannot be maintained for long if kept in the presence of fishes, which soon eat them. The "feathers" protruding from the head end of these worms are part of the animals' gill structures. Photo by Robert P. L. Straughan.

animal. The flower is in fact a mass of tentacles which collect plankton and other small edible material much as do those of the anemone. The main trouble in keeping sabellid worms is feeding them, but this difficulty is fairly readily overcome with the use of newly hatched brine shrimp. *Sabella* is very sensitive to sudden changes in light or sudden movement or jarring of the aquarium, and leaps back into the tube so quickly that the eye cannot follow the motion. This capacity doubtless helps it to avoid being eaten by fish in its natural environment, but regrettably in a tank containing fishes it does not go on avoiding them successfully enough and must therefore be kept on its own.

Various worms which live for the most part out of sight in the sand or under rocks are not very exciting as tank inhabitants because one so rarely sees them. They do not usually live long in a tank with fishes but they flourish quite well when kept on their own. There is however the danger of a large worm dying and polluting the tank. Some of these worms such as *Nereis* can inflict quite unpleasant bites and should be handled with care. They feed on decaying material. Some of them feed by ingesting the sand itself and getting what nourishment they can from the organic material it contains. One quite large worm, the so called sea mouse (*Aphrodite*) of the northern hemisphere is about the size its name suggests, quite fat and covered by iridescent hairs, a very attractive creature.

5. SEA SQUIRTS AND SPONGES

These are quite different creatures, but are coupled under the same heading because they are part of the encrustment which normally covers rocks in medium to shallow water and should be removed together with the portion of the rock on which they are found. The sea squirts come in a variety of species and size but share the same common habit of squirting sea water into the air when they are disturbed at low tide. They are good filters for marine water, living by extracting plankton and small particulate material from it. Their capacity to live in the aquarium varies from one species to another and it is not possible to generalize without the knowledge of the particular species available in each aquarist's locality. These creatures are rarely available commercially but are extremely plentiful along most coast lines. It is better to experiment with small ones since a large specimen dying in the tank can cause a lot of trouble.

Sponges are a very lowly order of animal life but can form beautiful additions to the salt water aquarium. They vary just as do the sea squirts in their ability to live for any great period and it must always be remembered that there is a natural life span to any of these organisms, and that in the case of the smaller encrusting sponges found in tide pools, this natural span may be quite short. The sponges come in all colors, some of them being a vivid orange, violet or even snowy white. Small specimens which

Sea squirts are interesting, and many are colorful, but they are very rarely offered for sale because of their relative unpopularity. Photo by Holzhammer.

can be removed in their entirety on a segment of rock are the most likely to flourish and if in the right conditions will grow quite rapidly. Some of these sponges are soft and others are silicious, meaning that they have hard spicules of silica which gives them a rough gritty texture. Sometimes a sponge will grow surprisingly in the tank and even spread rather alarmingly over the rock surfaces. However, it is more usual for it to decline rather than to flourish, unless amply supplied with clear oxygenated water and with food, again small particulate matter and plankton which they require for their sustenance. Sponges, like sea squirts, live by circulating the water through themselves and extracting nourishment from it.

6. MOLLUSKS

The so called univalve mollusks which comprise periwinkles, cone shells and various other snail-like marine creatures can be quite decorative in the aquarium, but should be included with caution since they all feed on other tank inhabitants, either vegetable or animal. Those like the limpet, which sits in a constant position on the rock and makes algae-eating expeditions from it at night will strip the aquarium of any growing algae in a very short time. Others like the whelk are carnivorous and bore through the shells of other mollusks and consume them. A few of the univalves per tank is clearly the most that can be accommodated.

The whelk (right) is an actively predatory univalve mollusk, whereas the marine snails shown below are harmless; univalves have their greatest degree of representation in marine aquaria through their shells, which are used for decoration and as prospective homes for hermit crabs. Photo of whelk by Doris Whitney; snails by New York Zoological Society.

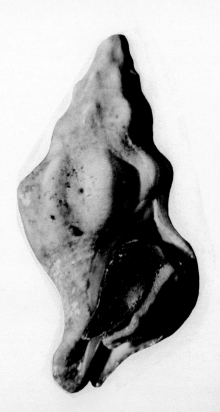

The bivalve mollusks, such as the oyster and the mussel, are filter feeders and do far less harm. The only problem is, as with the corals and sponges, to keep them adequately fed. There are sessile bivalves adhering to the rock surface for the whole of their lives after once having settled down from a motile larval stage. Other mollusks such as the scallop move around. The scallop is difficult to keep because it is also a plankton feeder but is well worth studying for as long as it will live since it is quite an evolutionarily advanced type of mollusk. Many species are also very colorful and can move around with a clapping motion of the shell, propelling themselves through the water at considerable speed. The scallop also has eyes placed around the edge of the fleshy material (mantle) just inside the shell. In addition to the eyes the scallop commonly has tentacles which

Bivalve mollusks like mussels and clams are hard to maintain, and if they die they can easily foul the tank; in or out of the aquarium, a bivalve's major enemy is the starfish, shown here preying on the mollusks. Photo by Gunter Senfft.

Scallops are less at the mercy of starfish than other bivalve mollusks, since they can move through the water and escape the comparatively slow-moving echinoderms. Photo by Dr. Herbert R. Axelrod.

protrude from between the valves of the shell. Although the eyes of the scallop are quite well organized, each having a lens and a retina, they do not appear to give the scallop a particularly clear picture of what goes on around it and it normally only reacts to changes in light and dark, i.e. shadows falling across it and warning it of a potential enemy.

All of the bivalve mollusks are characterized by a strong adductor muscle which enables them to close the two valves of their shell tightly against the elements or against a predator. However, the starfish can usually tire them by wrapping itself around them and pulling steadily against the adductor muscle until the bivalve opens its shell sufficiently for the starfish to insert its stomach. The everted stomach then pours gastric juices into the unfortunate mollusk, feeds upon it, and is then withdrawn again into the starfish. Lesson: One does not keep starfish and bivalve mollusks together with too great success.

It comes as a surprise to most of us to learn that the squids and octopuses are mollusks. Their shell is embedded inside their fleshy bodies and no longer performs the protecting function. The octopus has eight arms as its name suggests, whereas the squids and cuttlefish have 10 arms. Small specimens of either can be kept in an invertebrate tank, or preferably in a tank on their own, for considerable periods if the following precautions are taken. The tank must be very tightly closed or the octopus or squid is liable to escape by squeezing through even a quite small aperture. The tank must also be very well oxygenated and the creature must be supplied with food. This is for most species crabs or other crustacea. Many species of octopus are poisonous and some are capable of inflicting fatal bites. One of the most beautiful and attractive small octopus of the Pacific coast line is deadly. They should therefore be handled with considerable caution.

Although a number of octopuses can be kept in a tank together they are liable to fight and to disturb each other sufficiently to stimulate the ejection of the so-called ink which these mollusks are capable of releasing into the water. The ink is not only very murky but also poisonous and liable to kill off any other creatures present in the tank. Cuttle fish are in general less of a nuisance in this direction and are also less liable to climb out of the tank.

The cephalopods make truly fascinating aquarium exhibits and are considered to be among the most intelligent of all marine life, but all are hard to keep and dangerous to other animals in their tank. The cuttle fish shown is *Sepia officinalis*. Photo by Gerhard Marcuse.

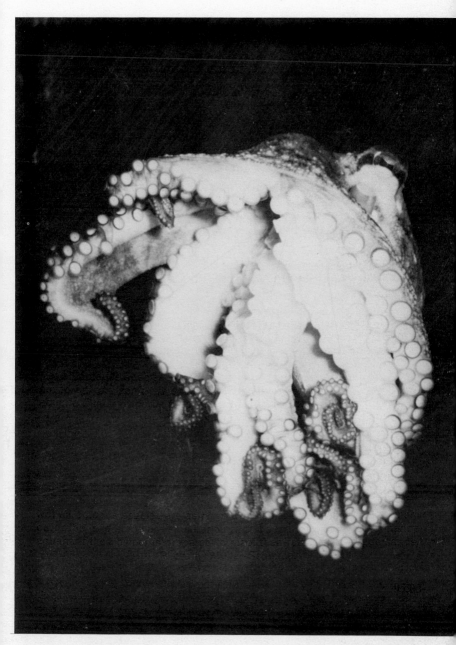

Not all octopus species are as large as popular imagination makes them out to be, and some are small enough to be maintained in home marine aquaria if their owner is prepared to meet their rather exacting demands. Photo by Muller-Schmida.

95.00

As these mollusks are rather dirty feeders and need good oxygenation, and because of their liability to release their ink it must be clear that their tank should be provided with strong adequate filtration with plenty of activated carbon to counteract their tendency to foul the water. Even so, do not in general expect them to live for very long.

In contrast to their land counterparts some of the sea slugs are outstandingly beautiful. Some are free swimming in the water and are particularly brightly colored and very often of a fairy-like diaphanous appearance which is to be seen to be believed. It is unfortunate that the more beautiful they are the more difficult they seem to be to keep and the more peculiar their feeding habits seem to be. Perhaps the most specialized feeder is the blue colored free swimming *Glaucus* which preys upon the blue bottle (a relative of the Portugese man of war) and feeds upon it. It is worth keeping some of these colorful creatures in the tank for the few weeks that they are likely to survive. Unfortunately they cannot be expected to live for any great length of time.

7. CRUSTACEANS

Crustacea of various kinds can adorn the invertebrate aquarium and can include the sessile forms, the various barnacles. The barnacle com-

Crabs are among the most adaptable of all invertebrates to life in a salt-water aquarium, but as a rule it is best to keep only small crabs and avoid large specimens, which are harder to keep and can do extensive damage. Photo by Hilmar Hansen.

Small hermit crabs are excellent scavengers for the marine aquarium, and they are often more interesting than fishes; they also are among the least expensive, hardiest and most easily available of all desirable marine invertebrates. Photos by Gerhard Marcuse.

mences life as a free swimming larval crustacean but settles down early on to the surface of a rock (or the hull of a ship) where it surrounds itself with a shell and from which it fishes with its feet. The legs of the barnacle project through an aperture at the top of its shell and actively sweep the water for small edible material. The commonest form of barnacle suitable for the aquarium is the acorn barnacle, often found encrusting rocks around the tide pools. It may also be found on the shells of mollusks and even on the shells of crabs or other living crustacea.

Crabs and shrimps or prawns of various kinds, even up to small lobsters, can be kept very easily in the marine tank, but the bigger they are the more nuisance they will be and the more destructive they will be, particularly the crabs. These will pick at algae, sponges, corals and even at small mollusks and gradually make a mess of a great deal of the tank if they are large enough to do so. It is advisable to include only a few small crabs or the scenery will suffer too much and the tank may become foul. The hermit crab has a soft body which it protects by inserting it into the empty shell of a univalve mollusk, but large ones cause just as much trouble as do their more normal cousins. Shrimps and prawns, particularly some of the tropical varieties, can be quite ornate and colorful and do not cause

Coral shrimp are more colorful than most other marine crustaceans available to hobbyists, and their interesting habits have made them popular. Photo by Hilmar Hansen.

Another interesting marine crustacean is the mantis shrimp, so named because of its resemblance to the terrestrial praying mantis. Mantis shrimps are active predators and can easily kill small fishes that they can catch. Photo by Gerhard Marcuse.

as much trouble as crabs. They are rather delicate feeders and are quite happy picking away at a small portion of fish or meat which can be left in the aquarium for them to feed on at leisure. Some of the prawns, out-standingly the pistol prawn, snap their claws in a quite alarming manner suggesting that the glass face of the aquarium has cracked. This is a form of defense.

8. ECHINODERMS

The echinoderms comprise the sea urchins, starfish and sea cucumbers amongst others, all of which are rather difficult tank inhabitants. We have already seen how the starfish feeds on bivalve mollusks. Other types of starfish, the brittle stars and feather stars, are feeders upon detritus or filter the sand and can be kept somewhat more successfully. The only trouble is that most of them are found under rocks or under the sand and tend to remain out of sight. The ordinary starfishes are quite slow in motion and move along the sand or glass of the tank with the aid of tube feet, of which many are normally present on the undersurface of the creature. The brittle stars however can be quite lively and move by pushing themselves around with their long slender arms. Some species do this quite quickly. Their main disadvantage is as their name suggests, their great liability to break up into fragments and it may be quite hard to collect intact specimens.

Sea urchins of various types are detritus feeders, passing sand through their bodies and extracting what they can. They also move by the aid of quite long tube feet which extend between their spines and are used to pull them over the sea bed. Some of them also have quite actively moving spines which are an alternative form of locomotion. In common with

This starfish's position on the aquarium glass provides an excellent view of its tube feet, which the starfish uses for locomotion. Photo by Dr. Herbert R. Axelrod.

Sea urchins usually do not live long in the marine aquarium, mainly because they are hard to feed. Photo by Holzhammer.

many detritus feeders it is difficult to keep them for very long in an aquarium because insufficient food is available to them. If an attempt is made to supply sufficient food it is liable to cause the tank to become foul.

Sea cucumbers are even worse than the starfish and sea urchins, and are even capable of exuding toxins. It is not worth risking their presence in the invertebrate tank.

The above is a very incomplete survey of some of the commonest types of creatures which may be included in the invertebrate tank. It will be seen that many of them are detritus feeders or plankton feeders and that their adequate nourishment depends upon the water containing sufficient of such material to supply them. The tank containing corals, mollusks, sea squirts should really have sufficient plankton to make the water quite cloudy, at any rate during the feeding period. This cloudiness will rapidly clear up as the inhabitants filter out their nourishment. Not all of them can depend on brine shrimp—some need small plankton or particulate matter. If the tank contains a reasonably but not too large population of rather messy feeders such as crabs, some degree of balance can be maintained since the crab in picking away at its feed tends to scatter particles all over the place and these in turn will be filtered off by the filter feeders. Generally speaking, however, the balance is difficult to maintain, but must be attempted in the absence of the constant artificial filtration that is used in the fish tank. Only experimentation can really guide the aquarist into achieving a suitable balance with the types of creatures available to him. Thus a very beautiful invertebrate set-up can be achieved at the start but it may prove extremely difficult to maintain for any length of time. Greater success can generally be achieved by severely limiting the variety of creatures present in the tank, so that a tank containing only algae and corals with perhaps a few sabellid worms or a tank containing algae and anemones and a few small crabs is more likely to be a success than one with a greater mixture.

9. FISHES

First a few words about the names of fishes. The scientific name of a fish normally consists of two words. The first, which starts with a capital letter, gives the genus to which the fish belongs. A genus is a group of fishes containing one or more species which are closely related to each other. The second part of the scientific name indicates the particular species of fish within the genus and this normally has a small letter to begin with, not, as often mistakenly printed, a capital letter, even if the specific name is that of a person or country. Finally the whole of this scientific name is normally written in italics and is followed by the name of the ichthyologist who first identified and named the species. Thus *Ostracion lentiginosum* (Bloch) is a trunk fish of the genus *Ostracion* species *lentiginosum*, first named by Dr. Bloch. Sometimes there will be three words in the scientific name, usually because a species has been split up by subsequent investigation into sub-species and instead of renaming, an additional indication has been added to the scientific name to differentiate the sub-species. If a particular fish is not fully identified one can write *Ostracion* sp. —meaning of unknown species, or even just *Ostracion*.

It is usually preferable to use the scientific name of the fish where possible, because the fish is then completely identified and there should be no ambiguity about which particular fish is being discussed. However nobody, even including ichthyologists, is perfect, and sometimes the same fish has been separately named by different authors; even the same fish caught in different localities has been known to be re-named as a different species by the same author. There is thus unfortunately still room for confusion, but we minimize this by using the scientific name and then if necessary giving a list of synonyms from the literature. When the scientific name is used or the generic name, such as *Dascyllus*, meaning the general group of fishes in the genus *Dascyllus*, it should not be preceded by the word "the." Do not write or say "the *Dascyllus* should be kept at a temperature of 75°F", simply "*Dascyllus* should be kept at a temperature of 75°" or one could say "the genus *Dascyllus*. . . ." Thus although it is correct to say "the Moorish idol" one does not say "the *Zanclus canescens*."

Genera of fishes are collected up into families which are collections of similar genera. Thus the family Pomacentridae or Damsel fishes comprise several genera including *Abudefduf*, *Chromis*, *Dascyllus*, *Pomacentrus* and some others. These are all somewhat alike in characteristics but contain groups with sufficient difference from one another to be included in individual genera. In the next section the characteristics of some of the most popular families will be considered, with remarks on their suitability for aquarium life and on the varieties seen within a family.

10. FAMILIES OF FISHES

Holocentridae

This is the family of squirrel fish found in most warm oceans of the world. They are large eyed stocky fishes frequently red in color and rather nervous in disposition. Many of them only grow to 6″ or 8″ in size and are therefore quite suitable for the larger size of marine tank even as adults. If captured as young specimens they will normally acclimatize fairly readily to the aquarium. They are of timid disposition, and omnivorous eaters, but will not harm other fishes unless they are small enough to be swallowed whole.

A squirrelfish *(Adioryx diadema)* of the family Holocentridae. Photo by Dr. Herbert R. Axelrod.

Monacanthidae

This family comprises the file fishes which much resemble the trigger fishes to which we shall come later. The file fish are so called because they have a hard abrasive skin which has actually been used as a file. These are small fishes very suitable in a mixed tank of fish, but are rather

Filefish of the genus *Monacanthus*, family Monacanthidae. Photo by G. Senfft.

difficult to keep. They will eat all kinds of food but need a fair amount of vegetable in their diet to flourish. Freeze-dried Tubifex with chlorella is ideal.

Ostraciidae

This is the family of trunk fishes or box fishes which mostly have a hard box-like shell formed of fused scales covering almost the entire body. Some are protected by spines as well as by this hard shell. The trunk fishes are often attractive and brightly colored, but they should be viewed with considerable suspicion as tank mates for some other species as at

Tetrasomus species, family Ostraciidae. Photo by G. Marcuse.

Diodon hystrix, family Diodontidae, showing puffed condition and erected spines. Photo by New York Zoological Society.

105.00

least some of them are capable of releasing poison into the aquarium when they are disturbed. This substance is of unknown composition and oddly enough sometimes kills not only all the other tank inhabitants but also the trunk fish itself. The fish may have been living quite harmlessly in the aquarium for weeks or months and then it is scared, perhaps by an attempt to catch it or one of its tank mates, and the damage is done. When catching trunk fish it can be fatal to put them in a container with others since from the same cause the whole lot will be dead within a few minutes. The family Diodontidae is related to the trunk fishes and contains the porcupine fishes which should be regarded with similar suspicion.

Chaetodontidae

This is a very large family comprising the butterfly and angel fishes, and containing some of the most beautiful fishes to be found in the ocean. The butterfly fishes, or chaetodons, are laterally compressed disc-shaped fishes which do not usually grow very large and are most desirable tank inhabitants. Unfortunately they vary in their capacity to survive in an aquarium and some of the most beautiful are also the most delicate. Food is often a problem and it may be necessary to supply them with live food, coral or coralline at least at first to get them acclimatized to tank life. The

Below: *Chaetodon larvatus*; right, *Chaetodon collare*, both species members of the family Chaetodontidae. Photo of *C. larvatus* by Gerhard Marcuse, *C. collare* by Klaus Paysan.

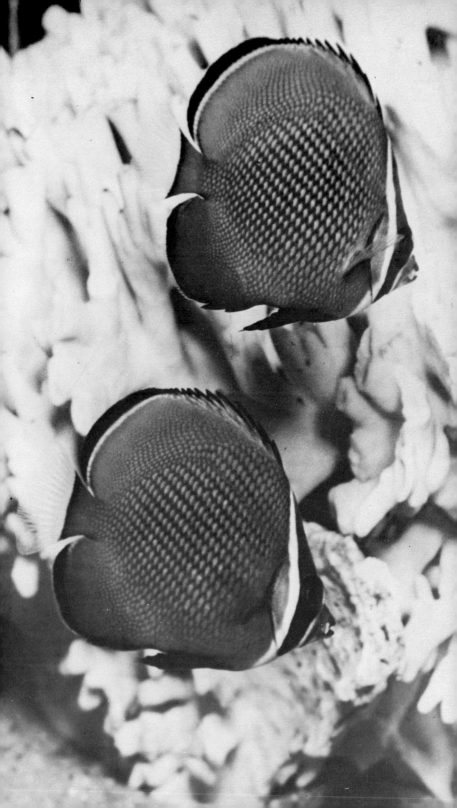

Chaetodon guttatissimus. Photo by Klaus Paysan.

weapon of the chaetodon is its spiny dorsal fin and it is quite prepared to use it for attack. Fortunately, chaetodons are not usually aggressive except to members of their own species and even then they usually settle down without too much trouble and without extensive damage.

Fortunately chaetodons are not usually attacked by other fishes and so they form good community tank members. It seems to be the general experience that chaetodons do best at a rather high temperature, at say about 80°F, a high salinity of not less than 1.025, and with sparklingly clear well-oxygenated water. Small specimens die quicker than bigger ones and the best chance of acclimatizing them seems to occur with specimens about 2″ in length, which are small enough to be adaptable and to learn to eat new foods and large enough to survive tank conditions. Chaetodons recommended to the beginner are *Chaetodon auriga, Chaetodon kleini, Chaetodon ephippium* and *Chaetodon vagabundus. Chaetodon trifasciatus, Chaetodon triangulum, Chaetodon plebeus, Chaetodon melanotus,* and *Chaetodon citrinellus* are fishes which are not recommended to the beginner and seem to be particularly difficult to keep.

The angel fishes are heavier bodied than their cousins the chaetodons. They have more character and get to know their owner and even come up to feed from his fingers or to have their backs scratched. They also tend to grow rather large but can be kept down to a reasonable size with restricted feeding. They vary in hardiness but generally speaking a reasonably large angel fish of say 4"–6" in length will settle down and live quite well if in a big enough tank. Smaller specimens sometimes give trouble, perhaps the hardest to keep for any length of time being *Centropyge bicolor*, an otherwise very desirable fish. Angel fish fight members of their own species unless there is a big discrepancy in size. A tank of angel fishes should therefore consist of different species which will then live relatively peacefully together after perhaps a settling down period. These fishes have a very sharp spine on the gill plate and their owner will discover it for himself if he does not handle them carefully. They can do considerable damage to one another with this weapon. Many of them flourish only if generously provided with a vegetable diet, and they readily eat frozen lettuce.

Antennariidae

These are the frog fishes, sometimes called fishing frogs, which are hardy and very interesting in the aquarium but fatal to anything they can swallow. The very flexible spine towards the front of the fish carries a bait which in some species actively wriggles, but in others is just waved towards the predator which is being stalked and is then swallowed in one gulp as it approaches to take the bait. Frog fishes will even swallow each other and so a tank of them should not only be on their own but contain specimens of much the same size.

Antennarius species, family Antennariidae. Photo by Gunter Senfft.

Zanclidae

The family of Moorish idols which includes the magnificent species *Zanclus canescens*. This is one of the most attractive aquarium fishes and unfortunately one of the most difficult to keep. The Moorish idol tends to ship badly and if it arrives in poor condition there is not much hope that it will survive for more than a few days. However, even when it arrives in good condition and eats straight away it has the most unfortunate habit of dying quite without warning and leaving its puzzled owner considerably out of pocket. Not a fish to be kept by the amateur or anyone who cannot afford to lose it.

Zanclus canescens, family Zanclidae. Photo by Rodney Jonklaas.

Balistidae

These are the trigger fishes, odd looking yet very attractive and often brightly colored. Unfortunately large specimens tend to be pugnacious and to attack and damage or kill their tank mates. Small specimens are attractive and relatively harmless but unfortunately they do not stay small. The trigger fish's weapons are two-fold: the dorsal trigger or spine after which he is named which can do a lot of damage, and his sharp teeth which can do even more. Really large trigger fish such as *Balistoides*

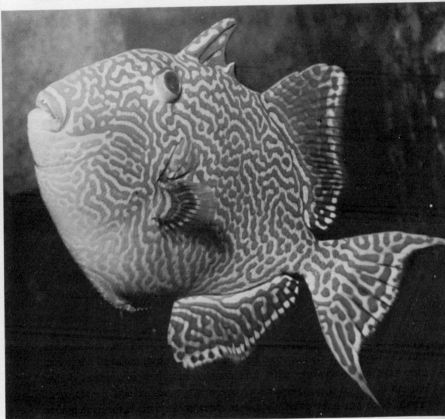

Pseudobalistes fuscus, family Balistidae. Photo by Miloslav Kocar.

conspicillum can form a beautiful exhibit singly in individual tanks, but care must be taken to protect air lines and electrical equipment which they will bite through with one crunch and either suffocate or electrocute themselves! The larger triggers seem to have their own views on the arrangement of their tank contents and rarely leave coral and rocks alone.

111.00

Amphiprion ephippium, family Pomacentridae. Photo by Klaus Paysan.

Pomacentridae

The family Pomacentridae is a very important family for the marine hobbyist, since it includes two of the most popular groups of salt-water fishes, the clown fishes and the damsel fishes. The clown fish species have perhaps lured more people into keeping salt water fishes than any other single family. These are the brightly colored, relatively small fishes living in association with tropical anemones. They are quite hardy and can live perfectly well without the anemones, but curiously enough the most commonly known and popular species, *Amphiprion percula*, is not by any means the easiest to keep. It is rather readily attacked by disease, tends to fight and to fade away rather easily. A very tough robust and beautiful clown is *Amphiprion ephippium*, which has set up a record in the author's tanks by living for $4\frac{1}{2}$ years. Despite their general hardiness, the clown fishes seem to be more liable than any other types

Chromis caerulea, family Pomacentridae. Photo by Klaus Paysan.

Dischistodus prosopotaenia, family Pomacentridae. Photo by Muller-Schmida.

113.00

Dascyllus trimaculatus, family Pomacentridae. Photo by Gerhard Marcuse.

to succumb to velvet disease, and may be used as indicators in a community tank that trouble is commencing. Treatment with copper is normally successful but the clowns are again one of the most susceptible families as far as copper poisoning itself is concerned, and again can be used as indicators of overdosage. Chronic overdosage in the clown fish causes popeye.

The damsel fishes are small and hardy, with many brilliantly colored varieties, and are perhaps the best type of fish for the amateur. They will eat anything. They are rather pugnacious, and in a few species even vicious, yet they may be kept successfully as a shoal. One or two dozen of the same species of damsel fish do better in a tank than a collection of odd specimens, and when there is a shoal of them individual fighting seems to be reduced.

Scaridae

The parrot fishes are allied to the wrasses but have a more pugnacious disposition and tend to become a pest in the aquarium. This is a pity because they contain some very beautiful species and are hardy and easy to keep and feed.

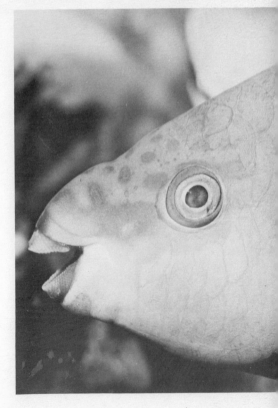

Above: *Scarus* sp.,
family Scaridae.
Right: Closeup of
head of parrot fish,
showing elaborate
dentition. Photos by
Gerhard Marcuse.

Canthigaster valentini, family Canthigasteridae. Photo by Gerhard Marcuse.

Canthigasteridae

These are the so called sharp-nosed puffer fishes, resembling the trunk fishes in body form but without the hard outer covering. They can also blow themselves up with air or water as the case may be when disturbed. They share with the trunk fishes, at least in some species, the capacity to poison other tank inhabitants and for this reason should be viewed with some caution.

Tetraodontidae

This family resembles the foregoing and contains the blow fishes which can also blow themselves up with air or water. They are poisonous to eat unless carefully prepared by someone who knows how to cook them, but they do not seem to be liable to poison the whole tank as do the Canthigasteridae.

Arothron reticularis, family Tetraodontidae. Photo by Gerhard Marcuse.

Canthigaster bennetti, family Canthigasteridae. Photo by Muller-Schmida.

Labridae

This family comprises the wrasses, another large group of fishes distributed throughout the world in tropical waters. Many of them burrow into the sand and may have trouble acclimatizing in its absence. Otherwise they are mostly reasonably hardy and harmless and contain some beautiful fishes. They are omnivorous and in general easy to keep. Some of the wrasses, the so called cleaner wrasses, as do some of the chaetodons, pick parasites from other fishes and can perform a useful task in the aquarium.

Thalassoma bifasciatus, family Labridae. Photo by Gerhard Marcuse.

Platacidae

This is the family of bat fishes, very fast growing rather intelligent and attractive fishes whose main drawback is that they do grow so fast. They are otherwise hardy, not particularly belligerent and attractive members of the community tank.

Platax orbicularis, family Platacidae. Photo by Gerhard Budich.

119.00

Brachirus zebra, family Scorpaenidae.

Scorpaena porcus, family Scorpaenidae. Photo by Gerhard Marcuse.

Scorpaenidae

These are the scorpion fishes or lion fishes, often called butterfly cod or zebra fishes. They are mostly hardy, attractive predators, harmless to other fishes unless these are small enough to be swallowed, whereupon they will be. Members of the family are characteristically provided with poisonous dorsal spines and must be handled with care. However, they rarely seem to cause trouble to other fish of large enough size.

Thus the scorpion fish may be a member of a community tank containing other large fishes as long as he is not crowded and is adequately fed. The food must usually be small live fish to begin with, but most species rapidly learn to swallow strips of dead fish or pieces of freeze-dried Tubifex.

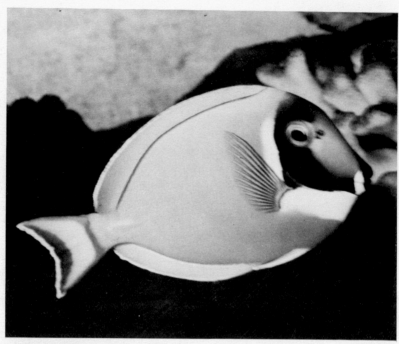

Acanthurus leucosternon, family Acanthuridae. Photo by Miloslav Kocar.

Naso brevirostris, family Acanthuridae. Photo by Gerhard Marcuse.

122.00

Zebrasoma scopas, family Acanthuridae. Photo by G. Marcuse.

Acanthuridae

Tangs or surgeon fishes are a group of fishes which tend to grow rather large, but some members of which are very beautiful in their juvenile stages. They are predominantly algae feeders, and must be given plenty of vegetable food to flourish. They are relatively peaceful and good community fishes although they are provided with a spine at the base of the tail which may be used as a weapon, even against their owner. Some of the best of the tangs tend to be rather expensive and rather delicate and therefore not for the amateur.

123.00

Hippocampus species, family Syngnathidae. Photo by Mildred D. Bellomy.

Syngnathidae

These are the sea horses and pipe fishes. They are attractive fishes which almost all marine aquarists feel they must keep at some stage or another. They should be kept on their own or with fish such as the lion fish which will not compete with them for food, as long as they themselves are too big to be swallowed. The reason is that sea horses and pipe fish are slow feeders and cannot compete successfully for food in the presence of other voracious fishes. They are quite harmless and most attractive in the salt water tank. The small pipe fish and the dwarf sea horses and juvenile members of other species should be fed on newly hatched brine shrimp, but larger members require mosquitoe larvae, daphnia, or better still large varieties of marine plankton. The sea horse is one of the few varieties of marine fish which has been bred in the marine aquarium. The male has a pouch into which the female deposits her eggs, and eventually he releases dozens or even hundreds of miniature replicas of himself into the water. These are immediately free-swimming and take up an independent existence.

124.00

This male sea horse's pouch has opened to allow the escape of young sea horses, a number of which can be seen swimming feebly around their father. Photo by Marine Studios.

Gobiosoma oceanops, family Gobiidae. Photo by Hilmar Hansen, Aquarium, Berlin.

Gobiidae

The Gobies are almost universally distributed, some inhabiting fresh water, They are bottom living, relatively lazy fishes not containing many members of outstanding color or appearance. They are not particularly pugnacious except perhaps sometimes to one another and are rather droll and interesting additions to a community tank.

Mullidae

Various members of the goatfish family are quite brightly colored yellow, greens, or reds and small usually juvenile specimens can look quite attractive in the aquarium. However, they are nervous and tend to dig up the sand and do not usually live outstandingly well.

Various other families of fish which will not be dealt with individually will be mentioned in the text of this volume, but they do not merit individual discussion. Most of them are of medium desirability from the point of hardiness and general suitability for community life, and none comprise particularly important genera.

11. PURCHASING FISHES

When you buy a fish, look for the following points:

(a) It should be breathing slowly and regularly, with steady unexaggerated gill movements and a half-closed mouth. Never accept a fish that is respiring rapidly or gulping water in any way.

(b) It should be swimming evenly in the water, with expanded fins and proper balance. However, it should not have rigidly extended fins, particularly not the dorsal fin, as this may be a sign of impending demise.

(c) Its color should be good, but not extreme for the species. Fishes that are brightly colored with a darkish hue over the body are often about to die.

(d) It must be eating. Ask the dealer to offer some food to the tank and see that the fish you intend to purchase takes some of it.

(e) It must be full-bodied. Never accept a fish with a hollow belly. It is on the way to fish heaven.

(f) Not only the fish you want, but every fish in the tank must be free of any obvious disease or distress. Distrust any fish from a tank containing suspect tankmates, and be prepared to quarantine it strictly for several weeks.

(g) It is not necessarily unwise to buy fishes newly received by your dealer. If he is not a first class marine aquarist, you may care for the fishes better than he can, and the sooner you get them the better. However, be aware of the situation, and treat for disease by giving a mild copper treatment rather than waiting fot it to appear.

IV

Alphabetical catalogue of fishes

Abalistes stellaris (Bloch and Schneider)

COMMON NAME: Flat-tailed Trigger Fish, Varken-vis.
PHOTOGRAPHED BY: Dr. Herbert R. Axelrod of a 9-inch specimen from Ceylon.
RANGE: Australia through the East Indies.
PREVIOUS SCIENTIFIC NAMES: *Balistes stellaris*.
MERISTIC CHARACTERISTICS: D.III, 27; A. 24–25. Grows to about 2 feet.

The genus *Abalistes* differs from other triggers by the shape of the caudal peduncle. When viewed from above, the caudal peduncle is flattened and it is thicker than it is high.

This is a very variable species as far as coloration is concerned. The Flat-tailed Trigger changes color pattern as it grows, but the three white blotches on the back are very typical, as is the light blotch at the caudal peduncle where the soft dorsal ends.

129.00

Photo by Dr. Gerald R. Allen.

Abudefduf amabilis (De Vis)*

Common Name: Orange Devil.
Range: Philippines, Japan, Micronesia and Polynesia to Australia.
Previous Scientific Names: *Glyphisodon amabilis, Glyphidodon brownriggii* var. *xanthozona*.
Meristic Characteristics: D. XIII, 12-13; A. II, 12-13; 19 tubes in upper section of the lateral line followed by 2-3 irregular pores; pores in straight section 8 + 1-3; 3 scales above lateral line.

As with most devils, this beauty requires that it be kept with fishes its own size or larger. Their color may vary in intensity with the environment, as they prefer to dart in and out of small coral crevices. Decorate their aquaria with as much living coral as possible; dried, clean coral is a suitable substitute. Plastic imitation coral is acceptable.

This fish is a good feeder. Supply them with canned Norwegian brine shrimp (*Calanus*), supplemented with freeze dried tubifex and brine shrimp. They need some vegetable matter in their diet, especially chlorella. Freeze dried tubifex worms with chlorella algae is available at most petshops. Give lettuce if this is not available but be careful not to pollute the aquarium.

* Now called *Abudefduf leucopomus* (Lesson).

Abudefduf aureus (Cuvier)

COMMON NAMES: Golden Devil; Golden Damsel.

RANGE: Indo-Australian Archipelago and tropical West Pacific as far east as Fiji and the Marshall Islands.

PREVIOUS SCIENTIFIC NAMES: *Glyphisodon aureus, Glyphidodon aureus, Glyphidodon (Amblyglyphidodon) aureus, Amblyglyphidodon aureus.*

MERISTIC CHARACTERISTICS: D. XIII, 12-14; A. II, 14 or 15; pectoral rays 17; tubed scales in lateral line 16. Attains a length of up to 4 inches.

This fish is quite beautiful, being an almost overall golden color sprinkled with bright blue spots on the head. The lower parts of the body may fade to a whitish color, leaving the upper yellow pale but with the pelvic and anal fins a very bright golden color.

The Golden Devil frequents depths of 50 to 150 feet, where individuals or small groups feed on plankton in the water column.

Abudefduf curacao (Bloch)

Common Name: Staghorn Damsel.
Range: East Indies, Oceania, China, Japan, Philippines.
Meristic Characteristics: D. XIII, 12-13; A. II, 13-15; tubed lateral
line scales 16 or 17. Maximum size to 90 mm standard length.

According to Dr. G.R. Allen in his book *Damselfishes of the South Seas*, the staghorn damselfish "Inhabits lagoons, outer reefs, coastal embayments and reef passages. Forms large feeding aggregations, frequently over growth of staghorn *Acropora* coral in one to 15 meters. The stomach of a specimen from Palau contained larval crabs and shrimps, fish eggs, and algae."

Abudefduf dickii (Lienard)

Common Name: Black-bar Devil.

Range: Tropical Indo-Pacific from Mauritius to the East Indies and Tuamotu Islands.

Previous Scientific Names: *Glyphisodon dickii, Glyphidodon dickii, Glyphidodon unifasciatus.*

Meristic Characteristics: Grows to about 5 inches. D. XII, 17-18; A. II, 14-16. There are 21 tubes in the lateral line and 6 + 1-2 pores in straight section; 3 scales above lateral line to spinous dorsal origin; 11 below.

This is one of the most colorful and well marked devils. It is easily recognized by the dark vertical band joining the soft dorsal and anal fins.

In the aquarium it is quite hardy and grows to a size larger than any that have been recorded from their natural habitat. They require an aquarium which has many hiding places amongst the coral backdrop, as they dart in and out of the holes in the coral snatching bits of food and moving with rapid, short movements.

They are nippers and aggravate fishes which venture near their "territory." They require worms, brine shrimp and vegetable matter in their diet. Freeze dried tubifex worms which has some chlorella algae in with it is highly recommended.

133.00

Abudefduf lacrymatus (Quoy and Gaimard)

Common Name: White-spotted Devil, Yellow-tail, Jewel Damsel.
Range: The Red Sea and tropical Indo-Pacific.
Previous Scientific Names: *Glyphisodon lacrymatus, G. nivosus.*
Meristic Characteristics: D. XII, 16; A. II, 13, i; 18-19 tubes in the
  lateral line.

   The Yellow-tail is an excellent prospect for beginners in the marine aquarium field. They are normally inhabitants of rocky pools and
subsist on a diet of algae and small invertebrates. It seems that the hardiest fishes are found in the tide pool environment. It's almost a sure
bet that anything that can withstand the extreme conditions which
tide pools afford will adapt perfectly to the marine tank. Tide pools
are often isolated at extreme low tide and temperatures may soar well
above 100° in the tropics or, during heavy rainfall the pools may become diluted to almost fresh water. Any fish which can withstand
these conditions has got to be rugged!

Abudefduf leucogaster (Bleeker)

Common Name: Yellow-belly Devil.
Range: East Indies, Philippines to Japan and Great Barrier Reef.
Previous Scientific Names: *Glyphisodon leucogaster, Glyphidodon leucogaster, Glyphidodontops unimaculatus* Bleeker.
Meristic Characteristics: D. XIII, 11-13; A. II, 12-14; 16 tubes in the lateral line, 9-10 below. Grows to 6 inches.

The eyes of most devils are interesting and contrasting. This fish has an iris which is pale yellow to grey. It seems that the larger the devils grow, the less colorful their eyes. While colors vary in almost every fish depending upon its diet, environment and condition, this fish has a fairly constant coloration.

It is scrappy and should not be kept with smaller fish. It behaves in a large aquarium if its territorial integrity is preserved and it has a few holes in the coral to hide in when danger threatens.

It must have some algae in its diet and freeze dried tubifex with chlorella has been found to be an ideal supplement to canned Norwegian brine shrimp. Add lettuce if tubifex with chlorella are not available but take care of pollution.

135.00

Abudefduf leucozona (Bleeker)

Common Name: Single-barred Devil, white-barred Damsel.
Range: Red Sea, Natal, East Indies, Philippine Islands, South Africa.
Previous Scientific Names: *Glyphisodon leucozona, Glyphidodon leu-cozona,* several authors use the species name *leucozonus, Glyphido-don florulentis, G. cingulatum, G. cingulatus, F. florentulus, Abu-defduf cingulum.*
Meristic Characteristics: To 4 inches in mid-Pacific; to 5 inches in the southern extremes of the range. D. XII-XIII, 15-17; A. II, 12-13; 21 tubes in lateral line; about 29 series of scales; 4 scales above later-al line, 10 below.

This is a very variable species whose color changes with age and environment. Small specimens are frequently seen in tidal pools and the author has collected specimens with a small dip net in coral tidal pools. Their normal color is brown or olive brown. Their vertical and ventral fins are golden brown or violaceous. Young specimens have a transverse white band from in front of the soft dorsal down ending be-fore the vent. The eye (iris) is purple-violet with a gold margin. There is the common eye-spot (ocellus) at the front of the soft dorsal and last dorsal spines with a white border (in some specimens?).

This species likes heat and its water can be comfortably 82° F. or higher. It is a common aquarium fish, though a bit nasty when it doesn't feel secure or has too much competition for food. Accepts can-ned Norwegian brine shrimp but requires freeze dried tubifex worms with chlorella algae imbedded in it.

136.00

Abudefduf phoenixensis L.P. Schultz

Common Name: Phoenician Devil.
Photograph By: Dr. John Randall of a specimen 2.8 inches from Eni-
    wetok.
Range: Marshalls and Marianas Islands, tropical Indo-Pacific.
Meristic Characteristics: D. XII, 16-17; A. II, 13-14; P. ii, 18-19; 27-
    29 scale rows from the upper edge of the gill opening to the base of
    the caudal rays. Specimens are usually under 3 inches.

   This is one of the newer, more rare species and none have ever
been kept in an aquarium. Though not evident in Dr. Randall's photograph, there is an ocellus in the outer margin of the dorsal. In the
photograph it shows as a black blotch. The dorsal of the dead specimen shown here is slightly damaged.

Abudefduf elizabethae Fowler

COMMON NAME: Blue-and-yellow Devil.

RANGE: Melanesia to Japan and possibly broader. Exact range problematical because of confusion with *Abudefduf cyaneus*.

PREVIOUS SCIENTIFIC NAMES: None.

MERISTIC CHARACTERISTICS: D. XIII, 12-13; A. II, 13-14; 16-17 tubed scales in lateral line.

This is a magnificent fish and one which rarely is correctly identified. Many variations are known especially in the amount of yellow or white on the body. This is an active species which loves to dart about the aquarium in and out of coral crevices.

138.00

Abudefduf saxatilis (Linnaeus)

Common Name: Sergeant Major.
Range: Throughout the world in tropical waters.
Previous Scientific Names: *Chaetodon saxatilis, Glyphisodon saxatilis, G. vaigiensis, G. rahti, G. tyrhitti, Abudefduf bengalensis.*
Meristic Characteristics: D. XIII, 12-13; A. II, 10-12; P. 18-19; 21 lateral line scales. Rarely exceeds 7 inches.

     This beginner's fish is found ". . . in the western Atlantic from Rhode Island to Paraguay. Abundant on Caribbean reefs. One of the most diversified of fishes in its food habits; feeds on colonial anemones (*Zoanthus*), benthic algae, copepods, pelagic tunicates, small fishes, larvae of various invertebrates and even adult nudibranchs. Often observed in aggregations well above the bottom when feeding on zooplankton; quickly retires to the shelter of reefs with the approach of danger. When guarding the eggs (visible as a deep red or purple patch of several inches in diameter on the sides of rocks or pilings), the adult male becomes dark bluish, the black bars thus less conspicuous on the body." (From *Caribbean Reef Fishes* by Dr. John E. Randall.) This is contrary to the author's experience.

Abudefduf sexfasciatus (Lacepede)

Common Name: Chinese Sergeant Major.

Range: Red Sea, Zanzibar, Natal, Mauritius, Persian Gulf, East Indies, Philippines, China, Japan, Melanesia and Polynesia.

Previous Scientific Names: *Labrus sexfasciatus, Glyphisodon coelistinus, Glyphidodon coelistinus, Glyphisodon sordidus, Abudefduf coelistinus.*

Meristic Characteristics: D. XIII, 12-13, i; A. II, 12, i; 19-21 tubes in the lateral line followed by 1-3 irregular pores. Grows to about 7 inches in the larger, more rare specimens.

This fish is distinguishable from *A. saxatilis* and *A. septemfasciatus* by the presence of dark streaks on the outer edges of the tail. Young specimens have a large dark blotch at the caudal base.

140.00

Abudefduf sordidus (Forskal)

Common Name: Kupipi.
Photograph By: Dr. Herbert R. Axelrod of specimens from Hawaii.
Range: Red Sea, Zanzibar, Mauritius, India, East Indies, China, Japan, Philippines, Polynesia, Micronesia and Hawaii.
Previous Scientific Names: *Chaetodon sordidus, Pomacanthus sordidus, Glyphisodon sordidus, G. geant, G. brownriggii.*
Meristic Characteristics: D. XIII, 14-15, i; A. II, 15-16, i; 21-23 pores in the lateral line. They grow to 8 inches.

Easily recognizable by the black spot on the caudal peduncle right behind the dorsal. Young specimens are almost everywhere to be found in Hawaii, especially in tide pools. The young are dark, while the adults are more gray.

Abudefduf xanthurus (Bleeker)*

COMMON NAME: Orange-tailed Devil.
PHOTOGRAPH BY: Earl Kennedy of a specimen from the Philippines.
RANGE: East Indies, Philippines.
PREVIOUS SCIENTIFIC NAMES: *Glyphisodon xanthurus, Abudefduf behni.*
MERISTIC CHARACTERISTICS: D. XIII, 14-16, i; A. II, 13-15, i; 15-17 tubes
    in the lateral line. Rarely exceeds 6 inches.

This is another of the magnificent devils and, luckily, one which is
exported fairly regularly by the famous collector, Earl Kennedy of the
Philippine Islands. Earl, who is of Chinese ancestry by the way, was
taught fish photography by the author and he has cooperated in the
completion of this book by helping with photographs of some of the
more rare fishes for the 12 years this book was in preparation.

Specimens of this species have been collected in about 100 different
locations which illustrates how common the fish is once you look for it.
Smaller specimens make wonderful additions to the marine aquarium.

* Now called *Paraglyphidodon nigroris.*

Acanthostracion quadricornis (Linnaeus)*

COMMON NAME: Scrawled Cowfish.

PHOTOGRAPH BY: Wilhelm Hoppe.

RANGE: Tropical Atlantic.

PREVIOUS SCIENTIFIC NAMES: *Cottus quadricornis, Oncocottus quadricornis, Acanthocottus labradoricus.*

MERISTIC CHARACTERISTICS: D. 10; A. 10; P. 11. Grows to 18 inches.

The cowfishes have a built-in defense against predators in the form of a hard bony armor with projecting spines. Nevertheless, the juveniles are sometimes among the stomach contents of larger fishes, such as tunas. However, once they reach several inches in length I doubt if they have any real enemies, with the possible exception of sharks (which will sometimes eat anything). This is one of the largest species occurring in the Atlantic Ocean.

Offer feedings of brine shrimp (live, frozen and freeze-dried), chopped fish and lean beef; and freeze-dried tubifex with chlorella algae.

* Now called *Lactophrys quadricornis.*

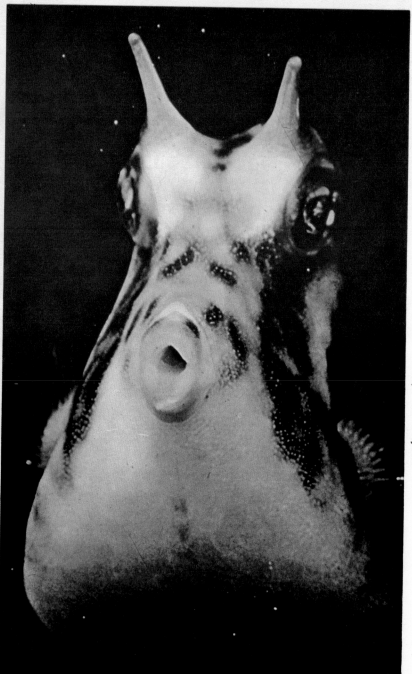

Scrawled Cowfish in frontal view; the horns and bovine expression have given rise to the name "Cowfish" for this species and its close relatives.

144.00

Photo by Dr. Gerald R. Allen.

Acanthurus achilles Shaw

COMMON NAME: Red-tailed Surgeon.

RANGE: Tropical mid-Pacific atolls, including Eniwetok, Bikini, Rongerik and Rongelap.

MERISTIC CHARACTERISTICS: D. IX, 30–34; A. III, 26–30; P. I, i, 14–15; 4–6 teeth in one side of upper jaw; 4–5 teeth in one side of lower jaw. Grows to over 7 inches.

The colors of this fish are variable with size (=age). It normally has the bright red spot when the fish reaches 3 inches. It is missing in smaller specimens. When about $2\frac{1}{2}$ inches color begins to appear in the fins and there is a red band in the base of the soft dorsal and anal fin rays. The margin of these fins has a blue line. The tail has a red margin. This is a fish which prefers heavily oxygenated water and its normal habitat is reefs where the surf breaks. Where they are found they are plentiful. They ship well and are very aggressive especially when competing for food.

They require copious amounts of freeze dried tubifex with chlorella algae if they are to prosper. This is a very large species but only smaller specimens should be kept in the home aquarium. I have seen specimens over 7 inches long.

145.00

Acanthurus bleekeri Günther

COMMON NAME: Striped Surgeon.
PHOTOGRAPH BY: Klaus Paysan.
RANGE: Philippines, Marshalls and Marianas; probably more widespread.
PREVIOUS SCIENTIFIC NAMES: *Harpurus gnophodes*.
MERISTIC CHARACTERISTICS: D. IX, 25–26; A. III, 23–24; P. I, i, 13–15;
   grows to more than one foot long.

The various color patterns described for *bleekeri* fit fairly closely with this species except for the blue lines which radiate from the eye. Most scientific descriptions take note of 9–10 dark lines coming from the eye to the lower edge of the gill cover.

This fish is very closely associated with *Acanthurus coeruleus*. The obvious difference between the two species is the gold iris in *bleekeri* and its more elongated body. *A. coeruleus* has a blue iris and is rounder.

Acanthurus coeruleus Bloch & Schneider

COMMON NAME: Blue Tang.

RANGE: Tropical western Atlantic from Bermuda to Brazil.

PREVIOUS SCIENTIFIC NAMES: *Acanthurus Broussonnetii; Acanthurus caeruleus; Acanthurus violaceus; Acanthurus brevis; Acanthurus caeruleatus; Teuthis helioides; Hepatus pawnee.*

MERISTIC CHARACTERISTICS: D. IX, 26-28; A. III, 24 to 26; pectoral rays 16 or 17. Attains a length of just over 9 inches.

This species is very popular with aquarists, part of its popularity being due to the color changes it undergoes when growing up. The aquarist gets two colorful fishes in one, so to speak. The juveniles are a bright yellow in color. This has raised many an eyebrow in aquarium stores when the owner referred to this bright yellow fish as a "blue" tang. But as the fish grows the yellow color disappears and a very pleasing blue color appears. The size at which the blue replaces the yellow color is variable and is probably more age-dependent than size-dependent.

This is the intermediate color stage of the transformation from the bright yellow juvenile to the blue adult. For those who are not aware of this color change reference to the yellow juvenile as the blue tang seems ridiculous. Photo by H. Hansen, Aquarium Berlin.

The food of the Blue Tang is entirely algal, and this should be taken into account when feeding aquarium specimens. Although other food is accepted, this fish does not do well unless there is a considerable amount of vegetable matter in its diet.

Acanthurus dussumieri Cuvier and Valenciennes

COMMON NAME: Palani; Hawaiian Surgeon.

RANGE: Southern Japan through the Philippines and East Indies to Australia and across the Indian Ocean to South Africa. Oddly, it only occurs in Hawaii in all Oceania.

PREVIOUS SCIENTIFIC NAMES: *Acanthurus undulatus, Acanthurus Lamarrii, Acanthurus grammoptilis,* and *Acanthurus bariene.*

MERISTIC CHARACTERISTICS: D. IX, 25-27; A. III, 24-26; pectoral rays 16 or 17. Grows to a length of about 16 inches.

This species is very common in Hawaii, and every trap you set will produce a few. The caudal peduncle spine is very sharp, and the fish should be handled with care. The spine and/or the area immediately surrounding it is often colored in a way that makes it very obvious and visible.

It does well in captivity and soon grows to more than a foot in length. It eats a variety of foods but must have some vegetable matter in its diet to prosper. This is one of the three largest species of *Acanthurus.*

149.00

Acanthurus guttatus Bloch and Schneider

COMMON NAME: Mustard Surgeon.

PHOTOGRAPH BY: Dr. John Randall of a specimen 8 inches from Eniwetok.

RANGE: Indo-Pacific coral reefs including Eniwetok, Bikini, Rongerik, Guam, Saipan and Rota. Common in the Philippines.

MERISTIC CHARACTERISTICS: Grows to about 10 inches. D. IX, 26–28; A. III, 23–26; P. I, i, 14; 4–6 teeth on one side of upper jaw, 4–7 on lower jaw (one side).

Prefers highly oxygenated water and can be found on the reef close to where the surf breaks.

This fish grows rather large for the aquarium and its color fades the larger it gets. It grows very quickly in the aquarium if it is properly fed. Algae is extremely important in its diet and unless freeze dried tubifex worms with chlorella algae is offered, lettuce must be given daily.

This is a dangerous fish to keep in an aquarium with *larger* fishes. It often attacks them without provocation, using its razor sharp spines located just in front of the caudal peduncle. It usually sidles next to them and whips itself against the body of the larger fish, making a deep gash. This is especially true when the fish is a newcomer to the aquarium. When placed into a tank in which the larger fish is an older inhabitant, it usually ignores the larger fish providing it can find a bit of free territory in which it can feel secure.

150.00

Acanthurus leucosternon Bennett

COMMON NAME: Powder-blue Surgeon
PHOTOGRAPH BY: Klaus Paysan.
RANGE: Tropical Indo-Pacific.
PREVIOUS SCIENTIFIC NAMES: None.
MERISTIC CHARACTERISTICS: D. VII–IX, 26–29; A. III, 25–26; P. I, i, 14.
  Grows to about one foot.

This is one of the most popular surgeon fish. Because it is so wide-spread and so hardy, it is stocked by marine fish dealers all over the world. Once it has settled down, the fish becomes very sociable and eats huge quantities of canned Norwegian brine shrimp and freeze-dried tubifex worms.

There is a possibility that there are two species. One seems to be found only in deep lagoon waters in the Indo-Pacific, while reports of it being found in shallow reefs persist. The meristic counts given by Smith for the African *leucosternon* varies considerably from the counts of the Bikini fishes, for example. A more thorough statistical analysis might show two species as aquarists know that some of them are very easy to keep (the shallow water forms) while the deep water forms are difficult to acclimate.

Acanthurus lineatus (Linnaeus)

COMMON NAME: Clown Surgeon
PHOTOGRAPH BY: Hans and Klaus Paysan.
RANGE: Tropical Indo-Pacific.
PREVIOUS SCIENTIFIC NAMES: *Chaetodon lineatus.*
MERISTIC CHARACTERISTICS: D. IX, 27–29; A. III, 26–27; P. I, i, 14–15.

This is a very colorful and beautiful fish for the home aquarium *if you are fortunate enough to get young specimens.* After the fish is about $1\frac{1}{2}$ inches it begins to take on a change in form and its adult coloration, even though sexual maturity isn't reached until the fish is about 3 inches long, or longer.

For the public aquarium, this fish is a must. It is extremely colorful and very hardy, taking almost all kinds of foods. It is especially fond of Norwegian brine shrimp (canned) when it is small (up to 6 inches), but it takes freeze-dried tubifex and brine shrimp readily. It is a very photogenic species and the markings in the center of the tail have been interpreted in various ways. This caudal pattern changes as the fish gets larger and as far as is known has no sexual connotations.

152.00

Acanthurus nigricans (Linnaeus)*

Common Name: Gray Surgeon.
Photograph By: H. Hansen.
Range: Throughout the tropical Indo-Pacific, to South Africa.
Previous Scientific Names: *Acanthurus gahmoides, Hepatus nigricans.*
Meristic Characteristics: D. IX, 23-28; A. III, 22-28. Grows to about 18 inches.

The surgeonfishes are extremely difficult to identify, even for the experts. Certain very obvious markings which you feel certain are characteristic of a species suddenly appear and disappear so quickly that you often wonder about the validity of a species.

Every careful worker who has studied the limited material available on certain groups of surgeonfishes has remarked how unsure they were about their identification of the Acanthurids.

I'm uncertain here, too, for the three specialists who have assisted me in identifying this fish from its photograph have all given different names to the fish.

It doesn't really matter that my description is wrong, for finally, someone has published a color photograph which can be used to compare with other living specimens. The color pattern and color combinations change so rapidly and from population to population, that identification is very uncertain.

*Red Sea species; the Indo-Pacific species is now called *A. nigricaudus.*

Photo by D. Terver, Nancy Aquarium, France.

Acanthurus olivaceus Bloch and Schneider

COMMON NAME: Olive Surgeon.

RANGE: Mid-Pacific atolls including Eniwetok, Bikini and Rongerik. Common on the Great Barrier Reef of Australia, from Queensland to the Capricorns.

PREVIOUS SCIENTIFIC NAMES: *Acanthurus nigricans* var. *olivaceus*.

MERISTIC CHARACTERISTICS: D. IX, 23–25; A. III, 22–24; P. I, i, 14–16. Grows to at least 9 inches.

A dangerous fish to handle due to its free use of the sharp spines forward of its caudal peduncle. This is not a fish for the small aquarium. It does very well in large, deep public aquariums. Small specimens are attractive and peaceful enough for a 50 gallon tank if they are properly fed and housed. They require large amounts of algae in their diet and several specimens we have had thrived and grew rapidly on a diet of freeze dried tubifex worms and chlorella algae, canned Norwegian brine shrimp and freeze dried brine shrimp. It appreciates heavy aeration in the aquarium. Keep it with fishes smaller than itself. Never introduce new fishes to its aquarium which are larger than *olivaceus* as it might attack the newcomer especially if it unwittingly intrudes upon the "private" territory of the *olivaceus*.

Acanthurus pyroferus Kittlitz

COMMON NAME: Chocolate Surgeon.

RANGE: Tropical Indo-Pacific.

PREVIOUS SCIENTIFIC NAMES: *Hepatus pyroferus, Acanthurus armiger, Acanthurus celebicus,* and *Acanthurus tristis.*

MERISTIC CHARACTERISTICS: D. VIII, 27 or 28; A. III, 24-26; pectoral fin rays 16. Grows to a length of about 10 inches or more.

In this very interesting surgeonfish the young are bright yellow in color and mimic the small angelfishes *Centropyge heraldi* and/or *C. flavissimus.* When the surgeonfish has its dorsal and anal fins spread it is relatively easy to tell them apart, but when the fins are folded the resemblance is striking.

Like other surgeonfishes, the diet should be varied and must include a good percentage of vegetable matter. This is one of those species with a gizzard-like stomach that acts as a food grinder.

155.00

Acanthurus triostegus (Linnaeus)

COMMON NAME: Convict Tang.
PHOTOGRAPH BY: Dr. Herbert R. Axelrod of a Ceylonese specimen.
RANGE: Wide ranging throughout the tropical Indo-Pacific.
PREVIOUS SCIENTIFIC NAMES: *Chaetodon triostegus, Teuthis troughtoni*.
MERISTIC CHARACTERISTICS: D. IX, 22–24; A. III, 19–21; P. I, i, 13.

The fish illustrated here is one of the subspecies of *Acanthurus trio-stegus*. It does not resemble any of the color patterns of the markings on and below the pectoral fin base figured by Schultz and Woods in Bulletin 202 *Fishes of the* Marshalls and Marianas Islands.

In very small specimens under one inch in length, the stripes are missing. This is a good fish for the home aquarium if small specimens can be found. They acclimate readily and take canned Norwegian brine shrimp, freeze-dried tubifex and brine shrimp.

156.00

Acanthurus xanthopterus Valenciennes*

COMMON NAME: Purple Surgeon
PHOTOGRAPH BY: Denmarks Aquarium, Charlottenlund.
RANGE: Oceania, mainly Hawaii, ranging widely from the Pacific Coast of Mexico to South Africa.
MERISTIC CHARACTERISTICS: D. IX, 27; A. III, 26.

This highly retouched photograph is, unfortunately, not too exact. I have never seen a specimen quite resembling it. This is one of the largest fishes in the genus, growing to almost two feet in length. It is easily recognized by the yellow in the outer part of the pectoral fins (accurately shown in this photograph.) The body is usually purple, but not nearly as intense as shown here.

In Hawaii the fish is often taken on hook and line. Small specimens appear irregularly in the home aquarium because they are not as desirable as other surgeonfishes.

* Now called *Zebrasoma xanthurus* (Blyth).

Adioryx caudimaculatus Rüppell

COMMON NAME: Tahitian Squirrel.
RANGE: Red Sea, Seychelles, East Indies, Samoa and Tahiti.
PREVIOUS SCIENTIFIC NAMES: *Holocentrus* (sometimes *Holocentrum*) *caudimaculatus, H. spinifer, H. leonoides, H. rubellio, H. bowiei.*

The Tahitian squirrelfish is rarely, if ever, kept in home aquaria. Its care and feeding should be no different from any of the other squirrelfishes.

This species is easily recognized by the white patch or saddle on top of the caudal peduncle although at times the whole peduncle and some of the adjacent parts of the body may also turn white.

Adioryx coruscus (Poey)

COMMON NAME: Reef Squirrelfish.
PHOTOGRAPH BY: Dr. John Randall of a 4.5-inch specimen from the Virgin Islands.
RANGE: Bermuda, Florida and the West Indies.
MERISTIC CHARACTERISTICS: D. XI, 12; A. IV, 8; P. 13; 41–45 scales in the lateral line. Grows to 5 inches.

   This is one of the best species for the aquarium since small specimens are usually available and they rarely grow once they have been acclimated to the aquarium. They have a very pleasant color which is almost a rusty red and their scales are very reflective. Not very obvious in the photograph is a large black spot covering the first 3 or 4 spines in the dorsal.

Adioryx diadema (Lacépède)

COMMON NAME: Barred Squirrel.
RANGE: Indo-Pacific including the atolls of Bikini, Eniwetok, Rongelap, Rongerik and Likiep.
PREVIOUS SCIENTIFIC NAMES: *Holocentrus diadema.*
MERISTIC CHARACTERISTICS: D. XI, i, 12–13; A. IV, 9; P. ii, 11–13; 48–49 perforated scales in the lateral line.

Like all squirrelfish, *diadema* is nocturnal in habit. It has found a place in public aquariums from time to time, but it rarely is seen in the home aquarium because it grows rather quickly and eats anything small enough to ingest in one piece (smaller fishes.) It prefers a dimly lit aquarium and is very hardy if properly fed and housed. It is not a finicky eater.

The basic color of this species is from a deep blood red to a light orange red. It has red lips and a red snout.

Feeding is simple and it eats almost everything offered to it which is alive. Feed it at dusk or in subdued light. It does better with several of its own species or mixed with other squirrelfish.

160.00

Adioryx lacteoguttatus (Cuvier)

COMMON NAME: Pink Squirrel.

RANGE: Throughout the Indo-Pacific including Eniwetok, Bikini, Rongelap, Rongerik, Kwajalein, Guam and Rota Island. Ranges to South Africa.

PREVIOUS SCIENTIFIC NAMES: *Holocentrus lacteoguttatus*, *H. lacteoguttatum*.

MERISTIC CHARACTERISTICS: Grows to more than 5 inches. D. XI, i, 12; A. IV, 9; P. ii, 13; 43–46 perforated scales in the lateral line.

This is a smaller species of squirrelfish which may make a good addition to the home aquarium if kept with larger fishes and several other squirrelfishes. Unfortunately it does not have the intense red coloration of most squirrelfishes; its basic color is silvery white. The brick red band on the dorsal is attractive, but it often fades to light orange.

This species eats most live foods, especially small fishes, so don't keep it with smaller fishes that can be gobbled down in one gulp. They are mostly nocturnal in habit and should best be kept in a subdued light.

Adioryx microstomus (Günther)

COMMON NAME: Bikini Squirrel.

PHOTOGRAPH BY: Dr. John Randall of a specimen 5.6 inches from outside reef S.E. Teavaraa Pass, Tahiti.

RANGE: Common throughout the Indo-Pacific including the atolls of Bikini, Rongerik, Eniwetok, Rongelap, Kwajalein, Likiep and Guam.

PREVIOUS SCIENTIFIC NAMES: *Holocentrus microstomus, Holocentrum microstoma.*

MERISTIC CHARACTERISTICS: D. XI, i, 12; A. IV, 9; P. ii, 12–13; 49–52 perforated scales in the lateral line. Grows to at least 7 inches.

The basic coloration of this species ranges from a brick red to a bright orange. It has tinges of brown at times. All squirrelfishes are nocturnal as is obvious from their rather large eyes (their bodies are usually 25–30% of their total body height.)

They should be kept in subdued light and not maintained with fishes smaller than themselves. They eat most living foods including smaller fishes which they usually devour at night when the smaller fishes cannot escape. Keep them in large aquariums with fishes of their own size and preferably with other squirrelfishes.

Adioryx rubra (Forskål)

COMMON NAME: African Squirrelfish.

RANGE: Widespread throughout the tropical Indo-Pacific to South Africa.

PREVIOUS SCIENTIFIC NAMES: *Holocentrus rubrum.*

MERISTIC CHARACTERISTICS: D. XI–XII, 12–14; A. IV, 8–10; 33–36 scales in lateral line. Grows to about 8 inches.

A beautiful red species with silvery stripes running along the body. Fairly variable in the intensity of the red. This species has a very wide range and specimens have been collected as far south as Durban, South Africa.

It has never been kept in the home aquarium as far as we can ascertain, but it is probably nocturnal and not safe with smaller fishes.

163.00

Adioryx spinifer (Forskål)

COMMON NAME: Long-jawed Squirrel Fish.

RANGE: Reefs of the Indo-Pacific, from the Hawaiian Islands to the Red Sea.

PREVIOUS SCIENTIFIC NAMES: *Sciaena spinifera, Holocentrum binotatum, Holocentrum unipunctatum, Holocentrus spinifer.*

MERISTIC CHARACTERISTICS: D. XI, i, 13–14; A. IV, 9–10; 40–44 tubed scales in lateral line. Grows to about 18 inches.

This species gets its common name from its protruding lower jaw. Additional characters which distinguish this species from other members of the genus are the lack of stripes on the body and the large size which the adults reach.

The care and feeding of this species is the same as that prescribed for the other Squirrel Fish species in this book.

Adioryx tiere (Cuvier and Valenciennes)

COMMON NAME: Palau Squirrel.

RANGE: Tropical mid-Pacific including Tahiti, Solomons, Bikini, Rongerik, Eniwetok, Kwajalein and Guam.

PREVIOUS SCIENTIFIC NAMES: *Holocentrum tiere, Holocentrus tiere, Holocentrum erythraeum.*

MERISTIC CHARACTERISTICS: D. X-XII, i, 13; A. IV, 9; P. ii, 13; 47–51 perforated scales in the lateral line. Grows to about 12 inches in length.

In specimens over 3 inches, the ground color of the head and body varies from a yellow red to a deep blood red. In smaller specimens the body is very deep red with numerous minute brown dots and with the lengthwise lines following each scale row iridescent purple. The dorsal spine count is variable and tends to increase in number with the temperature of the water. XII dorsal spines has been found on Johnston Island fish.

This is not a species for the home aquarium, though a group of them in a public aquarium makes a spectacular sight. They eat anything that moves, especially small fishes which they attack at night.

165.00

Adioryx vexillarius (Poey)

COMMON NAME: Dusky Squirrelfish.

PHOTOGRAPH BY: Dr. John Randall of a 3.9-inch specimen from the Virgin Islands.

RANGE: Bermuda, Florida and the West Indies in the Caribbean.

MERISTIC CHARACTERISTICS: D. XI, 13; A. IV, 8–10; P. 15; 40–44 scales in the lateral line. Grows to 7 inches in Bermuda. Smaller in Florida and the West Indies.

This is a very common aquarium fish because it is so plentiful in small sizes close to shore and near very shallow coral reefs. It is very frequently mis-named by aquarists, as are most of the squirrelfishes.

166.00

Adioryx tieroides Bleeker

Common Name: Fringed Squirrel.
Range: East Indies, Melanesia and Micronesia.
Meristic Characteristics: D. XI, i, 12; A. IV, 9; pored scales in the lateral line about 42.

    This species is one of the less well known Pacific squirrelfishes. Its general requirements can be considered similar to those of other species of *Adioryx*.

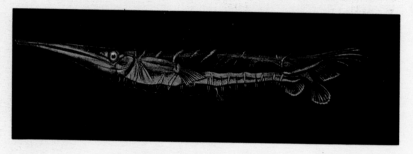

Aeoliscus strigatus (Günther)

COMMON NAME: Shrimpfish.
PHOTOGRAPHED BY: Paysan.
RANGE: Persian Gulf to the East Indies, Japan, Solomon Islands, Hawaii (known by 4 specimens found in 1909).
PREVIOUS SCIENTIFIC NAMES: *Centriscus, Amphisile, Amphisile komis.*

This is one of the weird fishes of the world. It is closely associated with the pipefishes and many articles and discussions revolve about how it swims, where it fits into the general pattern of fish evolution and why it swims upside down all the time with the "tail" being a dorsal ray.

One thing is known, it rarely is found far from sea urchins.

They do surprisingly well in captivity and feed perfectly on dried fairy shrimp (which have been boiled to make them sink), or canned Norwegian brine shrimp.

In the May, 1964 issue of *Tropical Fish Hobbyist* magazine, Dr. Klausewitz details the many ichthyological problems involved with this fish.

The Shrimpfish, *Aeoliscus strigatus* (Gunther) normally swim in a vertical position with the head pointed downward. Photo by Klaus Paysan.

Alectis ciliaris (Bloch)

COMMON NAME: Threadfin, Ulua kihikihi, Kagami ulua, Pennant Tre-
vally.

PHOTOGRAPH BY: Dr. Herbert R. Axelrod.

RANGE: Throughout tropical Indo-Pacific to Australia, and western
Atlantic.

PREVIOUS SCIENTIFIC NAMES: *Blepharis ciliaris*, *Zeus ciliaris*, *Caranx
ciliaris*.

This beauty grows to about 15 inches and is almost always sought as a
display fish for public aquariums. There were more than one dozen on
display in Hawaii when I took this photo.

Their bodies are strongly compressed (very flat), rhombic in shape,
and with 5–6 rudimentary spines in their dorsal. The soft dorsal and anal
rays extend in long filaments and the larger the fish the smaller are the
filaments as expressed in percentage of total body length.

The main difference between this fish and *Alectis indica* is that *indica*
grows to 5 feet, the distance from the eye to the mouth is more eye
diameters in *indica* than in *ciliaris*, but more important, in *ciliaris* only
the dorsal and anal produce long filaments while in *indica* long filaments

Juvenile *Alectis indica* have dorsal, anal, and pelvic fins with filaments. Photo by H. Hansen.

are produced by all fins, both paired and unpaired, except the tail.

In the aquarium, they should be fed anything they will eat, but they prefer bits of fish and meat that fall through the water.

Alectis indica (Rüppell)

COMMON NAME: Threadfins, Old Maid, Mirrorfish, Moonfish.
RANGE: East Africa to the East Indies to Hawaii and Australia.
PREVIOUS SCIENTIFIC NAMES: *Scyris indicus, Citulla gallus, Caranx gallus.*
MERISTIC CHARACTERISTICS: D. I, 19; A. I, 16; 36 scutes in straight
   section of lateral line.

For differences between this fish and *Alectis ciliaris*, see the writeup of *ciliaris*. This fish grows too large for most home aquaria. Day said the fish grows to 1525 mm (about 60 inches). I have never seen any larger than two feet, however, and smaller ones are very common. This is one of the startling forms found in the sea.

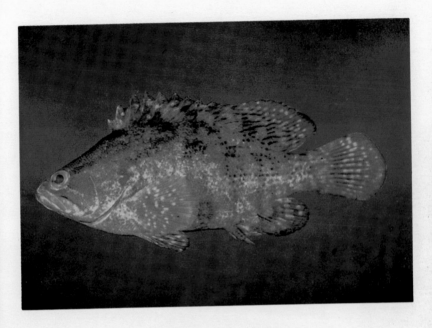

Alphestes afer (Bloch)

COMMON NAME: Mutton Hamlet.
PHOTOGRAPH BY: Dr. John Randall of a 9.2-inch specimen from the
Virgin Islands.
RANGE: Tropical western Atlantic.
MERISTIC CHARACTERISTICS: D. XI, 18–19; A. III, 9; reaches 12 inches in
length.

This is one of the few groupers suitable for the aquarium which rarely
dives into the coral to find a secure place. It prefers to hide among the
plastic plants which modern marine aquarists have found to be so
beneficial to their fishes sense of security.

It is often sold for aquarium purposes because of the great amount of
red in the fish, though it often fades under poor feeding and even poorer
aquarium management. Feed this fish chunks of freeze-dried tubifex
worms and Norwegian brine shrimp.

173.00

Alutera scripta (Osbeck)

COMMON NAME: Scribbled Trigger, O'ili lepa, Ohua.

RANGE: Hawaii to Marshall and Marianas, throughout the tropical seas to Caribbean.

PREVIOUS SCIENTIFIC NAMES: *Balistes scriptus.*

MERISTIC CHARACTERISTICS: D. I, 45; A. 48; P. 14. Grows to about 2 feet.

Unfortunately, the color photograph doesn't show the broom-like tail, but this common Hawaiian fish makes a very attractive addition to the larger marine aquarium.

It acts like the usual triggerfish and though they are plentiful in Hawaiian waters, few are to be found in European aquariums. Very rare in the Virgin Islands.

Amanses sandwichiensis (Quoy and Gaimard)*

Common Name: Sandwich Trigger.
Range: Worldwide distribution in the warm tropical seas.
Previous Scientific Names: *Monacanthus* or *Cantherhines* (sometimes spelled *Cantherines) pardalis* (as well as *sandwichiensis*).
Meristic Characteristics: D. I, 34-36; A. 30-31. Grows to 15 inches.

The reason this fish is so widespread is its ability to be almost perfectly camouflaged in Sargassum weed as can be seen in the accompanying photograph. The fish lays among the weed and is carried throughout the world on the various currents.

* Now called *Cantherhines sandwichiensis*.

175.00

The young Sandwich filefish remains near the protection afforded by the *Sargassum*. When it hovers among the fronds it is very difficult to spot. Photo by Shammie Wong.

Tiny fish live on plankton and depending upon their diet and age, coloration is varied.

In the aquarium they thrive on any foods. The author has been successful feeding them fairy shrimp (dried), freeze-dried tubifex with chlorella, and canned Norwegian brine shrimp.

Amblyapistus taenianotus (Cuvier and Valenciennes)

Common Name: Rouge Fish.
Photograph By: Hilmar Hansen.
Range: Tropical Indo-Pacific.
Previous Scientific Names: *Apistus taenianotus, Tetraroge crista-galli, Tetraroge taenianotus.*
Meristic Characteristics: D. XVII, 7-8; A. III, 5; about 90 lateral line scales. Attains a length of 5 inches.

This unusual fish scarcely resembles the graceful long-finned turkey fishes of the genus *Pterois*, but they are all members of the same family. It is not known whether or not the dorsal spines are poisonous, like so many of the other scorpion fishes. At any rate, it is best to handle them with caution, just to be on the safe side. This attractive little species will thrive on a diet of live brine shrimp and guppy fry. Since they are relatively inactive, a small tank is suitable provided ample aeration is furnished.

Amblycirrhitus pinos (Mowbray)

COMMON NAME: Redspotted Hawkfish.

RANGE: Tropial western Atlantic.

MERISTIC CHARACTERISTICS: D. X, 11; A. III, 6; P. 14; 41–44 scales in the
lateral line. Grows to about 3½ inches.

One of the common "rarities" for the aquarium. While fairly plentiful in
open waters over hard bottoms, this is not a real coral reef dweller. It
does well in the aquarium but is not a favorite.

Amblygobius phalaena (Cuvier and Valenciennes)

COMMON NAME: Banded Goby.
RANGE: Tropical Indo-Pacific.
PREVIOUS SCIENTIFIC NAMES: *Gobius phalaena.*
MERISTIC CHARACTERISTICS: D. VI, I–14; A. I, 14. Grows to about 4–5 inches.

A. phalaena is a hardy member of the goby family which is seen from time to time in pet shops. The Gobies can be identified by examining the pelvic fins, which are fused together and form a sucking disc. This helps them cling to the steep rocks where they are often found. This species acclimates to aquarium life in a hurry, and there is a strong possibility of getting them to spawn if you are lucky enough to obtain a mated pair. Provide plenty of rocky shelter to help them feel at home. Feed canned Norwegian brine shrimp and freeze-dried tubifex with chlorella algae.

Photo by Dr. D. Terver, Nancy Aquarium, France.

Amphiprion akallopisos Bleeker

COMMON NAME: Skunk-striped Anemone Fish.
RANGE: Tropical Indo-Pacific.
PREVIOUS SCIENTIFIC NAMES: *Prochilus akallopisos*.
MERISTIC CHARACTERISTICS: D. X, 18–19; A. II, 12–13; P. 17–19.

The coloration of various *Amphiprion* fishes is extremely important because they change very little from adult coloration during their life cycle. Feedings of freeze dried brine shrimp seem to make the light orange turn a bit deeper red, but perhaps this is imagination on my part.

This is one of the easiest marines to keep. They eat all freeze-dried foods, as well as most others, but beware of fouling the tank with frozen foods, especially brine shrimp, as it is 90% or more water.

This fish seems to behave peculiarly about certain anemones and it has often rejected Florida anemones, while it has accepted Philippine anemones.

Photo by Dr. Herbert R. Axelrod.

Amphiprion chrysopterus Cuvier and Valenciennes

COMMON NAME: Orange-Finned Anemone Fish.
RANGE: Tropical South and Central Pacific.
PREVIOUS SCIENTIFIC NAMES: *Amphiprion bicinctus, A. papuensis.*
MERISTIC CHARACTERISTICS: D. X–XI, 15–17; A. II, 13–14; P. 19–20.
 Grows to 5½ inches.

 This species has been confused with *A. bicinctus* of the Red Sea and western Indian Ocean. It is evidently restricted to the islands of the Pacific as far east as the Tuamotus. They are often found associated with anemones of the genus *Condylactis.*

Amphiprion ephippium (Bloch)

Common Name: Saddle Anemone Fish.
Photograph By: Dr. Herbert R. Axelrod.
Range: Tropical Indo-Pacific.
Previous Scientific Names: *Lutjanus ephippium, A. tricolor, A. ruppelli, A. rubrocinctus, Prochilus ephippium.*
Meristic Characteristics: D. X-XI, 15-18; A. II, 13-15; P. 18-20. Grows to 5 inches.

This species is restricted to the eastern Indian Ocean and westernmost portion of the Indo-Australian Archipelago. The juveniles have a thin white bar on the head which disappears at an age of approximately 2 months. The adults have no bars on the head and body and are distinguished by a large black saddle on the posterior part of the back. The entire interorbital area is scaled.

Amphiprion frenatus Brevoort

Common Name: Red Clown.
Range: Philippine Islands, Okinawa, Japan, Singapore.
Previous Scientific Names: *Prochilus polylepis, Amphiprion polymnus, A. macrostoma.*
Meristic Characteristics: D. IX-X, 16-18; A. II, 14; P. 18-20.

Unlike *A. ephippium*, with which it is often confused, this species always retains the head bar in adulthood, and the interorbital is scaled only halfway. This species has a wide latitude of body color, with young specimens usually bright reddish and large adults brownish or blackish, with reddish fins and breast. The young often have a mid-body bar which disappears with age. *A. frenatus* usually has 9 dorsal spines (60-70% of all specimens), while *A. ephippium* has 10 spines (occasionally 11).

There are a number of theories available which account for the immunity of the anemone fishes against the deadly tentacles of their host. The most popular of these involves the mucus secretion of the fish, which supposedly protects the fish.

Experiments have shown that if the mucus is scraped off, the anemone fish will become just another victim of the anemone.

183.00

The young have a mid-body bar which disappears with age. Here, the mid-bar is all but gone. Photo by Klaus Paysan.

The dark outline to the white head bar distinguishes this species from *A. rubrocinctus*, and the light pelvic fins differ in color from the blackish pelvics of *A. melanopus*, the two other species which might be confused with this one. Photo by Klaus Paysan.

Amphiprion polymnus (Linnaeus)

Common Name: Saddle Back Clown.
Photograph By: Earl Kennedy.
Range: Tropical Indo-Pacific.
Previous Scientific Names: *Amphiprion bifasciatus, A. laticlavius, A. unimaculatus, Perca polymnus, Prochilus bifasciatus.*
Meristic Characteristics: D. X-XI, 15; A. II, 12-14; P. 17-19.

    Although *A. polymnus* is mainly an Indo-Pacific species, scattered reports locate it close to the Philippines. It doesn't seem to be as hardy as *A. percula*, but it accepts bits of freeze-dried food. It might be an anemone-tentacle eater. I must theorize that the fact that all *Amphiprion* species eat tentacles from time to time might have something to do with their seeming imperviousness to the poison contained in the tentacles.

185.00

Amphiprion ocellaris Cuvier.

Common Name: Clown Anemone Fish.
Photograph By: Douglas Faulkner.
Range: Widespread throughout tropical Indo-Pacific.
Previous Scientific Names: *Lutjanus percula, Amphiprion tunicatus, Prochilus percula, Anthias polymna, Actinicola percula, Amphiprion bicolor.*
Meristic Characteristics: D. XI, 14-15; A. II, 11-13; tubed lateral line scales 32-41. Grows to about 3¼ inches (female); males are about ½ inch smaller.

   This species was long known to marine hobbyists under the name *Amphiprion percula*, but in his book *Anemonefishes* Dr. Gerald R. Allen has pointed out that *A. percula*, although very similar in appearance and meristics, is actually a different and infrequently seen species.

   Much is known about this fish, one of the mainstays of the marine aquarium hobby. It even has been one of the comparatively few marine species that has spawned regularly under aquarium conditions. The parent fish spawn like substrate-spawning cichlids after meticulously cleaning a site (usually at the base of a *Stoichactis* anemone) for depositing the eggs. The male tends the approximately 200 eggs, which hatch usually within a week. The young are free swimming almost as soon as they hatch, or within 48 hours at any rate. They leave the area and search for plankton at the surface of the water. In a week or two they search for an anemone for their home.

This is the real *Amphiprion percula* which normally has only nine or ten dorsal fin spines compared to eleven for *A. ocellaris*. Photo by Dr. Gerald R. Allen.

Amphiprion ocellaris are school fish. They swim about the aquarium in schools and they may inhabit a single anemone in schools. I have observed them on rare occasions to actually drop bits of food into the tentacles of *Stoichactis*. I have also observed them eat the excretion of *Stoichactis* as well as food which the anemone regurgitated. On more than one occasion I have seen them bite and eat bits of the tentacles of the anemone in which they dwelled. No one has ever found this fish very far from an anemone, and whenever they are frightened, they immediately rush into the tentacles of the anemone for protection. They frequently mouth the tentacles of the anemone either removing microscopic organisms from the tentacle, or eating its slime. The fish gets along well without anemones, and the anemone gets along well without the fish, but both *seem* to do better together. I have never been successful in getting *A. ocellaris* to inhabit a Florida anemone. At times, I have placed new *Stoichactis* in a tank with this species. They immediately left their previous "hosts" and teased the newcomer until it opened its tentacles and allowed them in.

Amphiprion perideraion Bleeker

Common Name: False Skunk-striped Anemone Fish.
Range: Tropical Indo-Pacific.
Meristic Characteristics: D. X, 16; A. II, 12-13, p. 17.

    This fish differs from *Amphiprion akallopisos* by the white vertical bar, about two scales wide, from the "skunk" stripe to the edge of the gill cover. It prefers Pacific anemones, though it frequently dashes close to the tentacles of Atlantic species.

    This is the only species of anemonefish in which Allen was able to distinguish the sexes. The males are reported to have a narrow edge of bright orange on the soft dorsal fin and upper and lower margins of the caudal fin. The female lacks the orange edges and has only plain whitish or translucent fins. The color differences appear in individuals larger than 35 mm (about 1½ inches).

Amphiprion perideraion tending its eggs which were laid near the anemone for protection. Photo by Dr. Gerald R. Allen.

Amphiprion xanthurus Cuvier and Valenciennes*

Common Name: Yellow-Tailed Anemone Fish.
Photograph By: Dr. Herbert R. Axelrod.
Range: Indian Ocean, Indo-Australian Archipelago and tropical western Pacific.
Previous Scientific Names: *Amphiprion clarckii, Amphiprion japonicus, Amphiprion chrysagurus, Amphiprion boholensis, Amphiprion debojer, Amphiprion melanostolus, Amphiprion snyderi, A. sebae.*
Meristic Characteristics: D. X, 17; A. II, 14; tubed lateral line scales 36-44. Attains a length of 5-6 inches.

There are a number of theories available which account for the immunity of the anemone fishes to the deadly tentacles of their host. The most popular of these involves the mucus secretion of the fish, which supposedly protects the fish. Experiments have shown that if the mucus is scraped off, the anemone fish will become just another victim of the anemone.

This species is one of the most widespread members of the genus. It ranges from the Persian Gulf to the Caroline Islands in the western Pacific and northwards to southern Japan.

* Now called *Amphiprion clarkii.*

In older specimens of *A. clarkii*, such as the one shown above, the white mid-body bar stops at the base of the dorsal fin. In young specimens, as the one shown below, it does. The specimen on p. 190.00 is intermediate. All photos by Dr. Herbert R. Axelrod.

192.00

Above: An individual of *Amphiprion clarkii* literally "bathes" in the tentacles of its anemone keeping a watchful eye out for any danger. Photo by Dr. Herbert R. Axelrod.

Opposite: The caudal fin may be a solid white or yellow or may have a pattern of yellow against the white like this one. Photo by Dr. Shih-chieh Shen.

Anampses caeruleopunctatus (Ruppell)

Common Name: Blue-green Wrasse.
Range: Widespread in the Indo-Pacific area from Red Sea to Easter Island.
Previous Scientific Names: *Anampses diadematus, Anampses caeruleopunctatus.*
Meristic Characteristics: D. IX, 12; A. III, 12; 29 scales in the lateral line.

    This species looks very similar to several of the parrot fish species at first glance. However, an inspection of the teeth quickly tells us we are dealing with a wrasse. Nearly all the parrot fishes have their teeth fused into a solid beak-like structure, while the wrasses have individual teeth in the jaws.

    The various species of wrasses are fond of frozen and live brine shrimp, and freeze-dried mosquitoe larvae and fairy shrimp. They should be fed these items regularly.

Anampses cuvieri Bennett

Range: Hawaiian Islands and Johnston Atoll.
Meristic Characteristics: D. IX, 12; A. III, 12; P. ii, 11.

This photograph was taken in Hawaii. The fish looks very much like Randall's *A. chrysocephalus* except for the tail. The tail is red in that species.

The juveniles are differently colored being pale green and having black ocelli in the last rays of the dorsal and anal fins. The spots are also absent in the smaller individual of this species.

195.00

Photo by Aaron Norman.

Anampses rubrocaudatus Randall *

RANGE: Hawaii.

This fish is found only in Hawaii. Its habitat seems to be in waters of about 100 feet deep and the specimens usually shipped out as aquarium fish have been identified as *Anampeses cuvieri*, called Opule or Hilu by the Hawaiians.

The *Anampses* are very colorful, probably the most colorful of all Hawaiian fishes. They are rare and expensive, but they rarely grow larger than 4 inches, thus they will make valuable additions to the marine home aquarium. They have only four teeth in their mouths; two in the upper jaw and two in the lower jaw, making them very easy to recognize from other Hawaiian fishes. These teeth are probably used for scraping bits of food from living coral, but they thrive on freeze-dried tubifex worms which has chlorella added to it.

* Now called *Anampses chrysocephalus* Randall.

196.00

Photo by Aaron Norman.

Anampses twistii Bleeker

RANGE: East Indies, Polynesia.
PREVIOUS SCIENTIFIC NAMES: *Anampses fidjensis*.
MERISTIC CHARACTERISTICS: Grows to about 6 inches.

According to Fowler (*Fishes of Oceania*) *A. twistii* resembles *Anampses pteropthalmus* by its having a black ocellus (eye spot) on the last dorsal and anal rays and a head without spots. It differs in the large scales, 28 to 30, and the dotted color of the trunk, tail and vertical fins. It differs from all the other species in the black posterior border to the gill opening and black blotch at the base of the pectoral fin. It has been confused when juvenile, and Sauvage identified a young *twistii* as a new species he called *Anampses fidjensis*. His specimen was about 3 inches.

Photo by Alimenta-Brussels.

Anarhichas lupus

COMMON NAME: Atlantic Wolffish.
RANGE: Atlantic Ocean.

This is not a fish for the home aquarium, but some people keep them anyway. There are three Atlantic species and two Pacific members of this family Anarhichadidae. The Pacific *Anarhichthys ocellatus* grows to 8 feet long and ranges from California to Alaska. They are vicious and have been known to attack bathers. They can live for months without food and they prefer live clams which they crush in their powerful jaws.

Anisotremus surinamensis (Bloch)

COMMON NAME: Black Margate.
PHOTOGRAPH BY: Dr. John E. Randall.
RANGE: Florida, Gulf of Mexico to Brazil.
MERISTIC CHARACTERISTICS: D. XII, 16–18; A. III, 8–10; P. 18–19.
  Grows to two feet.

Not a very suitable fish for the small aquarium, but specimens find
their way into most large public aquariums, or get sold as "something
new" when they are an inch or two long.
  They are not recommended for the home aquarium. They eat everything.

Photo by Dr. Walter A. Starck II.

Anisotremus virginicus (Linnaeus)

COMMON NAME: Porkfish.

RANGE: Tropical western Atlantic. Introduced to Bermuda.

MERISTIC CHARACTERISTICS: D. XII, 16–17; A. III, 9–11; P. 17–18. Grows to about 12 inches long.

The young Porkfish have been reported to pick parasites from the bodies of other fishes. They are school fish and are found in packs around reefs. They are commonly caught on hook and line.

Anisotremus virginicus showing the dark areas in the spinous dorsal and lateral stripes which form at night. Photo by Dr. Walter A. Starck II.

A daytime school of porkfish. *(Anisotremus virginicus)* Photo by Dr. Walter A. Starck II.

Photo by James H. O'Neill.

Antennarius bigibbus (Lacepede)

COMMON NAME: Pygmy Angler.

RANGE: Tropical Indo-Pacific.

PREVIOUS SCIENTIFIC NAMES: *Lophius bigibbus, Chironectes tuberosus, Chironectes reticulatus, Antennarius tuberosus.*

MERISTIC CHARACTERISTICS: D. I–I–I–12; A. 7; P. 11. Grows to 3 inches.

This is one of the most desirable of the angler fishes to keep in an aquarium. They are colorful and their small size makes them relatively easy to satisfy when it comes to feeding. The color of this species varies from tan to a gorgeous reddish-pink with black mottling. It's a common species in the Hawaiian Islands, often found inside heads of dead coral or under rocks. *A. strigatus* is an almost identical species from the eastern Pacific. Live fish and shrimp are the best foods in captivity.

Antennarius chironectes (Lacépède)

COMMON NAME: Toad Fish, Fishing Frog.

PHOTOGRAPH BY: Dr. John Randall of a specimen 4 inches from Kaaawa Oahu.

RANGE: Throughout the central tropical Indo-Pacific, including Natal, South Africa.

PREVIOUS SCIENTIFIC NAMES: *Lophius sandvicensis, Chironectes rubrofuscus, Chironectes niger, Antennarius laysanius, A. leprosus* and *A. commersonii.*

MERISTIC CHARACTERISTICS: D. I + I + I, 13–14, first spine with simple flap; A. 7–8. Grows to less than 12 inches; probably 10 inches.

These are difficult fishes to identify as can be seen by the various scientific names under which this species is known. They are an extremly variable species, changing colors almost in front of your eyes. They are not very active fish, but they are almost the most entertaining when they stalk their food. The author (HRA) kept one in a solitary aquarium; the only other inhabitants were food fishes (locally found killies) which disappeared one at a time as they were lured to their end by the dangling spine on the snout.

A single specimen in a small aquarium is very hardy and interesting. They should be transported alone without other fishes and this makes them expensive, though they are far from rare and easy to collect since they move so slowly. They are capable, however, of fast darting movements to capture prey.

Photo by Allan Power.

Antennarius coccineus Lesson and Garnet

COMMON NAME: Toad Fish or Fishing Frog.
RANGE: Widespread throughout the tropical mid-Pacific from Tahiti to South Africa.
PREVIOUS SCIENTIFIC NAMES: *Antennarius leucus* among others.
MERISTIC CHARACTERISTICS: D. $1 + 1 + 1$, 12–13, first dorsal spine bulbous at the tip; A. 7. A small species that grows to about 5 inches.

The toad fishes, and this one is no exception, must almost always be kept by themselves. They can eat anything that moves (swims) up to and including their brothers about the same size as they are. They must have living foods and the best way to keep them is to have them in with marine baitfish available at most cities along seacoasts. They are interesting in their habits, but this species seems to be particularly susceptible to *Ichthyophonus* disease. The colors are very variable and they are easily misidentified by scientists and hobbyists alike.

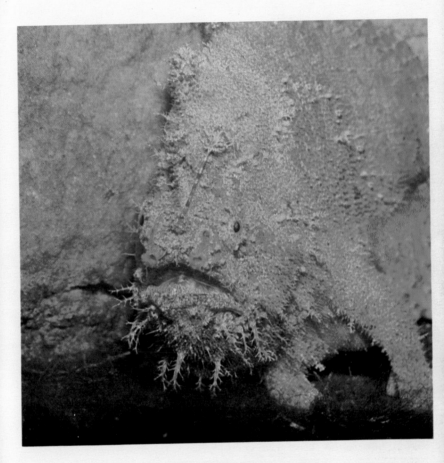

Antennarius hispidus Bloch

COMMON NAME: Anglerfish, Toad Fish, Fishing Frog.
PHOTOGRAPH BY: Dr. Herbert R. Axelrod.
RANGE: Tropical Indo-Pacific.
MERISTIC CHARACTERISTICS: D. I + I + I, 12; A. 7. Grows to 8 inches.

This fish is beautiful because it is so ugly. It can only be kept by itself or with fishes twice as large as it is. Not recommended for the home aquarium.

Antennarius nummifer

COMMON NAME: Scarlet Angler.

PHOTOGRAPH BY: Dr. John Randall of a specimen 2.2 inches from Teavaraa Pass, Tahiti.

RANGE: Throughout the tropical Indo-Pacific to the Australian Barrier
Reef. Collected as deep as 55 fathoms.

PREVIOUS SCIENTIFIC NAMES: *Antennarius drombus, A. coccineus.*

MERISTIC CHARACTERISTICS: Grows to about 6½ inches. D. I + I + I, 12;
A. 7; P. 10; V. 12.

The specimen collected and photographed by Dr. Randall in Tahiti
would have made a beautiful fish for a small 5 gallon aquarium. Unfortunately there has never been a successful aquarium with a muddy
bottom, for this fish would probably do well half buried in the mud with
only his head sticking out ready to snatch anything that passes.

They have voracious appetites and many specimens have been observed which had choked on several fishes being jammed into their
throats, or one large fish, too big to swallow, being stuck in their gullets.

In the aquarium they like to "nest" in a flowerpot laid on its side.
They can eat fish equal to their own size and weight.

Antennarius phymatodes Bleeker

COMMON NAME: Wart-skin Frogfish.
PHOTOGRAPH BY: Earl Kennedy.
RANGE: Philippines, Indian Ocean, Indo-Australian Archipelago.
PREVIOUS SCIENTIFIC NAMES: *Antennarius oligospilos.*
MERISTIC CHARACTERISTICS: D. I–I–I; 12; A. 7; P. 10; body with warts.
   Attains a length of at least 4–5 inches.

Here is one of the most bizarre members of a most unusual group of fishes. Most of the frogfishes have skin which is somewhat smooth in appearance and when examined under a microscope is seen to be covered all over with thousands of short denticles or "prickles." The Wart-skin Frogfish has these denticles, but in addition the body is covered with warts, which lend to an already ghastly appearance. However, the species has a beauty all its own, as the aquarist soon finds out.

If one decides to keep any of the frogfishes it is best to maintain an additional 3–10 gallon tank for the purpose of keeping a ready supply of live bait food. Frogfishes, or anglerfishes as they are sometimes called, are noted for their gigantic appetites, and a 3-inch specimen will devour 4 or 5 half-inch fish per day. Live brine shrimp may be substituted, but large amounts are required to keep this voracious beast satisfied. Aquarists in certain southeastern states and Hawaii may find a ready food supply for their pets in nearby local streams and ponds. For example, in Honolulu there are several streams which abound with young mollies and mosquito fish, perfect fare for the Wart-Skin Frogfish.

207.00

Antennarius striatus (Shaw)

COMMON NAME: Striped Angler, Toadfish, Fishing Frog.
PHOTOGRAPH BY: Paysan.
RANGE: Central tropical Indo-Pacific.
MERISTIC CHARACTERISTICS: D. I + I + I, 12; A. 7. Grows to 7 inches.

This fish, along with most anglerfishes, have the ability to inflate their body with air and float among driftwood or weeds. This is the manner in which they became distributed all over the Pacific. They are so hardy that several reports have it that they were eaten by groupers. The groupers were caught and while cleaning the fish the living angler was found.

They are interesting fish for the large public aquarium. Not recommended for the home aquarium unless you want one in a tank all by itself.

Antennarius species

COMMON NAME: Anglerfish.
PHOTOGRAPH BY: Gerhard Marcuse.
RANGE: Tropical Indo-Pacific.
PREVIOUS SCIENTIFIC NAMES: Not available.
MERISTIC CHARACTERISTICS: Not available.

It is impossible to tell for sure which species this is, for there are nearly 60 different kinds of tropical anglerfishes (family *Antennariidae*). For a positive identification it would be necessary to have an ichthyologist examine an actual specimen, since many of the species look very much alike and there is even considerable variation of color in individual species.

This angler makes a beautiful aquarium fish, but may require a tank all to itself, depending on its size. Needless to say, it will eat anything as big as itself. Live foods (fish and brine shrimp) are a must.

Anthias squamipinnis (Peters)

COMMON NAME: Lyretail Coralfish.

RANGE: Central tropical Indo-Pacific.

PREVIOUS SCIENTIFIC NAMES: Numerous references, mainly *Anthias lepidolepis*, *A. cheirospilos*, *A. nobilis*, *A. ardens*. Also referred to the genus *Franzia* as *F. ardens*, *F. affinis*, or *F. rubra*.

MERISTIC CHARACTERISTICS: D. X, 17–18; A. III, 7–9; 40–44 scales in the lateral line. Grows to 4 inches.

This is a very beautiful fish for the marine aquarium. It is agile and continuously moving about. Its color changes a bit from a yellow to yellow-orange to pink, but in all color phases it is beautiful.

It can be kept in the orange phase by heavy feeding of brine shrimp, either freeze dried or canned Norwegian.

They seem to get along well with fishes their own size.

Apogon binotatus (Poey)

COMMON NAME: Barred Cardinalfish.
RANGE: Bermuda, southern Florida and the Caribbean.
MERISTIC CHARACTERISTICS: D. VI + I, 9; A. II, 8; 23-25 scales in the
   lateral line. Grows to 4 inches.

This cardinalfish is often found in shipments due to its small size and lovely color. According to Boehlke and Chaplin it is one of the most abundant cardinalfish in the Bahamas; it has been taken from near the shore to deeper waters (75 feet). The pallid areas of the body can vary from very pale, to light pink, to red.

These are not related in any close manner with the freshwater cardinal, *Cheirodon axelrodi.*

Apogon conklini (Silvester)

COMMON NAME: Freckled Cardinalfish.

PHOTOGRAPH BY: Dr. John Randall of a 2.4-inch specimen from Puerto Rico.

RANGE: Caribbean, West Indies especially.

MERISTIC CHARACTERISTICS: D. VI + I, 9; A. III, 8; 23–25 scales in the lateral line. Grows to about 2 inches.

While this is a common species in the West Indies, it doesn't appear very frequently on the market because of its lack of color. An occasional specimen sneaks in with other fishes.

Apogon erythrinus Snyder

COMMON NAME: Cardinalfish.

PHOTOGRAPH BY: Dr. John Randall of a specimen 1.7 inches from Eniwetok.

RANGE: Widely scattered throughout the Indo-Pacific.

PREVIOUS SCIENTIFIC NAMES: *Apogon doryssa.*

MERISTIC CHARACTERISTICS: A small fish usually under 2 inches. D. VI + I, 9; A. II, 8; P. 13; 23 vertical scale rows.

The intensity of the red in this fish is very variable. Some appear light pink, while others might be a deeper red. They do very well in the aquarium, though they are nocturnal in habit. This is obvious from their rather large eyes.

It has been suggested that they are mouthbreeders, as are other members of the family, but they have never been bred in the aquarium, nor have specimens been collected with eggs in their mouth. They have very large mouths. They hide quite a bit, especially under coral pieces, but they do come out when the light is subdued. They eat freeze-dried brine shrimp and tubifex worms. Several specimens have been raised to larger sizes on canned Norwegian brine shrimp (*Calanus*) which was supplemented with freeze-dried tubifex with chlorella algae. It is not a finicky eater usually.

Apogon exostigma (Jordan and Starks)

COMMON NAME: Cardinalfish.

RANGE: Tropical mid-Pacific including Samoa, Bikini, Rongelap, Rongerik and Moorea.

PREVIOUS SCIENTIFIC NAMES: *Amia exostima, Apogon frenatus.*

MERISTIC CHARACTERISTICS: Grows to about 4 inches. D. VII + I, 9; A. II, 9; P. ii, 9–10, i–ii; 24–25 vertical scale rows.

Not one of the most beautiful cardinalfish, this specimen shows very little in the red for which the cardinal fishes got their popular name. This species has never become a favorite for the hobbyist, though it appears in mixed collections in public aquariums because it is not as nocturnal as most of the other cardinalfishes. When on display in large aquariums, I have seen it remain motionless for long periods of time, moving only when another fish approaches it.

It thrives on canned Norwegian brine shrimp and freeze-dried tubifex with chlorella algae.

Apogon fasciatus (Shaw)

COMMON NAME: Cardinalfish.
PHOTOGRAPH BY: K. Paysan.
RANGE: Australia and tropical Indo-Pacific.
PREVIOUS SCIENTIFIC NAMES: *Mullus fasciatus.*
MERISTIC CHARACTERISTICS: D. VII + I, 9; A. II, 8; 25–27 scales in the
lateral line. Grows to about 5 inches.

This fish occurs with many subspecies amongst Australia's Great
Barrier Reef. According to several authors, there are so many subspecies
in both form and color that it is doubtful that all cardinals on the reef
aren't one big, diverse variety of the fish shown here.

Cardinals are excellent aquarium fishes, especially when they are small.
Most are very colorful and eat freeze-dried foods.

215.00

Apogon fraenatus Valenciennes

COMMON NAME: Cardinalfish.
RANGE: Tropical mid-Pacific, New Guinea, Guam, Bikini, Tahiti.
PREVIOUS SCIENTIFIC NAMES: None.
MERISTIC CHARACTERISTICS: D. VII + I, 9; A. II, 8; P. ii, 10–11, ii–iii;
23–24 vertical rows of scales. Grows to about 4 inches.

This is one of the more popular Cardinalfish, but it is not often offered on dealer price lists. It seems a bit hardier than most cardinalfishes, but it is nocturnal in habit. If kept in a large aquarium with many other fishes they prefer to hide under pieces of coral or rocks, but in the evening they are usually seen free swimming. They have a habit of standing motionless in open waters at dusk and at dawn.

They do well on canned Norwegian brine shrimp and freeze-dried tubifex worms and chlorella.

216.00

Apogon leptacanthus Bleeker

COMMON NAME: Cardinalfish.

RANGE: Marshall Islands, East Indies, Philippines and Guam.

PREVIOUS SCIENTIFIC NAMES: *Apogon graffei, Amia hypselenota, Minorus graeffei.*

MERISTIC CHARACTERISTICS: (From a single specimen) D. VI + I, 9; A. II, 9; P. 13; 23 vertical scale rows.

Only a few specimens of this species has been studied. They were all under 2 inches. None has ever been kept in an aquarium to the best of our knowledge, though there seems to be no good reason for this other than their rarity.

It has a beautiful long, thin filamentous extension of the second spiny dorsal spine. Its body is more laterally compressed and deeper than most members of the genus.

Intuitively, we feel that this cardinal might have other characteristics which might make it a very useful aquarium fish. Its small size and lack of startling color, though, are against it as small marine fishes are not as much appreciated as small freshwater fishes.

217.00

Apogon maculatus (Poey)

COMMON NAME: Flamefish.

RANGE: Tropical western Atlantic.

MERISTIC CHARACTERISTICS: D. VI + I, 9; A. II, 8; 23–25 scales in the lateral line. Grows to about 4 inches.

This is one of the most common cardinalfishes in the West Indies. Many are shipped to marine aquarium dealers from that area and also from Florida.

They are secretive during the day, hiding in caves or holes in the reef or under large rocks. Collectors in Florida find them by lifting rocks up from one side to expose them and chasing them with a net held in the free hand.

The mouthbrooding habits of cardinalfishes are well known but there are still questions as to which sex carries the eggs. In *Apogon maculatus* a male was found with eggs in his mouth at Tortugas.

Although bright red in nature, aquarium specimens may fade to a light pinkish if not happy or if kept in bright light.

Apogon maculiferus Garrett

COMMON NAME: Spotted Cardinal.
PHOTOGRAPH BY: Dr. Herbert R. Axelrod.
RANGE: Hawaii.
PREVIOUS SCIENTIFIC NAMES: *Amia maculiferus.*

In the shallow, dead reefs which are so common in the Hawaiian Islands, I was fortunate to collect several hundred of these which I promptly shipped back to the mainland U.S.A. in the hopes of making a sale. Of the 245 I sent, 11 were sold in 30 days. This concludes that the fish isn't popular.

They are very common in Hawaii and they are easily maintained in the usual aquarium. They grow rather large (up to 6 inches) for the home aquarium.

Apogon novemfasciatus Cuvier and Valenciennes

COMMON NAME: Cardinalfish.

PHOTOGRAPH BY: Dr. John Randall of a specimen 3.1 inches from Western Samoa.

RANGE: Throughout the tropical mid-Pacific including Samoa, Bikini, Eniwetok, Rongelap, Rongerik, Guam, Rota, the East Indies, Philippine Islands, South Africa.

PREVIOUS SCIENTIFIC NAMES: *Amia novemfasciata, Amia* or *Apogon melanotaenia, A. taeniophorus.*

MERISTIC CHARACTERISTICS: Grows to more than 3 inches. D. VII + I, 9; A. II, 8; P. 14; 24–25 vertical scale rows.

This is a very variable fish, not only in its coloration, but in its habitat. Specimens have been collected living under stones close to shore as well as in water up to 60 feet deep. The W-shaped markings formed by the dorsolateral, ventrolateral and midbody stripes on the tail is the chief distinguishing characteristic of this species from some very similar species.

It has been kept in marine aquaria for long periods of time where it was a rather uninteresting member of the community. It hides under coral or rocks during most of the day. At dusk or dawn it may be found standing perfectly still in open waters as though in a daze. It is a fast swimmer, however, and moves quickly if disturbed by an approaching fish or a shadow. It eats most foods offered it, especially canned Norwegian brine shrimp (*Calanus.*)

Apogon orbicularis Cuvier and Valenciennes

COMMON NAME: Orbiculate Cardinalfish.

RANGE: Indo-Australian Archipelago, Philippines, Hong Kong and Caroline Islands.

PREVIOUS SCIENTIFIC NAMES: *Apogon nigromaculatus, Amia orbicularis, Amia nigromaculata, Apogon nematopterus, Amia nematopterus.*

MERISTIC CHARACTERISTICS: D. VI–I, 9; A. II, 8; lateral line scales 25–26. Grows to 4–5 inches.

This is the most attractive of the over 85 species of cardinalfishes found in tropical seas. A marine tank which houses several *A. orbicularis* makes a dazzling display. Unlike most of the other *Apogon* species, which are shy, it prefers to parade its colorful finnage out in the open. This fish is highly recommended for beginners and "old hands" alike.

A "starter" diet of live brine shrimp is advised and may eventually be replaced with such items as canned Norwegian or frozen brine shrimp, freeze-dried tubifex and dry flake preparations.

Apogon sealei

COMMON NAME: Four-striped Cardinal Fish.
PHOTOGRAPH BY: H. Hansen.
RANGE: Central Indo-Pacific to Africa.
PREVIOUS SCIENTIFIC NAMES: *Amia quinquestriatus*, *A. quadrifasciatus*.
MERISTIC CHARACTERISTICS: D. VII + I, 9; A. II, 8; 25–27 scales in the
lateral line. Grows to 4 inches.

There are many species of *Apogon*, probably about 100. Many of them
have the bar through the eye, as this species. They all act well in the
aquarium and seem to be fairly hardy. While they are colorful and diverse, their main claim to fame is their ability to get along with other
cardinals.

An aquarium of mixed cardinals is quite attractive. They eat most
freeze-dried foods.

Apogon savayennsis (Günther)

COMMON NAME: Cardinal Fish.

RANGE: Tropical mid-Pacific, including Tahiti, Bikini, Kwajalein, Rongelap and Rongerik.

MERISTIC CHARACTERISTICS: (Based upon 3 specimens). Grows to about 4 inches. D. VIII + I, 9; A. II, 8; P. ii, 9, ii; 23–24 vertical scale rows.

The author (HRA) has never experienced the metamorphosis of the dark saddle marking at the base of the tail as has been reported by some workers. They report that this saddle is characteristic of juveniles only and that when the fish is young it completely encircles the caudal peduncle. Specimens maintained alive for up to 6 months showed little, if any, change in the caudal marking.

This is a rather inactive species that spends most of the daylight hiding under rocks or remaining almost motionless in a corner of the aquarium. They become much more active at night or in very subdued light.

Feeding seems to be no problem. They take all types of dried, freeze-dried or frozen foods as well as live foods.

Apogon taeniopterus Bennett

COMMON NAME: Cardinalfish.

PHOTOGRAPH BY: Dr. John Randall of a specimen 4.7 inches from outside reef, S.E. Teavaraa Pass, Tahiti.

RANGE: Tropical Indo-Pacific.

PREVIOUS SCIENTIFIC NAMES: *Amia taeniopterus*.

MERISTIC CHARACTERISTICS: D. VII–I, 8–10; A. II, 8. Grows to a length of about 4–5 inches.

This species, like most of the other Cardinalfishes, is a dweller of dark holes and ledges. It is nocturnal in habit. *A. taeniopterus* is a species which prefers the deeper waters of the outer reefs and is not uncommon below depths of 50 feet. Feedings of a wide variety of live foods supplemented with frozen brine shrimp and finely chopped fish are recommended.

Archosargus rhomboidalis (Linnaeus)

COMMON NAME: Sea Bream.

PHOTOGRAPH BY: Dr. John Randall.

RANGE: New Jersey to Brazil, including the eastern Gulf of Mexico and the West Indies.

MERISTIC CHARACTERISTICS: D. XIII, 10–11; A. III, 10–11; 46–49 scales in the lateral line. Grows to over one foot long.

This is a fish which finds its way into the aquarium because so many aquarists catch them while seining in shallow water seagrass beds up and down the east coast of the U.S.A. from New Jersey to Florida and the Gulf. It is fairly colorful and very hardy, so the small specimens grow . . . and grow . . . and grow. They are excellent pan fish, but they have plenty of bones.

While not recommended for the home aquarium, they are fun if you can collect your own.

They take all kinds of food and seem to be especially fond of canned Norwegian brine shrimp.

Arothron meleagris (Schneider)

COMMON NAME: White-spotted Puffer.
RANGE: Micronesia, Polynesia, Hawaii.
PREVIOUS SCIENTIFIC NAMES: *Tetrodon meleagris, Tetraodon setosus, Ovoides latifrons.*
MERISTIC CHARACTERISTICS: D. I, 9; A. I, 9. Grows to one foot in length.

The white spots on this fish are very characteristic. The skin prickles are very tiny, but may get larger as the fish gets older. The spots never get larger than the eye and the favorite food of this fish is snails. I fed my own on live guppies, but they soon learned to take canned Norwegian brine shrimp.

There are some reports that this fish is poisonous when eaten, especially if their internal organs are ruptured during the cleaning process. This has not been verified.

226.00

Arothron nigropunctatus (Schneider)

COMMON NAME: Black-spotted Puffer.
RANGE: Zanzibar, East Indies, Melanesia, Micronesia and Polynesia.
PREVIOUS SCIENTIFIC NAMES: *Tetrodon nigropunctatus.*
MERISTIC CHARACTERISTICS: D. I, 8–9; A. I, 9–10; P. I, 17. Grows to
about 9 inches.

While the name of this fish can cause quite a problem (it is known in
the trade primarily as *Arothron*), it is not that often seen that we have the
problem. The black spots on the body are very variable, but none ever
get larger than the eye (pupil). As the fish gets older, its leathery skin
begins to get prickly, especially on the back. It has noticeable white
teeth and can take a bite on whatever is in reach. While it prefers coral
to chomp on, it settles for almost any food. It thrives on canned Norwegian brine shrimp.

227.00

Arothron reticularis (Bloch)

Common Name: Reticulated Blow Fish.
Range: Tropical Indo-Pacific.
Previous Scientific Names: *Tetraodon reticularis.*
Meristic Characteristics: D. 10-11; A. 10-11. Attains a length of 17
  inches.

The Reticulated Blow Fish is a homely creature that will win your heart in a very short time. It possesses the ability to inflate itself with water into the shape of a round ball. However, this behavior is rarely observed in the aquarium.

A closely related species, *Arothron hispidus*, is known to Hawaiians as Maki Maki or "deadly death", which refers to the extremely poisonous flesh. However, this same fish is specially processed in Japan and an intoxicating beverage called "fugu" is made from it. In spite of the special process, several hundred "fugu" poisonings are recorded annually.

Photo by K.H. Choo.

Aspidontus taeniatus Quoy and Gaimard

COMMON NAME: False Cleaner.

RANGE: From Guam, New Guinea to Tahiti and Fiji.

PREVIOUS SCIENTIFIC NAMES: *Petroscirtes taeniatus.*

MERISTIC CHARACTERISTICS: D. 39; A. 26. The first rays of the dorsal are not extended as in some related species. Grows to about 5 inches.

Aspidontus taeniatus is the species that mimics the cleaner wrasse *Labroides dimidiatus.* This can be easily seen by comparing the photos of the two species. The False Cleaner uses its "disguise" to approach fishes expecting to be cleaned. Even the undulating swimming motions of the *Labroides* is copied, enhancing the effect of the mimicry. In this way the False Cleaner can get close enough to the unsuspecting fishes to launch an attack. *Aspidontus taeniatus* will nip pieces off the fins of its victims or take a bit of mucus from their bodies.

The False Cleaner supplements its diet in nature with polychaete worms and perhaps other invertebrates. In an aquarium substitutes can be offered in the form of frozen and dried foods, which are accepted, as well as live foods, which are preferred.

229.00

Photo by Aaron Norman.

Astrapogon stellatus (Cope)

COMMON NAME: Conch Fish.
RANGE: Tropical western Atlantic.
PREVIOUS SCIENTIFIC NAMES: *Apogonichthys stellatus.*
MERISTIC CHARACTERISTICS: D. VII–I, 9; A. II, 8; scales 7–23. Reaches
slightly more than 2 inches.

This particular cardinalfish is not overly attractive but is interesting
to aquarists because of its most unusual dwelling habit. It lives as a
commensal within the mantle cavity of the Queen Conch. There is little
information available as to how long these fish can survive in the
aquarium without their molluscan host.

Balistapus undulatus (Mungo Park)

COMMON NAME: Undulate Triggerfish.
RANGE: Widespread throughout the tropical Indo-Pacific to South Africa.
PREVIOUS SCIENTIFIC NAMES: *Balistes undulatus, B. capistratus, B. porcatus,* and *B. lineatus.*
MERISTIC CHARACTERISTICS: D. III, 26–27; A. 23–24; about 24 scales between soft dorsal origin and anal. Grows to 12 inches.

This fish is one of my pets, and certainly one of the first fish I ever kept (HRA). I have a habit of trying to become "friendly" with fishes, and often I have them eating out of my hand and being tickled. This game is a bit dangerous with the Undulate Trigger, for their jaws can take a chunk of flesh out of my hand without too much exertion by powerful jaws that can chew up coral. The Undulate Trigger is dangerous. It can bite and it can slash with its spiny tail, so don't handle the fish.

Aside from their ability to do damage to their owner, they are mischievous in their aquarium. Don't bother setting it up in any decorative scheme for they will tear it all apart within a few days. I would also keep the tank bare of any tankmates, or they too will be torn apart. Just keep our friend all by himself and train him to eat from a pair of tweezers until you get enough courage to feed him from your fingers. Small specimens are much preferable to the larger ones . . . the smaller the better!

They eat anything, including dog biscuit, but they like pieces of boiled shrimp or something chunky.

Balistes bursa Bloch and Schneider*

Common Name: White-lined Triggerfish, Humuhumu lei.
Range: Widespread throughout tropical Indo-Pacific to Africa.
Previous Scientific Names: Many current books use *Sufflamen* and *Hemibalistes*.
Meristic Characteristics: D. III-ii, 25; A. I, 24; P. I, 13. 48 scale rows. 8 teeth in each jaw. Grows to 8 inches or slightly larger.

This is one of the more common triggerfishes and is found regularly in aquariums around the world. It is abundant in Hawaii, generally occurring at depths below 20 feet. They become tame in the aquarium and live a long time provided they are given ample shelter and proper feeding. They are hardy and feed upon most fish foods, especially canned Norwegian brine shrimp and fairy shrimp which is freeze dried.

* Now called *Sufflamen bursa*.

Balistes vetula Linnaeus

COMMON NAME: Queen Triggerfish, Old Wife, Old Wench, Cochino, Peje Puerco.

PHOTOGRAPH BY: Dr. Herbert R. Axelrod of a Bimini specimen.

RANGE: Caribbean area, sometimes ranging as far north as Massachusetts.

PREVIOUS SCIENTIFIC NAMES: *Guaperva* (1648), *Turdus oculo radiato* (1725), *Balistes bellus* (1792), *Chaliosma velata* (1839) and *Balistes equestris*.

MERISTIC CHARACTERISTICS: D. III, 29; A. 27; 63 scales.

This is one of the most common of all triggers, probably because it is so hardy and so inexpensive compared to the Pacific triggers. It is regularly available in the U.S.A. and England, as well as Europe, as the Caribbean reef fishes are collected with more regularity and by more dependable people than some of the South Sea species.

The Queen Trigger is not as friendly as the Undulate. It can be dangerous, as it has very sharp teeth and a vicious tail which it uses when annoyed. Some dealers report having difficulty in shipping this fish, but my experiences have been that it ships easily. Keep it alone in an aquarium and it will soon become friendly. It usually attacks other fishes if kept in a small aquarium. It feeds on canned Norwegian brine shrimp and chunks of freeze-dried tubifex worms which have algae added to it (Chlorella).

Balistoides niger (Bonnaterre)

COMMON NAME: Clown Triggerfish.
PHOTOGRAPH BY: Paysan.
RANGE: Rare throughout the tropical Indo-Pacific. Common in Maldives.
PREVIOUS SCIENTIFIC NAMES: *Balistes conspiculum, Balistoides conspiculum, Balistes niger.*
MERISTIC CHARACTERISTICS: D. III + ii, 25; A. i, 22; P. i, 13. 48 scale rows and 8 teeth in each jaw.

When asked which fish I think is the most beautiful, this one comes to mind. When the author (HRA) first came upon this fish in 1950, he brought the first specimen back . . . not alive! It took another three years before he was able to get it back alive and it eventually was sold for $650 in a petshop in Frankfurt, Germany.

This beautiful fish is the crowning glory of every public aquarium and they are in constant demand because they are so spectacular.

Feeding them is no problem. They readily take freeze-dried foods, canned Norwegian brine shrimp and fairy shrimp.

*Now called *Balistoides conspicillum* Schneider.

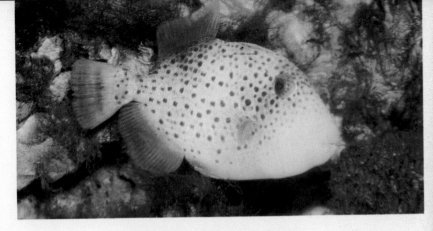

Balistoides viridescens (Bloch)

COMMON NAME: Spotted Triggerfish.
PHOTOGRAPH BY: H. Hansen.
RANGE: Widespread throughout the tropical Indo-Pacific.
PREVIOUS SCIENTIFIC NAMES: *Balistes viridescens.*
MERISTIC CHARACTERISTICS: D. III, 24–25; A. 23–24. About 18 scales
between beginning of soft dorsal and anal. Grows to two feet.

This species has been blamed for raiding oyster beds, especially the
kind which favor the growth of pearls. They are omnivorous and have
the teeth which would easily enable them to crush oyster shells.

In the aquarium they are not very spectacular. Young specimens are
often seen because they are so hardy, but they lack the dramatic color we
expect from exotic coral fishes.

Balistoides viridescens is one of the less colorful species of triggerfish both as adult (shown here) and juvenile (p. 235.00 top photo). Photo by Dr. Herbert R. Axelrod.

Blennius cristatus Linnaeus

COMMON NAME: Molly Miller.

PHOTOGRAPH BY: Marcuse.

RANGE: From Florida to Brazil; also the Gulf of Mexico.

PREVIOUS SCIENTIFIC NAMES: None.

MERISTIC CHARACTERISTICS: D. XII, 14–15; A. II, 16–17; P. 14. No scales. A mass of cirri about the anterior nostril and on top of the head.

Blennies, as a rule, are *either* herbivorous or carnivorous. This species does well on canned Norwegian brine shrimp and fairy shrimp once it falls to the bottom (HRA boils it first).

This species has been observed spawning in nature. They lay demersal eggs which are tended by the male who guards and fans them.

They are interesting fishes if kept by themselves in a small aquarium as they often like to climb out of the water. Plant their tank with rocks so they can spend some time in the open air. Cover the aquarium carefully or you might find them on the floor dried out.

Blennius nigriceps Vinciguerra

COMMON NAME: Carmine Blenny, Cardinal Blenny.
PHOTOGRAPH BY: Marcuse.
RANGE: Mediterranean.
MERISTIC CHARACTERISTICS: D. XII, 14–15; A. II, 15–17. Grows to about
  1½ inches.

All along the shallow rocky coast of the sunny Mediterranean where
the French, Spanish and Italian rivieras attract millions of sunbathers,
rocky ledges inhibit active beaches from becoming tourist havens. In
these rocky ledges live a variety of magnificently colored small blennies.
Few people are interested in blennies (except scientists like Dr. Victor
Springer of the U.S.N.M. who finds a great deal of beauty and fascination
in these slime or mucus fish, as the Germans call them); not even aquarists are interested in blennies. Hopefully these beautiful photos will
create some interest in the slimefish for they probably will be the easiest
of all marine fishes to breed.

The most beautiful of all blennies might be the carmine blenny, or
cardinal blenny. The next time you swim in the Mediterranean try to
catch a few. It took the author (HRA) three days to catch one alive as
they are very fast and quickly dart into a hole in the rocks. A small
electric-shock apparatus is what is needed.

Blennius pavo Risso

COMMON NAME: Peacock Blenny, Pfauenschleimfisch.
PHOTOGRAPH BY: Hansen.
RANGE: Mediterranean Sea, Black Sea, perhaps in the Atlantic Ocean close to the Mediterranean, but not as far north as England.
MERISTIC CHARACTERISTICS: D. XII, 21–24; A. II, 23. They grow to about 5 inches.

This blenny is popular in the smaller aquariums in Europe because it is one of the locally captured types. They live in rocky holes and may often be found in brackish water. The males have a fleshy crest on top of their heads; this is lacking in the females. The dark ocellus with the pale margin is characteristic of males of this species and seems to be diagnostic of the species as well. The females are less strongly marked.

In the aquarium they do well if they have plenty of rocks in which to hide. They like rather high temperatures, even though their natural waters are cooler. 75–85° F. is quite comfortable for them. Alkaline pH is required, from 7.4–7.6 being ideal. They breed fairly easily in the aquarium if they are given enough room. Males protect their "territories," so don't crowd them or fights will ensue. After spawning the male guards and aerates the eggs. Adults feed on Norwegian canned brine shrimp, freeze-dried brine shrimp or most freeze-dried foods. They also take live small fishes.

239.00

Blennius rouxi Cocco

COMMON NAME: Striped Blenny.
PHOTOGRAPH BY: Hansen at the Berlin Aquarium.
RANGE: Mediterranean Sea.
MERISTIC CHARACTERISTICS: D. 32–33; A. 23–25. Grows to 3 inches. The
dorsal and anal counts lump spines and rays together and are doubtful.

This beautiful, but rare, Mediterranean species would be more
plentiful if they weren't so difficult to capture. They hide among the
sea weed or huddle under a rock. They are rarely if ever found outside
in open waters and they seem to hug the coast in rocky, algae-strewn
habitats.

Not too much is known about this interesting fish and few specimens
have found their way into the home aquarium. They probably will be
simple to breed if a dozen specimens are kept in a 100 gallon aquarium
which is suitably outfitted with rocks and the fish are properly fed.

240.00

Blennius tentacularis (Brünnich)

COMMON NAME: Horned Blenny, Gehörnter Schleimfisch, Vavusella, Torillo.

PHOTOGRAPH BY: Hansen at Berlin Aquarium.

RANGE: Predominantly Mediterranean, Black Sea, and doubtfully reported from the Atlantic coast from Portugal to Dakar.

MERISTIC CHARACTERISTICS: D. XII, 20–23; A. II, 22–23. Grows to about 6 inches.

This beautiful blenny likes the algae beds on the rocky coasts off the Mediterranean. Skin divers also report this fish among sea grass, coral and detritus, but nowhere is it common.

Because of its pretty colors and the two "horns" projecting from the crest of its head, it is quite popular with aquariums all over the world. Scientists tell us that the "horns" or "cirrhi" are quite unique in that they are fringed on only one margin and that they are not to be described as "on the crest of the head" but rather as "occurring over each eye." Anyway this seems to be the only blenny with that characteristic so if you see a fish with a fringe on one side of the cirrhi you know it's this species.

Feeding is simple with canned Norwegian brine shrimp, fairy shrimp which has been boiled or soaked so it sinks, or small fishes.

Photo by Roger Steene.

Bodianus axillaris (Bennett)

Common Name: Coral Hogfish.
Range: Tropical Indo-Pacific.
Previous Scientific Names: *Lepidaplois axillaris, Lepidaplois albomaculatus.*
Meristic Characteristics: D. XII, 10; A. III, 12; lateral line scales 28.
Attains a length of 8 inches.

Many of the wrasses are known for their ability to drastically change coloration while growing from juvenile to adult. Often the basic juvenile livery may be retained by the adult female and is less spectacular than the brilliant coat of the male. There are a few species, however, which display different juvenile-female and male color patterns which are equally beautiful. Such a fish is *Bodianus axillaris.* The juveniles and females are velvety black with large white polka dots. It's hard to imagine that these two forms represent the same species.

This fish does well in the aquarium and will eat a variety of foods.

Bodianus bilunulatus (Lacepede)

Common Name: Pacific Hog Fish.
Range: Hawaii and Central Pacific.
Previous Scientific Names: *Labrus bilunulatus, Cossyphus albotaeniatus, Crenilabrus modestus, Lepidaplois strophodes, Lepidaplois
albotaeniatus, Lepidaplois modestus, Lepidaplois atrorubens.*
Meristic Characteristics: D. XII, 10; A. III, 12; scales 7-34-13. Attains
a length of about 2 feet.

    B. bilunalatus is a gorgeous species which is available to Ameri-
can aquarists via Hawaii, where it is very common. Juveniles are colored completely differently from the adults, presenting a striking combination of purple and yellow. The young are common during the summer months and are easy to capture with small dipnets and scuba
gear. This species is sometimes eaten, but is not rated as one of the better food fishes.
    Freeze-dried fairy shrimp, tubifex, daphnia and frozen and live
brine shrimp are ideal foods for this species, as is Norwegian brine
shrimp.

Photo by Dr. Patrick L. Colin.

Bodianus pulchellus (Poey)

COMMON NAME: Spotfin Hogfish, Cuban Hogfish.
RANGE: From the Carolinas to the West Indies.
MERISTIC CHARACTERISTICS: D. XII, 10; A. III, 12; about 30 scales in the
lateral line. Grows to 9 inches.

Young Spotfin Hogfish are yellow and they begin changing color when
they are about 2 inches long. They, like *Bodianus rufus* young, are
cleaners and can be found picking parasites from the bodies of larger
fishes.

This is a deep water fish, usually found below 80 feet. They do very
well in the aquarium and are extremely popular in European public
aquariums because they are so hardy.

Feed with canned Norwegian brine shrimp or fairy shrimp.

Photo by Ken Lucas, Steinhart Aquarium.

Bodianus rufus (Linnaeus)

COMMON NAME: Spanish Hogfish.
RANGE: Bermuda through the Caribbean and Gulf of Mexico.
MERISTIC CHARACTERISTICS: D. XI–XII, 9–11; A. III, 11–13; P. 15–16.
There are 29–31 lateral line scales. Reaches 24 inches.

Small specimens are interesting when kept with larger fishes for these are one of the cleaner fishes. They can be seen picking small ektoparasites, usually crustaceans, from the bodies of larger fishes. As they grow older their 8 strong canine teeth in the front of their jaws develop, and their appetites change to the more unpalatable diet of sea urchins, crabs, brittle stars, clams, mussels and even small lobsters.

In the aquarium they settle for fairy shrimp and canned Norwegian brine shrimp. Don't put any crabs or shrimp in their aquarium or they will kill them even if they don't eat them.

245.00

The upper anterior portion of the Spanish hogfish may be blue, violet, or even reddish purple. Very small individuals are violet anteriorly and yellow posteriorly, resembling somewhat the livery of the royal gramma. The younger individuals of the Spanish hogfish are part time cleaners. Photo above by Karl Probst; photo below by Klaus Paysan.

Bolbometopon bicolor (Rüppell)

COMMON NAME: Two-colored Parrot Fish

PHOTOGRAPH BY: Marcuse. The lower spotted fish is probably *Coris aygula*.

RANGE: Quite common throughout the tropical Indo-Pacific including the Red Sea.

PREVIOUS SCIENTIFIC NAMES: *Scarus bicolor, Chlorurus bicolor*.

MERISTIC CHARACTERISTICS: D. IX, 10; A. III, 9; 3 rows of scales on the cheek.

These are beautiful fish which change their color completely as they grow. The young fish illustrated here is characterized by the dark ocellated spot in the front part of the dorsal. The mature fish has lost

247.00

Adult male *Bolbometapon bicolor* which looks entirely different from the juvenile. Fortunately intermediates help bridge the gap. Photo by Roger Steene.

this spot and the yellow and white pattern and instead has an intricate pattern of pink, green, blue, etc.

This colorful parrotfish grows to a length of about 50 cm in nature but only the juveniles seem to be seen in home aquaria. It is a rare aquarist indeed who could raise one of these fish to maturity through all its intermediate color patterns. They do well on most marine aquarium foods, especially if some vegetable matter is included.

Bothus lunatus (Linnaeus)

COMMON NAME: Peacock Flounder.

PHOTOGRAPH BY: Dr. John Randall of an 11-inch specimen from the Virgin Islands.

RANGE: Tropical western Atlantic.

MERISTIC CHARACTERISTICS: D. 92–99; A. 71–76; pectoral rays on the eyed side: 11–12; 84–95 scales in the lateral line. Grows to about $1\frac{1}{2}$ feet.

The Peacock Flounder is a member of the family Bothidae. They have two eyes on one side, none on the other. They have unusually long dorsal and anal fins. In the aquarium they usually attach themselves to the glass sides so all you can see is their white bellies. If your aquarium has soft sand, you might find the Peacock Flounder almost completely buried in the sand, waiting for some small fish to come by which can be gobbled up. Though the Peacock Flounder is a true marine, there are quite a few flounders (usually they are more accurately referred to as "soles" as they do belong to the family Solidae) which are found in brackish water. At least one, from Brazil, is truly freshwater, the author having collected hundreds of them in various rivers deep inland in Brazil.

Though preferring small live fish as food, the Peacock Flounder and most other flatfish take almost any type of food if they are hungry.

249.00

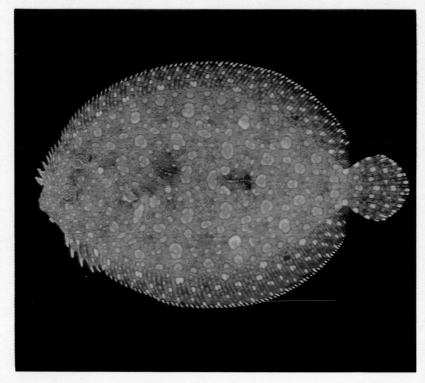

Bothus mancus (Broussonet)

COMMON NAME: Tropical Flounder.
PHOTOGRAPH BY: Dr. John Randall of a 5-inch specimen from Eniwetok.
RANGE: Widespread throughout the tropical Indo-Pacific, as far south as Durban, South Africa.
PREVIOUS SCIENTIFIC NAMES: *Platophrys mancua.*
MERISTIC CHARACTERISTICS: Grows to 16 inches. D. About 100; A. about 80.

The small tropical flounders are interesting inhabitants of the marine community aquarium. They attach themselves to the glass or almost bury themselves in the sand, waiting for a small fish to swim by they can gobble down. Males have longer pectoral fins than females, their pectorals reaching the caudal base. The females caudal is much shorter. They might be considered scavengers, as they take food from the bottom, but they are rarely seen to eat. Few if any starve.

By all means get small ones for your community aquarium if you see them in a dealer's shop.

Calamus bajonado (Bloch and Schneider)

COMMON NAME: Jolthead Porgy.
RANGE: Rhode Island to Bermuda to and throughout the West Indies.
MERISTIC CHARACTERISTICS: D. XII, 12; A. III, 10; P. 14–16. There are
50–57 lateral line scales. Grows to about 24 inches.

Small specimens of this fish are sometimes seen in public aquariums
and 2 and 3-inch specimens often find their way into home aquariums
when they are collected along the Atlantic coast in the summertime.

While they are not very beautiful, they seem to be friendly and often
learn to almost jump up and take food from your hand.

They do well on freeze-dried tuibfex worms, fairy shrimp, and canned
Norwegian brine shrimp.

251.00

Calamus calamus (Cuvier and Valenciennes)

COMMON NAME: Saucereye Porgy.

PHOTOGRAPH BY: Dr. John Randall of a 10.2-inch specimen from the Virgin Islands.

RANGE: Bermuda, Florida Keys, West Indies.

MERISTIC CHARACTERISTICS: D. XII, 12; A. III, 10–11; reaches over 14 inches in length.

The Saucereye Porgy looks very much like the Pluma, *Calamus pennatula,* but can be distinguished from that and other species by its cheek coloration which consists of a blue streak below each eye and many yellow spots on a blue background. The body is normally silvery but can become blotched apparently at will. The juveniles inhabit grass beds and the adults may be found in grass beds or occasionally on the reef. They feed on various crustaceans which they can crush with their molariform teeth.

The Saucereye Porgy does well in the home aquarium. It will accept most of the meaty foods such as chopped shrimp.

Callionymus bairdi Jordan

COMMON NAME: Lancer Dragonet.
PHOTOGRAPH BY: Dr. John Randall of a 1.7-inch specimen from the Virgin Islands.
RANGE: Tropical western Atlantic.
MERISTIC CHARACTERISTICS: D. IV, 9; A. 8; P. 19–20; C. 15. Grows to about 4 inches but the usual aquarium size is 2 inches.

This is a scavenger fish for the marine aquarium. It spends most of its time on the bottom of the tank scrounging food left over by other fishes. It should be easy to spawn if fed properly, but no one has recorded its spawning yet. Likes to play among rocks and formations on the bottom of the tank. Very uncomfortable in open tanks without some cover. Readily accepts canned Norwegian brine shrimp and freeze-dried foods which eventually sink.

Calloplesiops altivelis (Steindachner)

Common Name: Comet.
Range: Tropical Indo-Pacific.
Previous Scientific Names: *Barrosia barrosi, Calloplesiops niveus.*

    This species has become very popular in the aquarium trade. Once considered rare and commanding a very high price, this species is now available most of the time, and the price has dropped to within the range of most aquarists. It is easily kept and will eat almost anything (including smaller fishes in the tank).

254.00

Photo by Dwayne Reed.

Cantherhines macrocerus (Hollard)

COMMON NAME: Whitespotted Filefish.
RANGE: An uncommon fish from the tropical western Atlantic.
PREVIOUS SCIENTIFIC NAMES: *Monacanthus macrocerus.*
MERISTIC CHARACTERISTICS: D. II, 34–36; A. 29–32; P. 13–14. Grows to
  about 18 inches maximum.

This rare spotted beauty gets whiter spots the larger it becomes. There
are some who believe that mated pairs stay together all through life the
way certain freshwater cichlids *might*. Small specimens are expensive
as the fish is rare throughout its entire range. According to Randall
(*Caribbean Reef Fishes*) they feed mainly on sponges, but they also feed
upon hydroids, stinging coral, gorgonians and algae.

They have been successfully maintained in aquaria on dried fairy
shrimp, canned Norwegian brine shrimp and freeze-dried Tubifex with
Chlorella algae.

255.00

Cantherhines pardalis (Rüppell)

COMMON NAME: Brown Filefish.

PHOTOGRAPH BY: Dr. Herbert R. Axelrod in Ceylon.

RANGE: Red Sea, Zanzibar, Cape of Good Hope, East Indies, Melanesia, Micronesia and Polynesia.

PREVIOUS SCIENTIFIC NAMES: *Monacanthus pardalis, M. rüppelli, M. fatensis, M. spilosomus, Liomanacanthus pardalis.*

MERISTIC CHARACTERISTICS: D. II, 34; A. 29. Grows to about 8 inches.

This isn't one of the real beauties of the aquarium, but they are very hardy and because of their great range, they always turn up in the shipments received by aquarists as "substitutes."

They are fairly harmless in the aquarium and do well on most of the usual foods but they especially like freeze-dried Tubifex worms with Chlorella algae added to it before it was processed.

Smaller specimens are preferred.

Photo by Dwayne Reed.

Cantherhines pullus (Ranzani)

COMMON NAME: Tail-Light Filefish.
RANGE: The Atlantic from Massachusetts to Argentina to West Africa.
PREVIOUS SCIENTIFIC NAMES: *Monocanthus pullus*.
MERISTIC CHARACTERISTICS: D. II, 33–36; A. 29–32; P. 12–14. Grows to
  8 inches.

While not a raving beauty, this hardy filefish has been a favorite for
many years because of its availability and hardiness. It is often collected
and exported as a small specimen about 3 inches long for the smaller
fish seem to prefer open waters where they are more easily netted
(seined). Schools of one inch fish can be seen far out in the Gulf stream
on top of the water where they can be dipped out.

This is a vegetarian whose diet in nature is primarily algae and
sponges. In the aquarium they thrive on algi-flakes (a tropical fish flake
food) and freeze-dried Tubifex worms in which Chlorella algae has been
mixed.

Canthigaster bennetti (Bleeker)

Common Name: Bennett's Sharp Nose Puffer.
Range: Tropical Indo-Pacific.
Previous Scientific Names: *Tetraodon ocellatus, Tetraodon papua, Tropidichthys bennetti, Anosmius bennetti, Psilonotus bennetti, Canthigaster ocellatus, Psilonotus ocellatus, Tetraodon bennetti.*
Meristic Characteristics: D. I, 9; A. I, 9. Attains a length of 4-5 inches.

The Sharp Nose Puffers, like their cousins the blow fishes (family *Tetraodontidae*), possess the ability to inflate themselves with water. This is primarily a defense mechanism which serves to discourage would-be predators from swallowing them. This species is what is known as an opportunist feeder, that is, feeds on just about anything edible which it finds on the reef. Among the various items which have been found in the stomachs of dissected specimens are algal fronds, crustaceans, polychaetes, fish, sponges and coral fragments. The teeth are well developed for nibbling on the delicate tips of *Acropora* coral. This wide latitude of feeding habits is of advantage to the aquarist. Nearly any reasonable food will be accepted with enthusiasm.

258.00

Canthigaster cinctus (Richardson)

COMMON NAME: Israeli Puffer.

PHOTOGRAPH BY: Dr. Herbert R. Axelrod.

RANGE: From Hawaii to Tahiti to Guam to the Red Sea, then to Australia and Zanzibar.

PREVIOUS SCIENTIFIC NAMES: *Tetrodon cinctus, Tetraodon coronatus*, also confused with *C. valentini*.

MERISTIC CHARACTERISTICS: D. I, 9; A. II, 8. Grows to about 5 inches.

The photo doesn't clearly show the saddles running over the back in live specimens; when preserved these saddles are very distinct and closely resemble *C. valentini*. Alive, however, they are quite different fish.

This hardy puffer always looks emaciated and sick with its tail always pinched in (a normal symptom for impending disaster with most fishes) and its belly always sunken. Perhaps this sickly appearance has enabled it to survive and become distributed almost worldwide.

In the aquarium they thrive on dried fairy shrimp, freeze-dried Tubifex worms, brine shrimp and canned Norwegian shrimp.

259.00

Canthigaster jactator (Jenkins)

COMMON NAME: Hawaiian Sharp-nosed Puffer.
PHOTOGRAPH BY: Gene Wolfsheimer
RANGE: Hawaiian Islands.
PREVIOUS SCIENTIFIC NAMES: *Tropidichthys jactator*; often confused with *C. solandri*.
MERISTIC CHARACTERISTICS: D. II, 8; A. II, 8. Grows to about 3 inches.

This is the easiest of puffers to identify as the white spots on the dark background are characteristic. A similar looking fish is *C. solandri*, but this fish has lines radiating from its eye and has spotting on its tail while *jactator* does not.

Since this fish is so common in Hawaii, being the most common in the genus, it is exported on a regular basis. It is small and stays small. It is poisonous to eat unless properly prepared and its sharp mouth can rip your skin if you handle them.

They thrive on dried fairy shrimp, canned Norwegian brine shrimp and freeze-dried foods of all types.

Canthigaster rostrata (Bloch)

COMMON NAME: Sharpnose Puffer.

PHOTOGRAPH BY: Dr. Herbert R. Axelrod of a 3-inch specimen from Bimini.

RANGE: Both sides of the Atlantic in warm waters; in the Caribbean and from Bermuda to Florida.

PREVIOUS SCIENTIFIC NAMES: *Tetrodon rostratus*.

MERISTIC CHARACTERISTICS: D. 10; A. 9; P. 16–18 (including uppermost rudimentary ray). Grows to $4\frac{1}{2}$ inches.

A very common fish which is probably the least expensive of all puffers. They are hardy but not too colorful except for the brilliant white. According to Dr. Randall (*Caribbean Reef Fishes*), they feed on sea-grasses, sponges, crabs, mollusks, and crustaceans, polychaete worms, sea urchins, starfishes, hydroids and algae.

In the aquarium they are equally as easy to feed with dried fairy shrimp, canned Norwegian brine shrimp and any of the unified mass freeze-dried foods. Do not feed frozen products, such as frozen brine shrimp which is mostly brine shrimp "juice."

261.00

Canthigaster solandri (Richardson)*

COMMON NAME: Red Sea Sharp-nosed Puffer.
PHOTOGRAPH BY: Paysan.
RANGE: Hawaii (one specimen), Red Sea, Zanzibar, Mozambique, East Indies, China, Melanesia, Micronesia and Polynesia.
PREVIOUS SCIENTIFIC NAMES: *Canthigaster margaritatus, Tetraodon papua,* sometimes misspelled *solanderi.*
MERISTIC CHARACTERISTICS: D. I, 8; A. I, 8; P. II, 14. Very variable in the prickles. Grows to about 4 inches.

Sometimes confused as "males" of *jactator* because they are so similarly colored and have color in the tail and radiating lines about the eye.

The author (HRA) has never found any in Hawaii though most literature claims Hawaii as a part of the range based upon a single specimen. Since Hawaii is fished so regularly for live specimens for the aquarium trade, it is doubtful that Hawaii should be considered the eastern limit of the range since none have been found since the one.

They do well in the aquarium and are fairly common since they are shipped from almost every collecting point in the tropical Indo-Pacific where there are so many collectors.

They feed well on dried fairy shrimp, canned Norwegian brine shrimp and freeze-dried Tubifex.

* Now called *Canthigaster margaritatus* (Ruppell).

An adult *Canthigaster margaritatus* of about 4 inches in length on a reef at the Palau Islands. Note the different sized spots on the body when compared with the smaller specimen on the opposite page. Photo by Dr. Gerald R. Allen.

263.00

Canthigaster valentini (Bleeker)

COMMON NAME: Sharpnosed Puffer.

RANGE: Widespread throughout the tropical Indo-Pacific, to South Africa.

PREVIOUS SCIENTIFIC NAMES: *Psilonotus valentini, Tropidichthys valentini.*

MERISTIC CHARACTERISTICS: D. 9–10; A. 8–9; attains a length of 8 inches.

This scaleless beauty has a typical beak composed of two large plates in each jaw with a suture in front to form a strong beak which enables them to crunch coral if necessary. They can bite your hand painfully if you handle them, even when quite small. They like warm water over 80° F. and they are found in very shallow waters in their natural habitat. When young they have round blue and orange dots on the side. Typical of most puffers, they make croaking sounds when lifted from the water.

They do well in the aquarium and take freeze-dried Tubifex worms with Chlorella algae, as well as canned Norwegian brine shrimp. Freeze-dried brine shrimp is also a favorite.

264.00

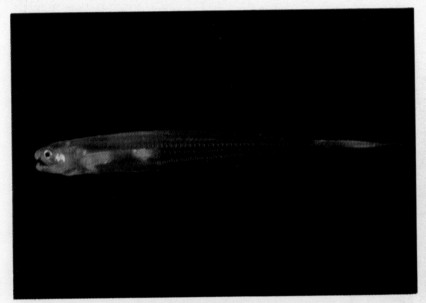

Carapus sp.

Common Name: Pen Shell Pearl Fish.
Photograph By: Dr. John Randall from a specimen 3.3-inches from
   Pen Shell.
Range: Moorea; Society Islands. Tropical South and Central Pacific.
Meristic Characteristics: Not available.

The pearl fishes are poorly known as far as their classification is concerned. These fish are small and often transparent. They are, however, among the most unique fishes by virtue of the fact that they dwell in the cloacal chamber of holothurians (sea cucumbers)! The pearl fish never wanders far from the sea cucumber and makes its entrance into its host by backing into the anus tail first. These creatures have a heavy coat of mucus covering the body and eyes. Therefore, they cannot see very well and depend primarily on chemical receptors to find their holothurian hosts. The mucus coat no doubt serves to protect the fish from abrasion when it wriggles into the relatively small anal opening of the cucumber.

The Pen Shell Pearl Fish is unique among this group, since it does not live in the sea cucumber but lives within Pen Shells. However, it is possible that this species may also dwell in sea cucumbers as well.

Little is known about the care and feeding of the species in captivity. They may prove to be impossible to keep without their native host. In fact, some species are known to feed upon the gonad material of the holothurians which harbor them.

Centropyge argi Woods and Kanazawa

COMMON NAME: Cherubfish, Pygmy Angelfish.
PHOTOGRAPH BY: Dr. John Randall of a 2.1-inch specimen from Curaçao.
RANGE: Bermuda, West Indies and the Gulf of Mexico.
MERISTIC CHARACTERISTICS: D. XIV–XV, 15–16; A. III, 17; P. 15–16.
32–34 lateral line scales. Grows to 3 inches.

This is a rare and expensive marine tropical which most aquarists hope to have someday. Odd specimens are collected in the shallow waters, but most of them are found in water over 100 feet deep . . . too deep for all but the real professional collectors.

The fish are reasonably hardy, especially the larger ones over 2 inches. They feed well on the usual diet of fairy shrimp, canned Norwegian brine shrimp, live brine shrimp and freeze-dried foods.

Centropyge bicolor (Bloch)

COMMON NAME: Two-colored Angelfish, Vaqueta de Dos Colores.
RANGE: Philippines, Fiji, Pago Pago.
MERISTIC CHARACTERISTICS: D. XIV, 16; A. III, 17. About 46 scale rows.
Grows to about 4 inches.

This is one of the more rare beauties of all the marine angelfishes. Earl Kennedy in Manila, P.I. ships them on rare occasions, but the price is always high and the larger public aquariums (with the highest budgets) always get them.

They seem to be fairly peaceful for an angelfish, but they are never to be trusted together as they usually fight.

Feeding them is no problem as they do well on dried fairy shrimp, canned Norwegian brine shrimp and the usual freeze-dried foods.

Centropyge bispinosus (Günther)

COMMON NAME: Dusky Angelfish.

RANGE: Widespread throughout the tropical Indo-Pacific to South Africa.

PREVIOUS SCIENTIFIC NAMES: *Holacanthus bispinosus, H. multispinis, H. somervilli.*

MERISTIC CHARACTERISTICS: D. XIV–XV, 16–17; A. III, 16–17; about 44–45 series of scales, counted lengthwise from the upper edge of the gill opening to the base of the caudal rays. Grows to 5 inches.

This is a very variably colored fish, from yellow to a dusky dirty coloration. The cross-bars are often vivid. It is well known to aquarists and has been very hardy if kept under proper conditions.

They feed on canned Norwegian brine shrimp or freeze-dried tubifex worms which has chlorella added to it. They are active and moderately peaceful if kept with fishes their own size. They do well in smaller aquariums up to 50 gallons in size. This might be one of the fishes which could be spawned in the home aquarium if a few were kept in their own tank and well fed.

They have not spawned in captivity to date.

Centropyge fisheri (Snyder)

RANGE: Hawaiian Islands

MERISTIC CHARACTERISTICS: D. XIV–XV, 16–17; A. III, 16–17; about 40–45 series counted lengthwise. A small species under 3 inches.

This is a fairly rare fish, but one that is so colorful that it commands a high price and collectors take pains to "bring it back alive." It has a place in every community aquarium, especially the small ones of about 20 gallons in capacity.

It feeds well on canned Norwegian brine shrimp and freeze-dried Tubifex worms with Chlorella algae added to it.

If possible, try to keep them in schools with as many specimens as possible. They might be induced to spawn if given proper conditions.

Centropyge flavissimus (Cuvier)

COMMON NAME: Lemonpeel Angelfish.

PHOTOGRAPH BY: Paysan.

RANGE: Tropical mid-Pacific, including the atolls of Bikini, Eniwetok, Rongelap, Rongerik and Kwajalein.

PREVIOUS SCIENTIFIC NAMES: *Holacanthus flavissimus*.

MERISTIC CHARACTERISTICS: D. XIV, 15–16; A. III, 16; P. I, i, 14–15; 44–50 scale rows in lengthwise series from the upper edge of the gill opening to the base of the caudal fin rays. Grows to about 4 inches.

This is a brilliantly colored fish suitable for the community aquarium. Smaller specimens have a round, ocellated spot, larger than the eye, on the middle of each side. Adults and young are a brilliant chrome yellow, some show the blue ocellus when young specimens are kept in good condition in the aquarium.

They feed well on canned Norwegian brine shrimp (*Calanus*), freeze-dried Tubifex worms with Chlorella algae and freeze dried brine shrimp. Keep several specimens together if possible. They do best in a small aquarium with a water temperature about 78° F. or slightly higher.

Centropyge heraldi Woods and Schultz

COMMON NAME: Golden Angelfish.

RANGE: Tropical mid-Pacific including Okinawa, Bikini, Rongelap and Tahiti.

PREVIOUS SCIENTIFIC NAMES: *Centropyge flavissimus.*

MERISTIC CHARACTERISTICS: D. XV, 15; A. III, 17; P. I, i, 12–14; 46–48 scale rows in lengthwise series from upper edge of gill opening to the base of the caudal fin rays.

This fish was named to honor Dr. Earl S. Herald, head of the famous Steinhart Aquarium in San Francisco, California.

It is a beautiful fish which is easily distinguished from all other members of the genus *Centropyge* by the color pattern of the head and fins.

271.00

Photo by James H. O'Neill.

Centropyge loriculus (Günther)

COMMON NAME: Flaming Angelfish.

RANGE: Society Islands, Hawaii.

MERISTIC CHARACTERISTICS: D. XIV, 16; A. III, 17; P. I, i, 11 (?). 28 scale rows.

There is doubt about whether there exists *Centropyge flammeus* which looks exactly like this fish except for certain physical characteristics. Woods and Schultz note that *loriculus* has broadly rounded hind margins of the dorsal and anal fins, while *flammeus* has sharply pointed ones, but this seems to be a sexual characteristic rather than a generic difference.

In any case, this is a magnificently colored fish, either species, and it doesn't matter which you have as both are equally easy to maintain.

They feed well on dried fairy shrimp, canned Norwegian brine shrimp and the usual freeze-dried foods.

Centropyge potteri (Jordan and Metz)

COMMON NAME: Russet Angelfish.
RANGE: Hawaii.
PREVIOUS SCIENTIFIC NAMES: *Holacanthus potteri*.

This is a familiar fish around Hawaii and specimens have been shipped regularly from this tropical paradise. According to Gosline and Brock this is "the only species of the genus in fact, the only chaetodontid of the group with a preopercular spine known from less than 60 feet of water in Hawaii."

It is quite well known and has been illustrated in color in various ichthyological publications. It is a favorite fish because it eats almost anything, including but not limited to canned Norwegian brine shrimp and freeze-dried Tubifex with Chlorella algae. It is always in good color, even when abused.

273.00

Centropyge tibicen Cuvier

COMMON NAME: Black Angelfish.
PHOTOGRAPH BY: Earl Kennedy.
RANGE: East Indies, Philippine Islands, Melanesia.
PREVIOUS SCIENTIFIC NAMES: *Holacanthus tibicen, H. leucopleura.*

There is considerable confusion in the literature about this fish. Kaup used this fish to describe the genus *Centropyge* in 1860; Cuvier described the fish, similarly, in 1830.

At any rate, the photograph shows a very young, small specimen about $1\frac{1}{2}$ inches long. The adults are mostly black with a brown head. The edges of the spiny dorsal and the lower border of the anal and all the paired fins are yellow. There is a large yellow blotch in adults; it is white in juveniles. It grows to about 5 inches.

Feeding is simple with fairy shrimp, canned Norwegian brine shrimp and freeze-dried foods.

Photo by K.H. Choo.

Cephalopholis argus Bloch and Schneider

COMMON NAME: Black Grouper.
RANGE: Tropical mid-Pacific, including the East Indies and the northern Marshall Islands, and Guam.
MERISTIC CHARACTERISTICS: D. IX, 15–16; A. III, 9; P. i–ii, 15–17; 95–100 scale rows above the lateral line; grows to more than 12 inches.

The normal coloration of the Black Grouper runs from a dark brown to a deep purplish black. It often has brilliant light blue specks on its body.

This is not a fish for the small aquarium unless very small specimens are available. They become very tame and can be trained to eat from your fingers. They also eat any small fishes in the aquarium.

Once acclimated to tank life, they do very well in the average home aquarium, but they are more at home in very large tanks.

Feed them freeze-dried Tubifex with Chlorella algae, canned Norwegian brine shrimp and chunks of cooked shrimp as they grow larger.

275.00

Cephalopholis aurantius (Valenciennes)

COMMON NAME: Spotted Grouper.

PHOTOGRAPH BY: H. Hansen at the Berlin Aquarium.

RANGE: East Indies to Tahiti.

PREVIOUS SCIENTIFIC NAMES: *Serranus* or *Epinephelus aurantius, analis,* or *roseus.*

MERISTIC CHARACTERISTICS: D. IX, 14–16; A. III, 8–10. Grows to about 14 inches.

Small specimens are more colorful as the larger specimens lack the white spots on the body. This fish is widespread in the central tropical Indo-Pacific, but nowhere is the fish plentiful, resulting in high prices for the smaller specimens. Larger specimens are eaten and are considered prime food.

They thrive on anything normally fed to marine fishes, especially smaller fishes.

Cephalopholis boenack (Bloch)

COMMON NAME: Boenacki Grouper.
PHOTOGRAPH BY: Dr. Herbert R. Axelrod. Photographed in Ceylon.
RANGE: Zanzibar, India, East Indies to China.
PREVIOUS SCIENTIFIC NAMES: *Bodianus boenack*, *Serranus boenack*, *S. boelang*, *Epinephalis boelang*.
MERISTIC CHARACTERISTICS: D. IX, 15, i; A. III, 8, i; 97–120 scales. Grows to about 12 inches.

This is a favorite amongst the grouper-lovers, for it stays relatively small and becomes fairly friendly. It retains the blue stripes but its identification has created some controversy among professional ichthyologists.

Some reports have it that the slime is toxic, but no aquarists has ever reported any problem, nor has the author had any problems with his (HRA).

Photo by Dwayne Reed.

Cephalopholis fulva (Linnaeus)

COMMON NAME: Coney.

RANGE: Tropical Western Atlantic.

MERISTIC CHARACTERISTICS: D. IX, 15–16; A. III, 9; P. 18. Grows to about 16 inches but rare over 12 inches.

There seem to be several color varieties of this fish; perhaps the same fish goes through several color changes during its lifetime. One color variety (or phase) is the bright yellow phase. A red phase and a very dark, almost black, form or phrase are also known. The phase illustrated here is the so-called "excitement phase."

This is a rare grouper in the aquarium because it is not very friendly.

278.00

Cephalopholis miniatus (Forskål)

COMMON NAME: Red Grouper.
PHOTOGRAPHED BY: Dr. Herbert R. Axelrod in Ceylon.
RANGE: Red Sea through tropical Indo-Pacific.
PREVIOUS SCIENTIFIC NAMES: *Perca miniata.*
MERISTIC CHARACTERISTICS: D. IX, 15; A. III, 9; P. ii, 17. There are
   about 111 scale rows above the lateral line. Grows to more than 8
   inches.

This is a very beautiful grouper which becomes fairly tame when they
are kept alone in a large aquarium. They soon learn to feed from your
hand. While they do take the usual freeze-dried Tubifex worms, they do
well on small goldfish or other living fishes, too.
   They should not be kept with fishes much smaller than themselves as
they can eat a fish half their size, which they do usually at night.
   They are not active fish and sometimes spend considerable time just
laying on the bottom under a bit of coral.

Cephalopholis urodelus (Bloch and Schneider)

COMMON NAME: Grouper.

RANGE: Tropical mid-Pacific including Tahiti, Bikini, Eniwetok, Kwajalein and Rota.

PREVIOUS SCIENTIFIC NAMES: *Percam urodetam.*

MERISTIC CHARACTERISTICS: D. IX, 15–16; A. III, 9; P. ii, 16–19; 93–105
scale rows above the lateral line. Grows larger than 8 inches.

This is an easily recognizable species by the oblique white streaks on
the caudal fin and by the occurrence of a black spot on the lower lip
opposite each canine tooth (according to L. P. Schultz.)

It is not a fish for the small aquarium, though small specimens do very
well in 50 gallon aquariums.

They become very tame if they are isolated and hand fed. Some recognize their feeder and refuse food from anyone else's hand. Feeding is
quite simple as they prefer freeze-dried Tubifex worms and Chlorella
algae. Canned Norwegian brine shrimp and the other usual diets for
marine fishes is greedily taken if the fish is fully acclimated. When large
they prefer chunky foods such as freeze-dried worms.

280.00

Chaetodon auriga Forskål

COMMON NAME: Threadfin Butterflyfish.
RANGE: From Queensland, Australia to the tropical mid-Pacific islands.
Common in Hawaii.
PREVIOUS SCIENTIFIC NAMES: None. Originally described in 1775.
MERISTIC CHARACTERISTICS. D. XII–XIII, 23; A. III, 21. Grows to about
9 inches.

This is one of the long-nosed *Chaetodons* which has been successfully
kept in marine aquaria all over the world. Reports of it being common in
the Red Sea, Australia and Hawaii makes it one of the most widely
distributed of the group. It is interesting that the usual maximum size in
Hawaii is about 6 inches, while in Australia it is found up to 9 inches.

This species thrives on brine shrimp, especially on the freeze-dried
variety. They love to be in an aquarium with living coral where they
may be seen picking at almost invisible bits of food. They are sensitive
to being moved and may go off their feed for a few days, but none have
starved to death if they were offered freeze-dried or live foods.

Chaetodon bennetti Cuvier

COMMON NAME: Bennett's Butterflyfish.
RANGE: Widespread throughout the Indo-Pacific.
MERISTIC CHARACTERISTICS: D. XIV, 17–18; A. III, 15–16; about 42 series
of scales; about 35 tubular; reaches 8 inches long.

This is a *Chaetodon* common to many waters, but it only rarely shows up in the aquarium because it is so sensitive to change if it is not handled properly during its period of acclimation from the reef to the aquarium. Like many butterflyfish, *bennetti* has the false eye pattern at the rear end of its body and is predominantly yellow. It is easily identifiable by the two diverging blue lines curving above and below the base of the pectorals. Reported from South Africa and the East Indies as well as Tahiti. Not reported from Hawaii.

This fish thrives on freeze-dried Tubifex and brine shrimp. The ideal size for the aquarium is 3 inches.

Chaetodon capistratus Linnaeus

COMMON NAME: Foureye Butterflyfish.
RANGE: Tropical Atlantic and Caribbean.
MERISTIC CHARACTERISTICS: D. XIII, 19–20; A. III, 16–17; 31–35 scales
in the lateral line. Grows to about 6 inches.

This is the most common butterflyfish in the West Indies and is also
the least expensive. Being very hardy, the Foureye has a reputed diet of
polychaete tubeworm tentacles and sea anemones (zoantherians). In
captivity they must be switched to other foods such as freeze-dried
Tubifex worms, canned Norwegian brine shrimp or live worms. If they
don't feed well they almost always die in 8 to 10 weeks.

The name *"foureye"* comes from the false eye in the rear end of the
fish which is supposed to confuse predatory fishes. The real eye is hidden
by the stripe through the eye, but this stripe is very common in most
chaetodons from the Caribbean.

283.00

Chaetodon xanthurus Bleeker

Common Name: Pearlscale Butterfly.
Photograph By: Earl Kennedy.
Range: Philippines to Japan.
Meristic Characteristics: D. XII-XIII,21-22; A. III,16-18. There are
about 33 scales in the lateral line. Grows to 6 inches.

This is one of the rare butterflyfishes which is exported on occasion by Earl Kennedy. This beautiful fish has often been confused in the popular aquarium books, but the identification here is probably correct.

284.00

Chaetodon citrinellus Cuvier

COMMON NAME: Speckled Butterflyfish.

RANGE: Common in northern Australia and rare in the tropical Indo-Pacific. Infrequently found in Hawaiian waters.

MERISTIC CHARACTERISTICS: D. XIV–XV, 20–21; A. III, 15–16; P. I, i, 13–14; 34–39 scale rows in lengthwise series from the upper edge of the gill opening to the base of the caudal rays.

This is one of the more rare butterflyfishes which shows up fairly often in aquaria because it is so hardy and so beautiful. It acclimates very quickly if it is kept with several members of the same species. The usual aquarium size is 3 to 4 inches, but 5 inch specimens have been reported from Hawaii.

They take most freeze-dried foods, especially brine shrimp. As with most butterflyfish, they gorge themselves on canned Norwegian brine shrimp (*Calanus*) and they should not be overfed. If possible maintain them in an aquarium with living corals so they can graze small edible bits off the coral from time to time.

285.00

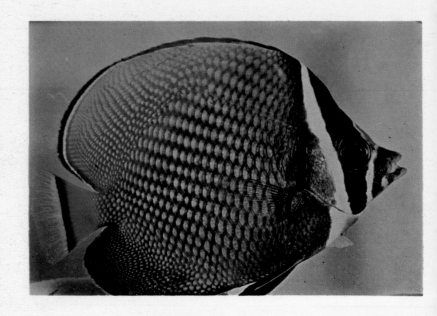

Chaetodon collaris Günther

COMMON NAME: Pakistani Butterflyfish.

PHOTOGRAPH BY: Dr. Herbert R. Axelrod in Karachi, Pakistan.

RANGE: This might be a local variety of *Chaetodon reticulatus* found near the bay in Karachi, Pakistan where this photo was taken.

MERISTIC CHARACTERISTICS: D. XII, 26, i; A. III, 20, i. About 3 inches.

Though almost completely different than *C. reticulatus* to the aquarist, scientists have always confused these two fishes.

They are fairly common in Karachi, Pakistan where they are exported as an aquarium fish. They are rather expensive, for some reason, but the public aquarium in Karachi has many of them.

They do well on fairy shrimp, canned Norwegian brine shrimp and freeze-dried foods.

Chaetodon ephippium Cuvier

COMMON NAME: Black-blotched Butterflyfish.

RANGE: Australia through the Indo-Pacific. Rare in Hawaii but common in the islands southwest of the Hawaiian Islands.

MERISTIC CHARACTERISTICS: Grows to about 12 inches, but the specimen photographed is one of the largest that can be kept in the home aquarium.

D. XIII, 24; A. III, 21; P. I, i, 14–15.

Easily identified by the large black blotch, this is a rare fish among aquarists. It does very well when properly acclimated. Should be maintained in a large aquarium; the larger the better, certainly not in an aquarium smaller than 20 gallons. Likes living coral in its aquarium. Feeds well on canned Norwegian brine shrimp, freeze-dried brine shrimp and freeze-dried Tubifex worms.

287.00

Chaetodon falcula Bloch

Common Name: Saddled Butterflyfish.
Range: Indian Ocean and Red Sea.
Meristic Characteristics: Grows to about 8 inches. D. XII-XIII, 24-28;
A. III, 19-23; about 25 scales in the lateral line.

This butterflyfish is easily confused with the Pacific species *C. ulietensis*. These two species are easily recognized by color pattern, as are all butterflyfishes, and can be distinguished from each other by the size and extent of the dark saddles. In *C. falcula* they are narrow and pointed, as shown in the photograph; in *C. ulietensis* they are broader and extend ventrally almost to the level of the pectoral fin base.

Small specimens occasionally appear in pet shops in Europe, but this Indian Ocean fish is rarely, if ever, imported into the United States.

Chaetodon fremblii

COMMON NAME: Bluestripe Butterflyfish.
PHOTOGRAPH BY: Dr. Herbert R. Axelrod of a 2-inch specimen from Hawaii.

This fish has been reported only from Hawaii, but it probably occurs in other areas. It is very common in the shallow waters around the Hawaiian Islands and reaches about 5 inches. It is easily identified by the lack of the bar through the eye and the narrow blue bars, usually about 8 in number, that run the entire length of the body. The Bluestripe Butterflyfish gets more elongate as it grows older, but the black spots on the caudal peduncle and dorsal fin, and the spot on the dorsal edge in front of the dorsal fin only get darker with age.

This fish is easily kept if fed freeze-dried Tubifex worms, canned Norwegian brine shrimp and freeze-dried brine shrimp.

Chaetodon kleinii Bloch

Photography By: Dr. Herbert R. Axelrod of a 2-inch specimen from
   Hawaii.
Range: Tropical Indo-Pacific.
Meristic Characteristics: Grows to about 5 inches in length. D. XIII,
   22-23; A. III,18-19; about 30 scales in a longitudinal series.

This species is fairly common over a very wide geographic area
from the Hawaiian Islands to the coast of Africa. It is not one of the
more colorful butterflyfishes but has a charm of its own and occasionally finds its way into home aquaria where it does better than most
butterflyfishes.

It takes time to acclimate it to captivity and it should not be
placed in tanks smaller than 20 gallons. Small invertebrates and occasional algae form the basis of its diet but it will take many of the prepared foods in home aquaria.

290.00

Chaetodon lineolatus Cuvier

COMMON NAME: Lined Butterflyfish.

RANGE: Hawaii and throughout the tropical Indo-Pacific. Found as far south as Durban, South Africa.

PREVIOUS SCIENTIFIC NAMES: Incorrectly known as *Chaetodon talii* Bleeker.

MERISTIC CHARACTERISTICS: Grows to about 12 inches long. D. XII, 24–28; A. III, 20–21; about 23 scales in the lateral line.

This is the largest of the butterflyfishes and is very common wherever it is found. Small specimens make excellent aquarium fish, while the larger specimens appear very commonly in public aquariums. This is one of the long-nosed butterflyfish which indicates it likes to poke about living coral for bits of edible material. It thrives on canned Norwegian brine shrimp as well as the usual freeze-dried brine shrimp and Tubifex worms.

Chaetodon lunula (Lacépède)

COMMON NAME: Red-striped Butterflyfish.

RANGE: Found throughout the Indo-Pacific, Hawaii and Australia.

PREVIOUS SCIENTIFIC NAMES: Originally described as *Pomacentrus lunula* and *Chaetodon lunulatus.*

MERISTIC CHARACTERISTICS: Grows to about 8 inches. D. XII, 23–25; A. III, 18–20; about 38 scales in the lateral line.

This is one of the more beautiful of the butterflyfish, especially when they are young. Specimens about 2 inches long are eagerly sought as aquarium specimens when they have the light bordered spot on their soft dorsal fin. As they grow larger, to about 5 inches, the spot disappears and is replaced by an indistinct vertical bar (according to Gosline and Brock).

These are shallow water fish which do well in the home aquarium. They eagerly accept canned Norwegian brine shrimp (*Calanus*), freeze-dried brine shrimp and Tubifex worms.

Chaetodon melanotus Schneider

COMMON NAME: Black-backed Butterflyfish.

RANGE: Throughout the coral reefs of the tropical Indo-Pacific from South Africa to Australia. Not reported from Hawaii.

PREVIOUS SCIENTIFIC NAMES: *Chaetodon dorsalis, marginatus* and *abhortani.*

MERISTIC CHARACTERISTICS: Grows to about 7 inches. D. XII, 19–20; A. III, 17–18; about 35 scales in the lateral line.

Though fairly rare in the usual areas from which many marine fishes are collected, the Black-backed Butterfly has been seen regularly among imports. It does very well in the home aquarium if it has been properly acclimated. It feeds heavily on canned Norwegian brine shrimp, freeze-dried brine shrimp and Tubifex worms. It likes a large aquarium, especially if there is some living coral in the background.

Some authors spell the species name with two *n*'s as *melannotus.*

293.00

Chaetodon mertensii Cuvier

COMMON NAME: Merten's Butterfly.
RANGE: Indo-Pacific atolls, including Eniwetok, Bikini and Rongelap.
PREVIOUS SCIENTIFIC NAMES: None, but easily confused with *C. chrysurus*.
MERISTIC CHARACTERISTICS: Grows to about 4 inches. D. XII–XIII, 21–23; A. III, 16–17; P. I, i, 13; about 32–36 scale rows in lengthwise series from upper edge of gill opening to the base of the caudal rays.

This is a fairly rare butterflyfish even though it has been known since 1831 when it was first.described. No one has successfully transported the fish alive for aquarium purposes, though odd specimens have been displayed in the tanks of some collectors who report that it eats well but refuses anything except canned Norwegian brine shrimp or live invertebrates.

It is probable that living specimens will reach the home aquarium as the fish is small enough and relatively easy to collect.

Chaetodon meyeri Bloch and Schneider

Common Name: Meyer's Butterfly.
Photograph By: Earl Kennedy, Manila, Philippine Islands.
Range: Philippine Islands, Moluccas and Marshall Islands, Indo-Pacific.
Meristic Characteristics: D. XII,23-24; A. III,19-21; 50 to 55 scales in lateral line.

Chaetodon meyeri is a fairly rare fish, but it is hardy and a few dozen specimens are collected every year from the Philippines and shipped to dealers. This is a very expensive butterflyfish only because of its great beauty and its rarity in Nature. Undoubtedly it will be found in greater concentrations and will become more available as time goes by and marine fish collecting becomes more sophisticated.

Small specimens thrive on canned Norwegian brine shrimp and freeze-dried brine shrimp, providing they are supplemented by freeze-dried Tubifex worms.

Chaetodon miliaris Quoy and Gaimard

COMMON NAME: Lemon Butterfly.
RANGE: Hawaiian Islands.
PREVIOUS SCIENTIFIC NAMES: None.
MERISTIC CHARACTERISTICS: Grows to about 6 inches. D. XIII 20–23;
A. III, 18–20; about 40 scales in the lateral line.

This fish is easily identified by the black spots forming about 11 vertical rows from the dorsal edge to the middle of the sides.

It is fairly common in aquaria because it is so easily shipped from Hawaii. It does well with a medium sized aquarium (about 20–50 gallons) and likes to graze on living coral as do most butterflyfishes. In nature it feeds almost exclusively on invertebrates and in the aquarium it thrives on canned Norwegian brine shrimp, freeze-dried brine shrimp and freeze-dried Tubifex worms.

296.00

Chaetodon multicinctus Garrett

COMMON NAME: Pebbled Butterfly.

RANGE: Hawaii.

PREVIOUS SCIENTIFIC NAMES: *Chaetodon punctatofasciatus.*

MERISTIC CHARACTERISTICS: Grows to over 4 inches. D. XIII, 24–25; A. III, 18–19; P. I, i, 13–14; 44–47 scale rows from upper angle of gill opening to the base of the caudal fin rays.

A fairly common Hawaiian species which is ideal for the home aquarium because of its rather small size. It is exported from Hawaii regularly, though it is sensitive to abrupt changes of water quality. When adult, it is often confused with *Chaetodon miliaris* and *citrinellus*.

Once acclimated, this species accepts canned Norwegian brine shrimp and freeze-dried brine shrimp eagerly. For such a small fish it eats ravenously when in good condition. It is often the first butterflyfish to perish when the water in an aquarium begins to break down. It cannot be kept successfully in the lower quality artificial sea salt mixtures.

Chaetodon ocellatus Bloch

COMMON NAME: Spotfin Butterflyfish.

RANGE: Massachusetts to Brazil. Common in the Caribbean; rare at the extremes of the range.

MERISTIC CHARACTERISTICS: D. XII, 19–21; A. III, 16–18; 33–34 scales in the lateral line. Grows to 8 inches.

An attractive, though not too colorful, butterflyfish which seems to have larger and more prominent scales than the other fishes in the genus, but this is only due to scalation marking. This is one of the common fish for American marine hobbyists since it can be found readily in Florida waters.

While it is difficult to feed at times, it does well on the usual freeze-dried foods and canned Norwegian brine shrimp.

Like most members of the family, it is very peaceful and does best when kept with other butterflyfish.

298.00

Chaetodon octofasciatus Bloch

COMMON NAME: Eight-banded Butterflyfish.

PHOTOGRAPH BY: Earl Kennedy in Manila.

RANGE: Reefs of the Indo-Australian Archipelago, Philippine Islands, coasts of India.

PREVIOUS SCIENTIFIC NAMES: *Tetragonopterus octofasciatus.*

MERISTIC CHARACTERISTICS: D. XI, 18–20; A. III, 16–17; 45–46 scale rows from operculum to base of caudal fin. Grows to approximately six inches.

The Eight-banded Butterfly belongs to a large family of fishes, well-known for their extravagance of colors and markings. Unfortunately the classification of these beautiful gems has not been so well known. Taxonomists of old have had the tendency to attach a new name on a particular species which comes into their hands without first making a thorough search to make sure the fish was not already named. The result is that many of the butterflyfishes carry a variety of scientific names, which is enough to baffle the scientific world, to say nothing of the layman and aquarist. Fortunately, Warren Burgess of the University of Hawaii is now engaged with the enormous task of reclassifying and putting the right names on the nearly 100 species of butterflyfishes. He has been working on this project for several years now and plans to finish and publish his results by next year. What a valuable contribution this will be to both ichthyologists and aquarists alike!

The feeding and care of this particular species is the same for the other members of this family.

299.00

Photo by K.H. Choo.

Chaetodon ornatissimus Cuvier

RANGE: Hawaii and the Indo-Pacific.

PREVIOUS SCIENTIFIC NAMES: *Chaetodon ornatus.*

MERISTIC CHARACTERISTICS: Grows to over 5 inches. D. XII, 25–27;
A. III, 20; P. I, i, 14–15; 50–58 scales in a lengthwise series from top of
opercular opening to the base of the caudal fin ray.

This is a beautiful species with a blunt nose and bright orange to red
bands in the middle of the body. It comes from fairly deep water and
young specimens are difficult to acclimate properly to small home
aquaria. It is sometimes shipped from Hawaii but these are usually
specimens collected in shallow waters which is not their usual habitat,
so the specimens might be sub-standard when collected. They thrive on
canned Norwegian brine shrimp (*Calanus*) and they eagerly accept
freeze-dried brine shrimp and Tubifex worms. They prefer larger
aquariums with large open areas for free swimming.

300.00

Chaetodon pelewensis Kner

COMMON NAME: Dot and Dash Butterflyfish.

RANGE: Marshall and Marianas Islands, as well as other Indo-Pacific atolls.

MERISTIC CHARACTERISTICS: D. XIII, 23; A. III, 18; about 45 scales in the lateral line.

A rare butterflyfish from the South Seas, sometimes reported from Queensland, Australia. It is reported to reach 5 inches in length and has never been kept in the home aquarium because it is so sensitive to water changes.

301.00

Chaetodon punctatofasciatus Cuvier

RANGE: Tropical Pacific around most atolls, including Bikini, Eniwetok and Rongelap.

PREVIOUS SCIENTIFIC NAMES: None.

MERISTIC CHARACTERISTICS: About 4 inches, though the largest specimen in the collection of the U.S.N.M. is about 3 inches. D. XIII, 22–25; A. III, 17–18; P. I, i, 12–13; about 35–40 scales in a lengthwise series from the upper edge of the gill opening to the base of the caudal fin rays.

At one time this was thought to be *Chaetodon multicinctus,* but a careful statistical comparison of specimens of *multicinctus* from Hawaii shows a great difference in scale counts.

This fish has rarely been captured alive since there are no commercial collectors working the atolls in its usual range. The few specimens which have been kept were difficult to keep alive because they were badly acclimated and mauled during transport. It is expected that future collectors will bring some back as the fish is not too uncommon in its range.

Chaetodon quadrimaculatus Gray

COMMON NAME: Neon-banded Butterfly.

RANGE: Tropical Indo-Pacific, including Hawaii.

PREVIOUS SCIENTIFIC NAMES: None.

MERISTIC CHARACTERISTICS: Grows to about 6 inches. D. XIV–XV, 21–22; A. III, 17–18; about 39–45 scales in the lateral line.

This is a common fish found in the shallow waters around Hawaii. It is shipped regularly and is a very colorful addition to the marine home aquarium. It is found in almost every coral atoll in the Indo-Pacific, especially Bikini, Eniwetok, Rongelap and Rongerik, as well as Tahiti.

Most specimens are under 4 inches. Hardy when kept under normal aquarium conditions. It thrives on canned Norwegian brine shrimp, freeze-dried brine shrimp and Tubifex worms. It enjoys grazing among the coral, especially living coral.

303.00

Chaetodon rafflesii Bennett

COMMON NAME: Latticed Butterflyfish.
RANGE: Indo-Pacific, including Australia.
MERISTIC CHARACTERISTICS: D. XIII, 21; A. III, 19; about 29 scales in
the lateral line. Grows to about 6 inches.

A fairly common Indo-Pacific butterflyfish which has been collected
in North Queensland, Australia. Live specimens are rarely exported, but
enough have been kept alive for extended periods of time (up to one
year) to generalize about their care. They are not particular about their
aquarium and perhaps they even thrive in old marine water. They take
canned Norwegian brine shrimp (*Calanus*) and they eagerly accept freeze-
dried brine shrimp. They prefer an aquarium with quite a bit of coral in
the background. They graze on living coral and they seem to feed on
invertebrates in their natural habitat.

304.00

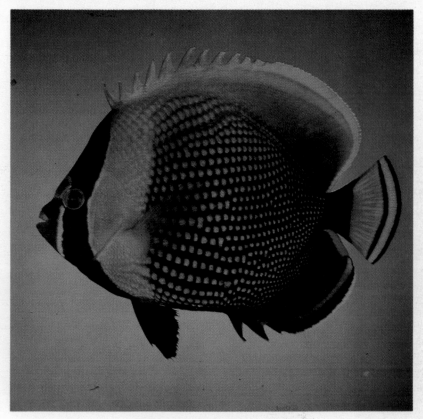

Chaetodon reticulatus Cuvier

COMMON NAME: Reticulated Butterfly.

PHOTOGRAPH BY: Dr. John Randall of a specimen 4.8 inches from Hitiaa, Tahiti.

RANGE: Hawaii and the Indo-Pacific. Common in most atolls, including Bikini, Eniwetok, Rongelap and Rongerik.

PREVIOUS SCIENTIFIC NAMES: None.

MERISTIC CHARACTERISTICS: Grows to about 5 inches. D. XII, 26–27; A. III, 20–21; P. I, i, 15–17; 41–43 scale rows in lengthwise series from the upper part of the gill opening to the base of the caudal rays.

This is a very dark fish which has been rarely collected. Only one shipment has been made from Hawaii and the specimens were fairly hardy. Observations from the Kona Coast of Hawaii have been noted.

They eat well on freeze-dried brine shrimp and canned Norwegian brine shrimp. They like warmer water, about 82° F. Their aquarium should be as open as possible with small coral build-ups in which they can hide should they be frightened.

305.00

Chaetodon sedentarius Poey

Common Name: Reef Butterflyfish.
Range: North Carolina to Brazil.
Meristic Characteristics: D. XIII-XIV,21-23; A. III,18-19; 36-39
scales in the lateral line. Grows to about 6 inches.

This is a deep water *Chaetodon* which is fairly common and widely
ranged throughout the Caribbean. During the summer months it
ventures far north to the Carolinas; other chaetodons go as far north as
Massachusetts.

This fish is almost always available from dealers in Puerto Rico and
Florida. It is one of the less expensive of the butterflyfishes, though it is
not one of the most eager feeders. Difficulty in getting this fish to feed on
freeze-dried Tubifex worms will result in it only living a few months at
most. Once it takes worms the battle is over. They do take freeze-dried
brine shrimp but this isn't substantial enough as a sole diet. Canned
Norwegian brine shrimp will also keep them alive and healthy if they
take it.

306.00

Photo by K.H. Choo.

Chaetodon semeion Bleeker

COMMON NAME: Golden Butterfly.
RANGE: Indo-Pacific atolls and tidal pools.
MERISTIC CHARACTERISTICS: Grows to over 7 inches. D. XIII, 25; A. III, 21; P. I, i, 14; about 32 scale rows in lengthwise series from the upper edge of the gill opening to the base of the caudal fin rays.

A pretty fish which has been known to science since 1855. It has been shipped on occasion and a well acclimated individual will live a long time if properly maintained. They take canned Norwegian brine shrimp (*Calanus*), freeze-dried brine shrimp and Tubifex worms. They prefer large aquariums and will perish if kept in tanks less than about 6 times as long as their bodies. They seem to be quarrelsome with smaller fishes when competing for territory or food.

Photo by Douglas Faulkner.

Chaetodon striatus Linnaeus

Common Name: Banded Butterflyfish.
Range: New Jersey to Brazil.
Meristic Characteristics: D. XII,21-22; A. III,16-18; 35-36 scales in
    the lateral line.

The banded butterflyfish is one of the few butterflyfishes that is banded as an adult. It is fairly common in the Caribbean and is often imported from that area or Florida. Occasional strays are reported from as far north on the east coast of the United States as New Jersey.
Young banded butterflyfish have an ocellated spot in the soft dorsal fin but this becomes lost in the banding with age.
As for other butterflyfishes, careful attention to acclimatization should be adhered to and feedings of a variety of foods should be tried.

Chaetodon tinkeri Schultz

Common Name: Tinker's Butterfly.
Range: Hawaii.
Meristic Characteristics: Grows to about 6 inches.

This species was named after Spencer Tinker, the director of the Waikiki Aquarium in Honolulu, by Dr. Leonard P. Schultz in 1951. It is a very rare fish, easily identified by the large black area behind the dorsal. It is doubtful that this fish will ever be owned by more than a few marine hobbyists, though it was relatively easily maintained in Hawaii. All known specimens have come from relatively deep water around the Hawaiian Islands.

Chaetodon trifasciatus Mungo Park

COMMON NAME: Redfin Butterflyfish.

RANGE: Tropical Indo-Pacific with specimens recorded from Bikini, Eniwetok, Tahiti, Rongelap, Rongerik, Guam, Likiep and as far as South Africa. Originally found in Sumatra in 1797.

PREVIOUS SCIENTIFIC NAMES: Mistakenly referred to as *Tetragonopterus*

(Rabdophorus) trifasciatus, *Chaetodon trifascialis*, *C. vittatus*, *C. taunigrum*, *C. bifascialis*, *C. bellus* and *C. ovalis*.

MERISTIC CHARACTERISTICS: D. XIII–XIV, 19–23; A. III, 19–20; P. I, i, 13–14; 38–44 scale rows in a line between the upper edge of the gill opening and the base of the caudal rays.

There might be a hint of sex difference in this beauty as some specimens, according to Woods (USNM Bulletin 202, p. 585), have an anal fin which is pink at the base of the spiny part.

Otherwise this beauty is well known and well appreciated as it is commonly found in many aquariums. It grows to 6 inches at the most, but the best aquarium specimens are about 4 inches.

Scientific descriptions of this fish as far as color pattern goes seem fairly uniform, but several authors have given "color when alive" descriptions which vary from the specimens we have seen. Woods (*op. cit*) also describes as orange the anterior part of the opercular flap. It is yellow in all the specimens I have seen. Perhaps in smaller specimens (the smallest I have seen alive is 4 inches) the flap is orange. This is a very peaceful fish and enjoys a large hole in the coral in which it can feel secure.

The juvenile *Chaetodon trifasciatus* with the characteristic two yellow spots on the caudal peduncle. Photo by Dr. Herbert R. Axelrod.

Chaetodon speculum

Common Name: One-spot Butterfly.
Range: Tropical Indo-Pacific.

    Chaetodon speculum is often confused with *Chaetodon unimaculatus* (see p. 313.00) because of the large black spot in the middle of the body of both species. The solid yellow color of *C. speculum* with no black edging to the trailing edges of the dorsal and anal fins and no black band around the caudal peduncle make the two easily distinguishable.
    This species is often included in shipments from the Philippines. It does fairly well in captivity once it begins feeding.

Chaetodon unimaculatus Bloch

Common Name: One-spot Butterfly.
Range: Indo-Pacific atolls, including Bora Bora, Bikini, Eniwetok,
  Rongelap and Rongerik in the Marshall and Marianas.
Meristic Characteristics: Over 4 inches. D. XIII, 21-23; A. III, 18-19;
  P. I, i, 13-14; 41-44 scales in a lengthwise series from the upper end
  of the gill opening to the base of the caudal rays.

  This is a butterflyfish which has been occasionally seen in the
home aquarium; it is hardy if kept under optimum aquarium conditions. It likes to graze on living coral, but it eagerly accepts canned
Norwegian brine shrimp and freeze-dried invertebrates such as brine
shrimp and Tubifex worms.
  It prefers large holes in coral where it can hide should it be frightened.

Chaetodon vagabundus Linnaeus

COMMON NAME: Vagabond Butterfly.
RANGE: Tropical Indo-Pacific including Guam, to South Africa.
MERISTIC CHARACTERISTICS: Grows to 8 inches. D. XII–XIII, 23–26;
A. 20–22; P. I, i, 14; 35 scale rows.

This is a very common aquarium fish, though relatively rare in its very broad range. The fish is very hardy and easy to capture. Specimens have been kept for long periods of time and they thrive on canned Norwegian brine shrimp and freeze-dried foods, especially brine shrimp and Tubifex worms.

They should be kept in as large an aquarium as possible and do well with other fishes. Specimens have been known to live for several years under ideal conditions.

Cheilinus undulatus Rüppell

COMMON NAME: Giant Labrid.
RANGE: Widespread throughout the tropical Indo-Pacific.
MERISTIC CHARACTERISTICS: This is probably the largest fish in the family Labridae. Reports of it reaching 8 feet long are probably slightly exaggerated, but it does reach 7 feet. D. IX, 10; A. III, 8.

This is certainly an interesting fish for the public aquarium, but not one for the home aquarium unless very, very young fish can be found and stunted. Even with dwarfing they will probably grow to more than 12 inches in length and this is too large for a fish with the kind of teeth found in this species.

They are extremely colorful for such a large species, and older specimens grow a hump on their head similar to many freshwater cichlids.

They feed on chunks of freeze-dried Tubifex worms, shrimp (well cooked and peeled), and the usual other fishfoods.

315.00

Cheilodipterus macrodon (Lacépède)

COMMON NAME: Big Teeth.
RANGE: Indo-Pacific region.
PREVIOUS SCIENTIFIC NAMES: *Centropomus macrodon, Cheilodipterus lineatus, C. octovittatus, C. heptazona, Paramia octolineata,* and *P. macrodon.*
MERISTIC CHARACTERISTICS: D. VI + I, 9; A. II, 8; P. ii, 9, ii; 23–26 vertical scale rows. Grows to over 8 inches.

One close look at the mouth of *macrodon* and you have a hint of what the strong, enlarged canine teeth can do to other fishes, living coral or your hand if you are one of those people who likes to handle fish without a net.

This is not a fish for the small aquarium, even though small specimens make interesting additions. Young specimens show an intense black spot on the caudal peduncle when they are active and in good condition, the spot fades as the fish matures or takes on its "frightened" color pattern. The dark color of the spiny dorsal and parts of the soft dorsal is missing in young specimens, and usually they have no color in their anal and pelvics until they are sexually mature.

316.00

Cromileptes altivelis (Cuvier and Valenciennes)

COMMON NAME: Polkadot Grouper.
PHOTOGRAPH BY: Hansen.
RANGE: Indo-Australian Archipelago.
PREVIOUS SCIENTIFIC NAMES: *Serranus altivelis, Serranichthys altivelis.*
MERISTIC CHARACTERISTICS: D. X, 18–19; A. III, 10; lateral line about 70.
Grows to about 14 inches.

This is by far the most popular of the many Indo-Pacific groupers. This fish is so docile it is almost unbelievable. They are unafraid and hover around collectors as if asking to be caught and are among the easiest of fishes to collect. As the fish grows the spots on the body become smaller and more numerous.

It's a perfect aquarium fish which prefers to be out in the open most of the time, unlike many of the groupers. Their peculiar habit of hovering off the bottom is most interesting to watch, and they seem to get along fine with other fishes in the tank providing they are not too small. Live foods are recommended, but canned Norwegian brine shrimp and frozen fish are good substitutes.

Chromis caeruleus (Cuvier and Valenciennes)

COMMON NAME: Blue-green Chromis.

PHOTOGRAPH BY: Hansen.

RANGE: Tropical Indo-Pacific and Red Sea.

PREVIOUS SCIENTIFIC NAMES: *Heliases lepisurus, Glyphisodon bandanensis, Heliases frenatus, Heliases caeruleus, Abudefduf amboinensis, Chromis lepisurus, Chromis axillaris, Haplochromis caeruleus.*

MERISTIC CHARACTERISTICS: D. XII, 10; A. II, 10; lateral line with 22–24 scales. Grows to 4 inches.

C. caeruleus is extremely abundant on the coral atolls of the South Pacific. They are a fantastic sight as they literally swarm over massive outcrops of living coral. The schools may number up to several hundred individuals. At Eniwetok, in the Marshall Islands, they spawn on pieces of filamentous algae which become snagged up on the coral. The male initiates courtship and lures the female to the chosen nest sight. After the eggs are laid the male guards and fans them until hatching, 3 or 4 days later.

This species is hardy and will accept a wide assortment of food items. Among its favorites are brine shrimp (live, frozen or canned), freeze-dried red worms (tubifex) and shrimp flakes.

Chromis cyanea (Poey)

COMMON NAME: Blue Chromis.

RANGE: Bermuda, southern Florida and Caribbean Sea.

PREVIOUS SCIENTIFIC NAMES: *Furcaria cyanae, Heliastes cyaneus.*

MERISTIC CHARACTERISTICS: D. XII, 12; A. II, 12; 16–18 lateral line scales. Grows to 5 inches.

The Blue Chromis is a favorite from the Caribbean area. It's the Atlantic counterpart of the Blue-green Chromis from the Pacific. The feeding and behavior of these 2 species are essentially identical.

319.00

Photo by U. Erich Friese.

Chromis dimidiatus (Klunzinger)*

COMMON NAME: Bicolor Chromis.
RANGE: Tropical Indo-Pacific.
PREVIOUS SCIENTIFIC NAMES: *Haliases dimidiatus.*
MERISTIC CHARACTERISTICS: D. XII, 12; A. II, 26 scales in lateral line.
Grows to 2–3 inches.

This species is a plankton feeder which forms large aggregations over
the bottom. They rely on the current to bring them the tiny invertebrates upon which they feed. Like other *Chromis,* they have a habit of
feeding on the freshly spawned eggs of their own species. Though live
foods are preferred they can be converted to dry flake and freeze-dried
items when kept in captivity.

*Now called *Chromis iomelas.*

320.00

THE WORLD'S LARGEST SELECTION OF PET, ANIMAL, AND MUSIC BOOKS.

T.F.H. Publications publishes more than 900 books covering many hobby aspects (dogs, cats, birds, fish, small animals, music, etc.). Whether you are a beginner or an advanced hobbyist you will find exactly what you're looking for among our complete listing of books. For a free catalog fill out the form on the other side of this page and mail it today.

. . CATS . . .

. . . BIRDS . .

. . . ANIMALS . . .

. . . DOGS . . .

. . FISH . . .

. . . MUSIC . . .

For more than 30 years, *Tropical Fish Hobbyist* has been the source of accurate, up-to-the-minute, and fascinating information on every facet of the aquarium hobby.

Join the more than 50,000 devoted readers worldwide who wouldn't miss a single issue.

Cirrhitichthys aprinus (Cuvier)

COMMON NAME: Spotted Hawkfish.

RANGE: Central tropical Indo-Pacific.

PREVIOUS SCIENTIFIC NAMES: *Cirrhites fasciatus, C. oxycephalus, C. graphidopterus, C. bleekeri, C. calliurus, C. aureus, C. indicus.*

MERISTIC CHARACTERISTICS: D. X, 12; A. III, 6, P. 6. About 40 scales in the lateral line. Grows to about $4\frac{1}{2}$ inches. Larger specimens have been reported but have not been verified.

Hawkfish are found every now and then in aquariums. They make their way in, usually, as small specimens which are hardy, but they gradually grow to about $4\frac{1}{2}$ inches in one year.

They are not very active fish and they like to stay close to the bottom. The color of their spots varies with locale and, probably, diet. They have an interesting fascination of red organ coral and if there is any in the aquarium, it is almost certain they will be close to it.

They eat the usual fishfoods including dried fairy shrimp, canned Norwegian brine shrimp and freeze-dried Tubifex worms.

Cirrhitichthys oxycephalus (Bleeker)

COMMON NAME: Spotted Hawkfish.

RANGE: Tropical Indo-Pacific and Red Sea.

PREVIOUS SCIENTIFIC NAMES: *Cirrhites oxycephalus, Cirrhites grandima-culatus, Cirrhites murrayi, Cirrhitichthys corallicola, Cirrhitichthys aprinus.*

MERISTIC CHARACTERISTICS: D. X, 12; A. III, 6; lateral line scales 41–45. Attains a length of 4–5 inches.

One of the most common species of hawkfishes in the Indo-Pacific, *C. oxycephalus* is an admirable aquarium addition. The Australians sometimes refer to them as "Curlyfins," which refers to the flexible pectoral fin rays and the short filaments on the end of each dorsal spine. They are hardy aquarium fish provided they are given live foods. Small fish and occasional feedings of brine shrimp are the best bet.

322.00

Clepticus parrae (Bloch and Schneider)

COMMON NAME: Creole Wrasse.

RANGE: North Carolina, Bermuda to the Caribbean.

MERISTIC CHARACTERISTICS: D. XII, 10; A. III, 12–13; P. 17–18. Grows to about one foot long.

This is one of the very rare violet fishes. It has found its way into public aquariums, especially the young which have 6 bars coming over the back. Many specimens show more yellow than the one illustrated here.

They are a common fish and are frequently exported, especially the smaller ones. They are hardy and feed well on fairy shrimp, freeze-dried foods and canned Norwegian brine shrimps.

According to Dr. Randall (*Caribbean Reef Fishes*) they feed on pelagic copepods, small jellyfishes, pteropods, pelagic tunicates and various invertebrate larvae.

323.00

Coradion chrysozonus (Cuvier and Valenciennes)

COMMON NAME: Coradion Butterflyfish.

RANGE: Indo-Australian Archipelago.

PREVIOUS SCIENTIFIC NAMES: *Chaetodon melanopus, Chaetodon chrysozonus, Tetragonopterus melanopus.*

MERISTIC CHARACTERISTICS: D. IX, 27–29; A. III, 19–21; lateral line with about 44 scales. Grows to 5 inches.

This is one of the many species of Far Eastern Butterflyfishes which have appeared on the pet market in recent years. Although it is not a member of the genus *Chaetodon*, it is a Butterflyfish nevertheless, as its appearance clearly shows. The care and feeding of this species is the same as that recommended for the other Butterflyfish species.

Coris aygula Lacépède

COMMON NAME: Clown Labrid.
PHOTOGRAPH BY: K. Paysan.
RANGE: Widespread in the tropical Indo-Pacific.
PREVIOUS SCIENTIFIC NAMES: *Coris* or *Julis aygula* and *cingulum*.
MERISTIC CHARACTERISTICS: D. IX, 12–13; A. III, 12. There are about
62–66 scales in the lateral line Grows to about 4 feet.

This is one of the most popular of the labrids because it is so easy to
obtain. They occur in small quantities all over the usual marine collecting
areas and most exporters have them from time to time.

Though they undergo extreme changes in coloration as they mature,
the two black ocelli in the dorsal always seem to be present. The orange
blotches on the back are more or less permanent, especially the rear
blotch.

They can be seen picking parasites from the bodies of larger fishes
and are thus dubbed "cleaners" by some authors.

325.00

Coris flavovittata (Bennett)

COMMON NAME: Hilu.
RANGE: Hawaii, perhaps as far as Guam.
PREVIOUS SCIENTIFIC NAMES: *Julis flavovittatus, J. eydouxi.*
MERISTIC CHARACTERISTICS: Reaches 18 inches.

This is a very plentiful fish, both in Hawaiian aquariums and fish markets. It is active in the aquarium, always on the move and thus is popular with the public aquariums because it grows fairly large and is relatively inexpensive. While it is the only *Coris* from Hawaii with a longitudinal band from the tip of the snout to the caudal peduncle, other *Coris* have similar characters.

It feeds on fairy shrimp, brine shrimp and canned Norwegian brine shrimp, as well as the usual freeze-dried foods.

326.00

Coris gaimard (Quoy and Gaimard)

COMMON NAME: Red Labrid.

RANGE: Throughout the tropical Indo-Pacific.

PREVIOUS SCIENTIFIC NAMES: *C. grenovii, C. pilcherrima.*

MERISTIC CHARACTERISTICS: D. IX, 12–13; A. III, 12–13; 70–80 scales in the lateral line. Grows to 15 inches.

This is the most expensive of the labrids and they are extremely popular because small specimens are easily shipped. They are hardy and make pests of themselves to larger fishes as they try to pick parasites from the bodies of their tankmates.

Juvenile *Coris formosa* closely resemble those of *C. gaimard* but have a dark spot in the dorsal fin which is absent in *C. gaimard.*

Coris julis (Linnaeus)

COMMON NAME: Mediterranean Wrasse.
PHOTOGRAPH BY: Paysan.
RANGE: Mediterranean.
MERISTIC CHARACTERISTICS: Grows to about 8 inches.

There is quite a bit of literature about this fish since it is the only *Coris* in the Mediterranean and most of the Italian and French scientists use this as a teaching aid.

According to Tortonese, *Coris julis* lives on *Posidonia* beds and near rocky or gravelly bottoms. In the winter it dives to 330 feet where it subsists on small invertebrates. It also does a job on the tough shelled fishes, mollusks, crabs, echinoderms, and crustaceans. Its jaws are powerful and their teeth are strong. They spawn in the spring and summer and lay eggs which are spherical and floating. They contain an oil globule and reach a diameter of 0.65 mm. They hatch out at a length of 2.3 mm.

In the aquarium they prefer heat or they dig into the sand and rest there with just their heads poking above the gravel. Perhaps this species is the same as *Coris giofredi*.

They eat most foods, especially fairy shrimp, canned Norwegian brine shrimp and the usual freeze-dried foods.

328.00

Coris rosea Vaillant and Sauvage

COMMON NAME: Malamalama.
PHOTOGRAPH BY: Dr. Herbert R. Axelrod at Waikiki Aquarium, Hawaii.
RANGE: Hawaii.
MERISTIC CHARACTERISTICS: Grows to about 10 inches long.

There is considerable doubt that this is a valid species as many authors consider this a synonym for *C. ballieui* which seems to be identical in every way except size and color. *rosea* is always light pink or rosy while *ballieui* is always blue and grows larger.

They are active fish and make excellent additions to the general large show aquarium. They are hardy, inexpensive and eat the general foods offered to marine fishes.

Coris variegata (Rüppell)

COMMON NAME: Variegated Wrasse.

PHOTOGRAPH BY: Dr. John Randall of a 4.1-inch specimen from Eniwetok.

RANGE: Red Sea through the East Indies almost to Hawaii. There are 2 specimens in the Bishop Museum caught by fishermen near Hawaii but none have been seen close to the islands.

PREVIOUS SCIENTIFIC NAMES: *Halichoeres variegatus.*

MERISTIC CHARACTERISTICS: D. IX, 12, i; A. III, 12, i. There are 40 scales in the upper section of the lateral line and 6–7 in the lower.

This is a small wrasse and one which appears in aquariums on very rare occasions. There is no record of the fish having been kept in a public aquarium but it is assumed that it will require the same care as other wrasses.

330.00

Ctenochaetus strigosus (Bennett)

COMMON NAME: Kole.
PHOTOGRAPH BY: Dr. Herbert R. Axelrod, of a Hawaiian specimen.
RANGE: Tropical Indo-Pacific, to South Africa.
PREVIOUS SCIENTIFIC NAMES: Often confused with *Ctenochaetus striatus,*
   Acanthurus strigosus, A. ctenodon.
MERISTIC CHARACTERISTICS: D. VIII–IX, 25–27; A. III, 23–25. Grows to
   about one foot.

   The author photographed this fish in Hawaii where it is quite common and is exported regularly. Smaller specimens make excellent
aquarium pets and when they are in good condition their coloration is
quite unique. There are small variations between specimens in terms of
the light blue body markings and reports of larger specimens being
completely unstriped have not been verified. It would be interesting to
photograph one specimen as it grew from one inch to one foot, but no
one has been able to do this because the fish doesn't live too long in the
aquarium. This short life span is quite unique for such a hardy fish and
it is probably due to the very poor handling of specimens.

Dactyloptena orientalis (?) (Cuvier)

COMMON NAME: Lolo-'oau, Purple Flying Gurnard, Tropical Sea Robin.

RANGE: Cape of Good Hope, Australia, East Indies, China, Japan, Hawaii and all intermediate points. Very common.

PREVIOUS SCIENTIFIC NAMES: *Dactylopterus, Cephalocanthus, Trigla.* Often confused with *Dactyopterus volitans = Dactyloptena orientalis.*

MERISTIC CHARACTERISTICS: D. I, I, V, I, 8; A. 6; 43–48 scales in lateral line. Grows to about 16 inches.

The long, spotted "wings", are not usually used for flying, though some shrimp fishermen along the Australian coast say they do fly. They are very common all along their range.

As small fishes they are interesting for the aquarium. They are hardy and eat everything. They do equally well in warm waters of 85° F. as in temperate waters of 65° F.

Dascyllus albisella Gill

COMMON NAME: Hawaiian Threespot Damsel Fish.
PHOTOGRAPH BY: Dr. Herbert R. Axelrod.
RANGE: Hawaiian Islands and Johnston Atoll.
PREVIOUS SCIENTIFIC NAMES: None.
MERISTIC CHARACTERISTICS: D. XII, 16; A. II, 15; vertical scale rows 27.
Grows to 8 inches.

This species is virtually identical to *Dascyllus trimaculatus*, which occurs throughout the rest of the tropical Indo-Pacific, but not reaching Hawaii. It probably represents a species which originally was of *trimaculatus* stock, but through the centuries became isolated at Hawaii. Perhaps one good difference between *albisella* and *trimaculatus* is the size of the white spot on each side of the body. In *albisella* juveniles it tends to be much larger, but this is a variable character which may even disappear altogether in the adults of both species. If your Threespot Damsel is from Hawaii you can be sure it is *D. albisella*.

Dascyllus albisella resembles *D. trimaculatus* but normally has a larger lateral spot. Unfortunately the spot is variable from specimen to specimen and may even fade out entirely. Photos of 3 inch (above) and 4½ inch (below) specimens by Dr. Herbert R. Axelrod.

Dascyllus aruanus (Linnaeus)

COMMON NAME: White-tailed Damselfish.

RANGE: Widespread throughout tropical Indo-Pacific. Doesn't reach Hawaii, though some authors report it from there. Specimens have been collected in the Red Sea, East Africa, India, Australia, China and Melanesia.

PREVIOUS SCIENTIFIC NAMES: *Chaetodon aruanus, Tetradrachmum aruanum, Pomacentrus emamo, P. devisi.*

MERISTIC CHARACTERISTICS: D. XII, 12–13; A. II, 12–13; about 25 scale rows. Grows to about $3\frac{1}{2}$ inches.

The beginner often confuses this fish with *Dascyllus melanurus* because of the similar black and white stripes, but a close look at the tail and there can be little chance for confusion as one has a white tail and one a black tail!

This is a popular aquarium fish and thousands are exported every year from the Philippines and Ceylon. They stay small and seem to have immunity to sea anemone's poisonous sting. The author has seen *aruanus* dive amongst the waving tentacles of a particular sea anemone

335.00

from time to time; it snubbed an adjacent anemone. Several experts advise that the fish does not go into an anemone unless it is being attacked by an external parasite (like *Ich*) and that the fish rids itself of parasites in this manner.

Like all damselfish, this pomacentrid has strong territorial claims and plenty of tank space should be afforded it if you are to keep peace and harmony in the aquarium.

This fish, like most other truly coral fishes ("untruly" coral fishes are those which find their way into brackish water), requires good quality artificial sea salts if they are to survive. Almost any coral fish can live for a few months in sea salts or "Kosher" salt solutions, but they cannot live there for long. The many trace elements necessary for coral fishes' health and welfare are found in only the best of sea salt mixtures.

They feed on small crustaceans in nature, and an ideal diet for them is canned Norwegian brine shrimp, fairy shrimp and freeze-dried brine shrimp.

Dascyllus aruanus lacks the black caudal fin of its closer relative *Dascayllus melanurus*. Shown is a very young specimen that is less than 20 mm long. Photo by Rudie Kuiter.

Dascyllus marginatus (Ruppell)

COMMON NAME: Marginate Damselfish.
PHOTOGRAPH BY: Dr. Herbert R. Axelrod of a 2½-inch specimen from the
Red Sea.
RANGE: Tropical Indo-Pacific.
PREVIOUS SCIENTIFIC NAMES: *Pomacentrus marginatus.*
MERISTIC CHARACTERISTICS: D. XII, 15; A. II, 14; lateral line 26. Attains
a length of 8 inches.

The Red Sea has a relatively high percentage of fishes which are found
nowhere else. However, many of these endemic forms, as they are called,
have close relatives in the nearby Indian Ocean. Sometimes the differences
between these closely related species are so slight it is difficult to deter-
mine whether we are dealing with a valid genetically isolated species
(or subspecies) or just a geographic variation of a widespread form.
Dascyllus marginatus presents this problem. It is very close in appearance
and meristic characters to *D. reticulatus,* which is widespread in the
Indo-Pacific, but doesn't occur in the Red Sea. For the time being we
shall consider it as a good species until ichthyologists shed more light
on the problem.

Dascyllus melanurus Bleeker

COMMON NAME: Black-tailed Humbug.
RANGE: Indo-Australian Archipelago.
PREVIOUS SCIENTIFIC NAMES: *Tetradrachmum melanurus, Pomacentrus onyx.*
MERISTIC CHARACTERISTICS: D. XII, 13; A. II, 13; lateral line scales 26. Grows to 4 inches.

This species is almost a dead ringer for *Dascyllus aruanus* but differs in one important respect as far as color is concerned. As the common name suggests, it has black on the tail, while that of *D. aruanus* is transparent. These two species are similar in behavior and feeding habits as well. It's a hardy species which will eat a variety of live, frozen and dry foods.

338.00

Dascyllus reticulatus (Richardson)

COMMON NAME: Reticulated Damsel Fish.

RANGE: Tropical Indo-Pacific.

PREVIOUS SCIENTIFIC NAMES: *Heliases reticulatus, Tetradrachmum reticulatum, Dascyllus xanthosoma.*

MERISTIC CHARACTERISTICS: D. XII, 15; A. II, 14; lateral line scales 26. Grows to 4–5 inches.

This *Dascyllus* is drab in comparison to the other members of the genus, but is nevertheless an excellent prospect for the marine tank. In their native habitat they are often seen living among lush growths of staghorn coral. The male prepares a nest by cleaning off a dead piece of staghorn with his mouth. He then goes through an elaborate "dance" which results in attracting a female to the nest site where the eggs are attached. The female is then driven off and the male guards the nest and cares for the eggs until hatching, which occurs in about 4 days. At this time the tiny (about 4 mm.) young are dispersed by the currents. It is estimated that it takes about 1 year for this species, which probably has a life span of 3–5 years, to reach maturity.

Feeding is no problem with the Reticulated Damsel. They accept a wide assortment of live, frozen and freeze-dried foods.

Dascyllus trimaculatus (Rüppell)

COMMON NAME: Three-spot Damselfish.
PHOTOGRAPH BY: Dr. Herbert R. Axelrod of a Ceylonese specimen $3\frac{1}{2}$ inches.
RANGE: Widespread from the Red Sea to East Africa and Polynesia. Not found in Hawaii where it is replaced by *Dascyllus albisella*.
PREVIOUS SCIENTIFIC NAMES: *Pomacentrus trimaculatus, Tetradrachmum trimaculatum, Dascyllus albisella, Dascyllus niger*.
MERISTIC CHARACTERISTICS: D. XI–XII, 13–16; A. II, 13–14; about 28 scale rows. Grows to 6 inches.

Mature specimens are almost impossible to differentiate from *Dascyllus albisella*, except they grow larger than 5 inches. The young are easy to differentiate as the white blotch on their sides extends lower onto the abdomen and they have a characteristic white spot on the forehead. The white blotches atrophy uniformly and by the time the fish is 5 inches long

340.00

Dascyllus trimaculatus will often share an anemone with clownfish. Photo by Dr. Gerald R. Allen.

there is no evidence of there having been any white blotches at all.

They are hardy, interesting coral fishes which live on the coral heads picking at small crustaceans. Their natural diet is small shrimps, *Calanus* and crab larvae. They often pick parasites from the bodies of larger fishes.

In the aquarium canned Norwegian brine shrimp (*Calanus*), fairy shrimp and the usual freeze-dried foods are accepted and the fish thrive on them.

Photo by Roger Lubbock.

Dascyllus species *

Common Name: Black Damselfish.
Range: Unknown. The only specimen taken was from Tahiti.

This apparently is a new species of *Dascyllus* and therefore does not yet have a name. It is very much like the other species of *Dascyllus* in body and head shape but differs in color pattern.

Species of *Dascyllus* react much the same in captivity and what has been said about other species will probably hold true for this new one. Feeding would therefore present no great problem, and a variety of live, frozen, and freeze-dried foods should be offered. Remember, damsels of all types are rather scrappy, and timid fishes should not be considered for their tank mates.

* This species is now known as *Dascyllus flavicaudus* Allen & H. Randall.

Dendrochirus brachypterus (Cuvier)★

COMMON NAME: Scorpionfish, Butterflyfish, Turkey Fish.
RANGE: Tropical Indo-Pacific to South Africa.
PREVIOUS SCIENTIFIC NAMES: *Pterois brachypterus*.
MERISTIC CHARACTERISTICS: D. XIII, 9–10; A. III, 6; about 45 series of
scales. Grows to 7 inches.

This is one of the less expensive Turkey Fish. Though it has nicely
contrasting shades, it doesn't have the long fins found in *Pterois*. This
species is dangerous. Their spines are poisonous (dorsal spines). They
require feedings of live fishes and the author (HRA) usually feeds an
adult one goldfish every few days when the baitfish (killies) are not
available. They slowly stalk their prey and then attack them ferociously,
attempting to swallow them whole.

This is a very quiet fish when not stalking food and it gets along well
with other fishes which are too large to be eaten. It is very hardy and
quite common in petshops.

★Now called *Brachirus brachypterus*.

343.00

Dendrochirus zebra Quoy and Gaimard*

COMMON NAME: Zebra Lionfish.
RANGE: Tropical Indo-Pacific.
PREVIOUS SCIENTIFIC NAMES: *Pterois zebra, Pseudomonopterus zebra.*
MERISTIC CHARACTERISTICS: D. XIII, 10 (11); A. III, 6 (7). Reaches a
length of about 8 to 9 inches.

This species, because of its coloration and finnage, is often confused
with species of the genus *Pterois*. However, members of the genus *Pterois*
have their pectoral fin rays relatively free, whereas species of *Brachirus*
have the pectoral fin membranes extending out to near the ends of the
rays.

Zebra Lionfish are relatively peaceful with other fishes and even with
their own kind, but be sure tankmates are large enough, for the Zebra
Lionfish will accept small fishes as food and will not discriminate between food fishes and tankmates.

The spines, like those of many other members of the family, have
venom associated with them and can produce a very painful wound.

*Now called *Brachirus zebra*.

344.00

Dinematichthys iluocoetoides Bleeker

Common Name: Yellow Brotulid.
Range: Indo-Pacific.

While little is known about the fish scientifically, even less is known by aquarists. Hopefully someone will collect and maintain this species and publish his knowledge.

Beautiful fishes like this one are bound to be shipped to aquarists. Hopefully future editions of this book will contain more information about this fish.

345.00

Diodon hystrix (Linnaeus)

COMMON NAME: Porcupinefish.
PHOTOGRAPH BY: Dr. Herbert R. Axelrod of a puffed-up specimen from Bimini 4 inches long.
RANGE: All over the world in warm seas.
MERISTIC CHARACTERISTICS: D. 15–17; A. 15–16; P. 25.

This fish is one of the most popular of fishes. It is sold in almost every souvenir shop in the mid-Pacific tourist belt, dried out in the swollen form. They make excellent lamp shades, decorations and curios. They have no other commercial value as they are nuisance fish. The tourist is usually disappointed, however, when their exotic souvenir washes up on their Jersey shore. In the aquarium they are oddities. Carefully taking one out of the water, they gasp for air until they swell themselves up. As they swell their spines become erect and would probably discourage a potential carnivore.

In nature they eat sea urchins, mollusks, crabs, hermit crabs and snails which they easily crush with their powerful jaws. They can inflict a painful bite when handled, so take care!

In the aquarium they eat anything usually offered to fish.

346.00

Doratonotus megalepis Günther

COMMON NAME: Dwarf Wrasse.

PHOTOGRAPH BY: Dr. John Randall of a 2.1-inch specimen from St. John, Virgin Islands.

RANGE: Bermuda, Florida, Caribbean to the eastern Atlantic.

MERISTIC CHARACTERISTICS: D. IX, 10; A. III, 9; P. 11–12. Grows to 3 inches.

This is probably the smallest of Atlantic wrasses and has only recently been discovered in the warm eastern Atlantic.

While it is not rare, it is difficult to find since it blends in so well with blades of turtle grass, its favorite habitat.

In the aquarium it does fairly well if it has a place to hide. The recent introduction of plastic aquarium plants suitable for seawater has made keeping this fish a lot easier.

In the aquarium it feeds upon canned Norwegian brine shrimp, fairy shrimp and the usual freeze-dried foods.

Drepane punctata (Linnaeus)

COMMON NAME: Spotted Drepanid.
PHOTOGRAPH BY: Marcuse.
RANGE: Tropical Indo-Pacific from the Red Sea to Samoa.
PREVIOUS SCIENTIFIC NAMES: *Chaetodon punctatus, Chaetodon longimanus, Chaetodon flacatus, Ephippus falcatus, Drepane longimana, Harpochirus punctatus, Harpochirus longimanus, Cryptosmilia luna.*
MERISTIC CHARACTERISTICS: D. VIII–IX, 19–22; A. III, 17–18; lateral line with 50–55 scales. Grows to a length of about 10 inches.

The drepanids are close relatives of the bat fishes (genus *Platax*) and are inhabitants of shallow reefs throughout the Indian and Pacific Oceans. This species, which is reasonably hardy, needs a large aquarium and will do well when fed a variety of freeze-dried foods.

348.00

Dunckerocampus dactyliophorus (Bleeker)

COMMON NAME: Zebra Pipe Fish.

RANGE: Indo-Australian Archipelago and Micronesia.

PREVIOUS SCIENTIFIC NAMES: *Syngnathus dactyliophorus, Acanthognathus dactyliophorus.*

MERISTIC CHARACTERISTICS: D. 21–25; A. 4; P. 19–21; about 36 tail and trunk rings. Attains a length of 6–7 inches.

The members of this genus have the most striking color patterns of all the pipe fishes. The males are characterized by the presence of a brood pouch, where they incubate the young in the same manner as the sea horses. The long snout is used to suck up small crustaceans which abound on the bottom. Newly hatched brine shrimp makes a good substitute food in captivity.

349.00

Echidna nebulosa (Ahl)

COMMON NAME: Snowflake Moray Eel.
RANGE: Tropical Indo-Pacific and Red Sea.
PREVIOUS SCIENTIFIC NAMES: *Muraena nebulosa, Gymnothorax echidna, Gymnothorax nebulosa, Muraena ophis, Echidna variegata, Thaerodontis ophia, Muraena variegata, Paecilophis variegata.*
MERISTIC CHARACTERISTICS: Grows to about 3 feet.

This beautiful fish is sometimes available and makes a stunning aquarium attraction. The snowflake-like blotches are diagnostic for the species. Many of the eels are most active at night, but *E. nebulosa* is often seen out in the open during the daylight hours, presumably in search of crustaceans which are a favorite food item.

350.00

Echidna zebra (Shaw and Nodder)

COMMON NAME: Zebra Moray.
PHOTOGRAPH BY: Paysan.
RANGE: Tropical Indo-Pacific and Red Sea.
PREVIOUS SCIENTIFIC NAMES: *Gymnothorax zebra, Gymnomuraena doliata, Muraena molendinaris, Gymnomuraena fasciata, Muraena zebra, Gymnomuraena zebra.*
MERISTIC CHARACTERISTICS: Attains a length of about 4.5 feet.

Here's a beast which is actually less ferocious than it appears. The teeth of this species are short and pebble-like in contrast to the sharp fangs which are characteristic of many of the other morays. *E. zebra* gets its common name from the bold pattern of bars which appear on the body. The girth of this eel is remarkably large in proportion to its length and often fools divers who try to estimate the length after only getting a glimpse of a portion of the body. This species is often seen out in the open during the daytime. Feed your eel sizeable portions of fresh frozen fish and shrimp.

351.00

Ecsenius bicolor (Day)

COMMON NAME: Bicolor Blenny.
RANGE: Tropical Indo-Pacific.
PREVIOUS SCIENTIFIC NAMES: *Salarias bicolor*.
MERISTIC CHARACTERISTICS: D. XII, 16–17; A. II, 18–20; P. 13-14.
   Grows to 4 inches.

The bright orange posterior and purplish head make *E. bicolor* one of the more handsome of the blenny species commonly seen in the aquarium. They are extremely abundant at Eniwetok Atoll in the tropical Central Pacific. Here they are found in the quiet lagoon waters, usually in depths in excess of 15–20 feet. Wherever there is shelter available in the form of a coral mound or shipwreck you will find the Bicolor Blenny darting from crevice to crevice. They succumb (temporarily) to quinaldine, which is a chemical anaesthetic now in wide use by collectors, and this is by far the easiest way to capture them.

Freeze-dried foods which are supplemented with chlorella algae make excellent fare for this species.

352.00

Ecsenius pulcher (Murray)

COMMON NAME: Rock Blenny.

PHOTOGRAPH BY: Paysan.

RANGE: Tropical Indo-Pacific.

PREVIOUS SCIENTIFIC NAMES: *Salarias pulcher, Salarias phantasticus, Salarias anomalus.*

MERISTIC CHARACTERISTICS: D. XII, 19–20; A. II, 20–21. Reaches 3 inches.

As is the case with many other hard-to-collect fishes, the Rock Blenny is most effectively captured with chemical anesthetics such as the widely used quinaldine. Many dealers are up in arms against chemically captured fish and absolutely refuse to handle them. It has been reported that fish caught in such a manner are in poor shape and have a drastically shortened life span. However, personal experience tends to disprove this theory. Specimens captured with quinaldine have lived over a year without showing any ill effects while net-captured specimens (of the same species) in the same tank have succumbed. There doesn't seem to be a correlation between the use of chemicals in capture and a shortened life in captivity.

353.00

Elacatinus oceanops (Jordan)*

COMMON NAME: Neon Goby
PHOTOGRAPH BY: Douglas Faulkner.
RANGE: West Indies to Floirda.

The Neon Goby is one of the most popular Florida fishes. They almost always are found on red coral and they spend a great deal of their time picking parasites from other fishes.

Several reports have been seen in the aquarium press about this fish having spawned, but to the best of my knowledge no one has ever raised any to the free-swimming stage.

They do well on canned Norwegian brine shrimp and most live foods.

* Now known as *Gobiosoma oceanops*.

354.00

Eleotriodes strigata (Broussonet)

COMMON NAME: Golden-headed Sleeper.
RANGE: Tropical Indo-Pacific.
PREVIOUS SCIENTIFIC NAMES: *Valenciennesia strigata.*
MERISTIC CHARACTERISTICS: Not available. Reaches about 6 inches.

This beauty is a member of the family Gobiidae and is distinguishable on the basis of its bright orange head with a light blue oblique line below the eye. In the tropical Central Pacific, *E. strigata* is a common inhabitant of atoll lagoons, usually found associated with sandy areas. These fish are bottom dwellers which live in burrows in the sand, often at the base of a rock or under dead coral. Large pairs are often seen together.

Provide them with a thick layer of sand on the bottom of the aquarium and add several good-sized rocks. They will accept feedings of frozen and live brine shrimp supplemented with freeze-dried foods. This species feeds primarily on small crustaceans in nature.

355.00

Epibulus insidiator (Pallas)

COMMON NAME: Long-jawed Wrasse.
PHOTOGRAPH BY: Dr. John Randall of a 1-inch specimen from Eniwetok.
RANGE: Tropical Indo-Pacific.
PREVIOUS SCIENTIFIC NAMES: *Sparus insidiator.*
MERISTIC CHARACTERISTICS: D. IX, 10–11; A. III, 8–9; lateral-line has
   22–27 scales. Attains a length of about 15 inches.

Here is a most unusual aquarium attraction. The jaws of this species
are protractile; that is, they can be thrust forward to form a funnel-like
feeding apparatus which aids them in picking up invertebrate food items
from hard-to-get-at crevices in the coral reef.

This species displays a variety of color patterns of which the juvenile
phase is the most spectacular. It has a purplish body with a series of
white bars radiating out from the eye, four vertical bars on the body and
several black spots on the dorsal and anal fins. Adults may be either
bright yellow or blackish with orange markings on the head. The pro-
trusible mouth is the best way to identify this wrasse, since it's the only
member of the family which has it.

The Long-jawed Wrasse should be given relatively large feedings of
frozen and live brine shrimp, freeze-dried daphnia and tubifex.

356.00

Epinephelus corallicola Valenciennes

COMMON NAME: East Indian Red Hind.
PHOTOGRAPH BY: Klaus Paysan.
RANGE: East Indies.
PREVIOUS SCIENTIFIC NAMES: *Serranus corallicola.*

Sometimes confused with *Epinephelus merra*, but there is a distinct difference in the shape of the red spots. The spots on *corallicola* are much more round.

This fish grows to 15 inches at least and is a common food fish in the range where it is found. Small specimens are often shipped to aquarists, but the fish keeps growing and growing.

They feed well on most chunky foods and they will eat small fish.

Epinephelus flavocaeruleus (Lacepede)

COMMON NAME: Blue and Yellow Reef-Cod.
PHOTOGRAPH BY: Hansen.
RANGE: Tropical Indo-Pacific.
PREVIOUS SCIENTIFIC NAMES: *Holocentrus flavo-caeruleus, Serranus flavocaeuleus.*
MERISTIC CHARACTERISTICS: D. XI, 15–17; A. III, 8; lateral line scales 75–77. Reaches 18 inches.

The delicate colors of this grouper make it an outstanding attraction. This species is relatively uncommon, usually being found in rocky areas which abound with dark ledges. In captivity they prefer live foods, but may gradually be switched to a diet consisting entirely of frozen fish and shrimp. After an adjustment period which varies with individual fish, these normally shy creatures will become quite tame and unafraid.

Epinephelus guttatus (Linnaeus)

COMMON NAME: Red Hind.
PHOTOGRAPH BY: Dr. John Randall of a 10-inch specimen from the Virgin Islands.
RANGE: Tropical western Atlantic from North Carolina north to Brazil.
MERISTIC CHARACTERISTICS: D. XI, 15–16; A. III, 8; P. 16–17. Grows to about 21.5 inches according to Randall.

This is the most common species of grouper found in the West Indies. They are easily taken on hook and line or by spear. I ate the first one I ever speared as grouper cutlet and I must admit it was one of the best fish I have ever eaten.

As an aquarium fish it is a gem, though very few aquarists care to bother. These fish become real pets. They seem to like people and readily turn to hand-feeding training.

Epinephelus hexagonatus (Bloch and Schneider)

COMMON NAME: Rock Cod, Groupa, Garoupa.

RANGE: Tropical mid-Pacific, including Tahiti, Bikini, Eniwetok, Rongelap, Rongerik, Kwajalein and Rota.

PREVIOUS SCIENTIFIC NAMES: *Holocentrus hexagonatus, Serranus hexagonatus, Serranus stellans.* Easily confused with *E. merra.* Called *E. merra* by J. L. B. Smith.

MERISTIC CHARACTERISTICS: D. XI, 15–16; P. ii, 16–18; 95–100 scale rows above the lateral line. Grows to about 18 inches.

The beautiful spots, most of which are hexagonal in shape, make this fish easy to recognize, even though L. P. Schultz confused them originally with *E. merra,* a mistake copied by J. L. B. Smith.

This is a very common fish in its range, with thousands of them inhabiting large reefs which afford holes and crevices in which they can seclude themselves.

In the aquarium small specimens are very friendly and soon learn to feed from your hand. The larger specimens like freeze-dried Tubifex worms in a unified mass. Smaller specimens tear it apart before eating it. They feed well on canned Norwegian brine shrimp and small fishes.

They will eat any fish small enough to be swallowed whole, so don't keep them in an aquarium with small fish. They should have a large aquarium. A 6-inch specimen should not be kept in less than a 20 gallon aquarium.

360.00

Epinephelus merra Bloch

COMMON NAME: Rock Cod, Groupa, Garoupa.

RANGE: Tropical mid-Pacific including Bikini, Eniwetok, Sea of Japan, Guam and Palau.

PREVIOUS SCIENTIFIC NAMES: Confused with *E. hexagonatus*.

MERISTIC CHARACTERISTICS: D. XI, 15–17; A. III, 8; P. ii, 16; 100–110 oblique scale rows above the lateral line.

It is easy to confuse this species with *E. hexagonatus* since they have the same basic color pattern with the hexagonal markings all over their bodies. It lacks the usual black blotches along the base of the dorsal fin and on the upper edge of the caudal peduncle.

It is extremely plentiful and found by the thousands in large coral masses which afford it ample holes and caves in which it can retire.

It is identical to *E. hexagonatus* in almost every characteristic including its great abundance.

361.00

Photo by Dr. Shih-chieh Shen.

Epinephelus tauvina (Forskål)

COMMON NAME: Garoupa, Groupa, Rock Cod.

RANGE: Red Sea, Zanzibar and Natal to India, East Indies, China to the Carolines to Hawaii.

PREVIOUS SCIENTIFIC NAMES: *Perca tauvina, Serranus tauvina, S. crapao, S. salmonoides, Epinephelus gilberti, Homalogrystes guntheri, Epinephelus fuscoguttatus* and *Serranus phaeostigmaeus.*

MERISTIC CHARACTERISTICS: D. XI, 14, i; A. III, 8, i; 108 scales in lateral line to caudal base and 7 on caudal base. There are 60 tubes in lateral line to caudal base and 3 on caudal base.

This is one of the most common fish in the Pacific Ocean and Red Sea. Small specimens seem to be more easily obtainable from the Red Sea and most of our aquarium specimens come from that source.

This fish becomes very large, with reports of 4 feet long specimens being common. The record is about 130 cm (1 inch = 2.54 cm). Small specimens are very friendly in the aquarium and they can usually be taught to feed from your hand. They like to hide in crevices among the coral, so be sure to make a place for them when you set up the aquarium.

Obviously they require an aquarium suitable to their size. A 6-inch fish must have a 20 gallon aquarium if it is to thrive. It takes freeze-dried Tubifex worms gluttonously.

Epinephelus truncatus (?)

PHOTOGRAPH BY: Dr. John Randall of a specimen 14.5 inches from Papeete Market, Tahiti.

The identification of this fish is tentative as the author has not seen the specimen nor could he verify its identification from the literature. Dr. Randall wasn't positive of the fish either as he didn't catch it, but bought it in the fish market in Tahiti.

Eques acuminatus (Bloch and Schneider)

COMMON NAME: Cubbyu or High Hat.
RANGE: Bermuda and South Carolina to Rio de Janeiro.
PREVIOUS SCIENTIFIC NAMES: *Grammistes acuminatus, Eques lineatus, Pareques acuminatus.*
MERISTIC CHARACTERISTICS: D. IX or X–I, 37–40; 45–50 lateral-line scales.

Robert P. L. Straughan has recently reported that the High Hat is now a member of that exclusive club of fishes which have been observed to spawn in the aquarium. He has described the spawning of a pair of 5–6 inch specimens of which the female had a belly quite visibly swollen with eggs. The female initiates the spawning and is the aggressor throughout. Actual spawning takes place during vigorous head-to-tail chasing at which time the fish swim rapidly in a circle until they come into bodily contact. At this moment there is a rapid quivering of the jaws and the eggs and sperm are released simultaneously. Unlike those of many other marine species, the eggs of the High Hat are demersal; that is, they are negatively buoyant and sink to the bottom. The eggs no doubt undergo heavy predation by the many species which dwell on or near the bottom. Unfortunately, Straughan was not able to hatch the eggs and raise the young due to the fact that they were laid in a large holding tank with many other fishes. Perhaps someday advanced aquarists will be able to spawn these spectacular beauties on a regular basis when all the factors which lead up to a successful spawning become known.

Equetus lanceolatus (Linnaeus)

COMMON NAME: Jackknife Fish or Ribbon Fish.

PHOTOGRAPH BY· Hansen.

RANGE: Bermuda and South Carolina to Brazil.

PREVIOUS SCIENTIFIC NAMES: *Chaetodon lanceolatus, Eques americanus, Eques balteatus.*

MERISTIC CHARACTERISTICS: D. XIII or XIV, 49–55; P. 15 or 16; lateral line scales 48–55. Grows to 9 inches.

This extremely attractive species is similar in appearance to *E. acuminatus.* However, it is not as common, usually being confined to deeper water. The members of the genus *Equetus* are sometimes called "High Hats" in reference to the elongate first dorsal fin. They are commendable aquarium fish, but slightly on the shy side.

365.00

Eupomacentrus partitus (Poey)

Common Name: Bicolor Damselfish.
Range: Caribbean Sea.
Meristic Characteristics: D. XII, 14-17; A. II, 13-15; about 18-21 lateral line scales. Reaches a length of about 4 inches.

This species is relatively abundant in Caribbean waters. It is often encountered in Florida on the outer reefs in shallow water around coral rubble. They are easily collected and make good (but scrappy) aquarium fishes. They are hardy and not too particular about food.

366.00

Eupomacentrus fuscus (Cuvier and Valenciennes)

COMMON NAME: Dusky Damselfish.

PHOTOGRAPH BY: Dr. Herbert R. Axelrod.

RANGE: Tropical western Atlantic.

PREVIOUS SCIENTIFIC NAMES: *Pomacentrus fuscus, Pomacentrus variabilis, Pomacentrus atrocyaneus.*

MERISTIC CHARACTERISTICS: D. XII, 14–17; A. II, 13–15; lateral line scales 18–21. Grows to a length of 6 inches.

E. fuscus lacks the colors which are displayed by so many other members of the damselfish family, but it is nevertheless an excellent aquarium fish, especially for the beginner. The juveniles have a large blue-edged black spot at the base of the dorsal fin and are not unattractive. They are one of the most abundant shallow reef fishes in the Caribbean. They are good eaters and will accept nearly all commercially prepared foods. The species is especially fond of freeze-dried tubifex and brine shrimp. Since it is an omnivorous species, algae should be made available.

Eupomacentrus leucostictus (Muller and Troschel)

COMMON NAME: Beau Gregory.

PHOTOGRAPH BY: Dr. John Randall of a 2.1-inch specimen from Puerto Rico.

RANGE: Maine to Brazil; also recorded from St. Helena and Sao Tome in the Gulf of Guinea.

PREVIOUS SCIENTIFIC NAMES: *Pomacentrus leucostictus, Pomacentrus caudalis, Pomacentrus xanthurus, Pomacentrus dorsopunicans.*

MERISTIC CHARACTERISTICS: D. XII, 13–16; A. II, 12–14. Reaches a maximum of 4 inches.

The Beau Gregory, a flashy little fellow, is recommended for beginners and advanced aquarists alike. They are fascinating to observe. They are continually on the move and will take over a small (sometimes not so small) patch of the aquarium and guard it against all comers. If several are present in one aquarium a regular "peck-order" will be established, usually with the larger fish dominating the smaller ones. They are eager beavers at the dinner table and may consume all the food before less aggressive species such as the butterfly fishes and wrasses can get their fill. This is one drawback of keeping damsels with the more delicate species.

They're not particular about what they are fed and will take all dry flake preparations and freeze-dried foods.

368.00

Eupomacentrus planifrons (Cuvier and Valenciennes)

COMMON NAME: Yellow Damsel Fish.
PHOTOGRAPH BY: Dr. Herbert R. Axelrod.
RANGE: Southern Florida and the Caribbean Sea.
PREVIOUS SCIENTIFIC NAMES: None.
MERISTIC CHARACTERISTICS: XII, 15–17; A. II, 13–14; lateral-line scales
18–20. Reaches a length of 5 inches.

The young of *E. planifrons* are extremely attractive and make excellent aquarium fish. They are hardy and will enthusiastically accept a wide variety of food items, including frozen and live brine shrimp, finely chopped fish, and freeze-dried tubifex. This diet should be supplemented with occasional feedings of algae or chopped lettuce.

Euxiphipops navarchus (Cuvier and Valenciennes)

COMMON NAME: Blue-girdled Angelfish.
PHOTOGRAPH BY: Earl Kennedy.
RANGE: Indo-Australian Archipelago.
PREVIOUS SCIENTIFIC NAMES: *Holacanthus navarchus, Heteropyge navarchus*.
MERISTIC CHARACTERISTICS: D. XIV, 17–18; A. III, 17–18; lateral scale
    rows 48–50. Grows to 12 inches.

This is the most spectacular member of the angelfish genus *Euxiphipops*. They are generally solitary in habit, but occasionally are found
in pairs, preferring the quiet and clear waters of offshore coral reefs.
Provide plenty of room for this gorgeous specimen; only shy, non-
aggressive species should serve as tank mates. Feed a diet which consists
of finely chopped fish and shrimp, tubifex (live and freeze-dried), brine
shrimp and chopped lettuce or spinach.

370.00

Euxiphipops sexstriatus (Cuvier and Valenciennes)

COMMON NAME: Six-barred Angelfish.

RANGE: Indo-Austrialian Archipelago, Western Caroline and Philippine Islands.

PREVIOUS SCIENTIFIC NAMES: *Holacanthus sexstriatus, Chaetodon resimus, Heteropyge sexstriatus.*

MERISTIC CHARACTERISTICS: D. XIII, 18–20; A. III, 18–19; about 50 scale rows. Attains a length of 20 inches.

The angelfishes can be distinguished from the closely related butterfly fishes by the presence of a stout backward projecting spine on the lower edge of the gill cover. In this species it may be extremely large, extending beyond the base of the pectoral. *E. sexstriatus* can be identified by the 5 or 6 dark bars on the body and its arrowhead-like shape. Provide your angelfish with as much room as possible. Approximately 25 gallons is recommended for one 4–5 inch fish, but this figure is flexible, depending on aeration and the temperament of individual fish. Feed as recommended for the other angelfish species.

371.00

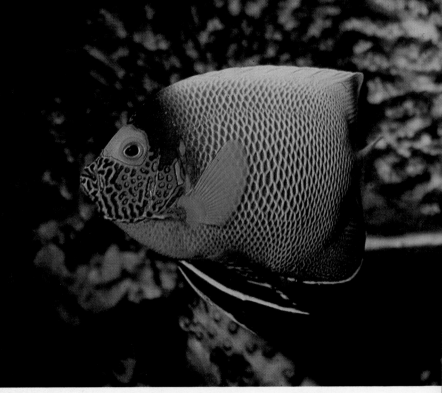

Euxiphipops xanthometapon (Bleeker)

COMMON NAME: Yellow-faced Angelfish.
PHOTOGRAPH BY: Gerhard Marcuse.
RANGE: Indo-Australian Archipelago to the Caroline Islands.
PREVIOUS SCIENTIFIC NAMES: *Holacanthus xanthometopon, Heteropyge xanthometopon.*
MERISTIC CHARACTERISTICS: D. XIV, 16–18; A. III, 16–18; scale rows 46–50. Grows to about 15 inches.

Another one of the magnificent angelfish species, *E. xanthometapon* is a much sought after aquarium fish. There is no other group of fishes which can compete with the angels and butterflies when it comes to wild colors and boldness of body markings. Many exhibit patterns which appear to have been literally painted on. Such a fish is the Yellow-faced Angel with its gaudy yellow face mask, scales outlined in gold and brilliant blue head markings and fin borders. It is one of nature's master-pieces! Give your treasure the attention it deserves. This means a tank all to itself or with only very small and peaceful neighbors. Live brine shrimp is a good "starter" food, but eventually they will accept such items as canned Norwegian brine shrimp, finely chopped beef, fish, and shrimp and freeze-dried tubifex.

372.00

Flammeo marianus (Cuvier and Valenciennes)

COMMON NAME: Longspine Squirrelfish.
PHOTOGRAPH BY: Dr. John Randall of a 4.6-inch specimen from the Virgin Islands.
RANGE: West Indies. According to Randall this fish appears to be the most common squirrelfish in depths of 100 feet or more.
MERISTIC CHARACTERISTICS: D. XI, 12–14; A. IV, 9; P. 14; 45–47 scales in the lateral line. Grows to about 7 inches.

This is a rare squirrelfish for the aquarium because it rarely gets into shallow water but prefers the deeper waters where aquarium collectors fear to tread. When small specimens are available they make magnificent additions to the home aquarium and can be said to be peaceful and interesting especially if kept in a large aquarium with plenty of hideouts and dim light.

Hobbyists vacationing in the Caribbean often bring some of these beauties home after they catch them on hook and line!

373.00

Flammeo opercularis (Valenciennes)

COMMON NAME: Black Finned Flammeo.
RANGE: Tropical Indo-Pacific.
PREVIOUS SCIENTIFIC NAMES: *Holocentrus opercularis.*
MERISTIC CHARACTERISTICS: D. X, I, 11–12; A. IV, 9; perforated scales
in lateral line 37–39.

The squirrelfishes have recently been divided by taxonomists into
three different genera, namely *Adioryx, Flammeo* and *Holocentrus.*
Most of the squirrels are now called *Adioryx.* There are only 2 species
of *Holocentrus,* and these occur in the Atlantic. The genus *Flammeo*
consists of 4 species, of which *F. opercularis* stands out by having an
almost entirely black dorsal fin. However, don't confuse this species with
Adioryx diadema, which also has a black dorsal. *Diadema* has alternating
red and white stripes on the body, which *F. opercularis* lacks.

These are attractive aquarium fish which live a long time when
properly cared for. They do best if fed live foods.

Flammeo sammara (Forskal)

Common Name: Blood-spot Squirrelfish.
Range: Tropical Indo-Pacific, from Hawaii to the coast of Africa and
the Red Sea.
Previous Scientific Names: *Sciaenia sammara, Labrus angulosus,
Holocentrus sammara, Holocentrus tahiticum, Holocentrus fusco-
striatus, Kutaflammeo sammara.*
Meristic Characteristics: D. X, I, i, 10-11; A. IV,8; lateral line 40-44.

    The common name refers to the dark spot in the anterior part of
the dorsal fin. This dorsal fin pattern is one of the characters which
distinguishes the Blood-spot Squirrelfish from the Black-finned Flammeo, *Flammeo opercularis.*
    The Blood-spot Squirrelfish is occasionally imported from the
Pacific and does very well in captivity. It eats almost anything and a
variety of frozen, dried, flake, or freeze-dried foods will suffice. They
tend to be shy in an aquarium at first but with time will show itself
more and more, especially at feeding time. Subdued light will also
help squirrelfish acclimate to new environments as will plenty of
hiding places.

Flammeo scythrops (Jordan and Evermann)

COMMON NAME: Hawaiian Squirrelfish.
PHOTOGRAPH BY: Dr. Herbert R. Axelrod.
RANGE: Hawaiian Islands.
PREVIOUS SCIENTIFIC NAMES: *Holocentrus scythrops*.
MERISTIC CHARACTERISTICS: D. XI, 13–14; A. IV, 9; 44–45 tubed lateral-line scales. Grows to 10 inches.

The Squirrelfishes of the genus *Holocentrus* have recently been divided into three different genera or groups. Most of the species which formerly were called *Holocentrus* are now recognized as belonging to the genus *Adioryx*, with the former name being valid for a couple of species which occur in the tropical Atlantic.

F. scythrops is endemic to the Hawaiian Islands, that is, it occurs nowhere else outside this island chain. Like the other members of the family, the Hawaiian Squirrelfish is an inhabitant of dark holes and ledges and must be provided with plenty of shelter. Small live fish and earthworms make excellent food for this species, and the diet may be supplemented with frozen brine shrimp and chopped fish.

Forcipiger flavissimus Jordan and McGregor

Common Name: Long-nose Butterflyfish.
Range: Widespread in the tropical Indo-Pacific from the Red Sea and
 coast of East Africa to Easter Island, Hawaii and coast of Mexico.
Previous Scientific Names: *Forcipiger longirostris* (in part), *Chelmon
 longirostris*.
Meristic Characteristics: D. XI to XIII)usually XII), 21-25; A. III,
 17-19; lateral line scales 68-78. Grows to 6 inches.

It was formerly thought that there was only one kind of long-nose,
but there are 2 distinct species involved. Both are very similar in appearance, but there are some minor differences which will enable you
to tell them apart. *F. flavissimus* is by far the most common species,
and 99 times out of 100 this will be the one encountered in pet shops.
It is similar in appearance to *F. longirostris* but usually has 12 dorsal
spines instead of 10 or 11 spines which the latter has. Also the snout is
much more exaggerated in *F. longirostris*. *Forcipiger longirostris* also
has a phase in which it is entirely black in coloration in contrast to its
yellow brothers. It is a rare species, occasionally sighted by divers on
the Kona Coast of Hawaii.

The Long-nose is a brilliant attraction which will thrive in the
aquarium. Feed a variety of freeze-dried foods and live brine shrimp.
It may prove difficult to keep with others of its own kind since they are
prone to fighting.

Photo by Ray Allard.

Gobiodon citrinus (Ruppell)

Common Name: Lemon Goby.
Range: Tropical Indo-Pacific.
Meristic Characteristics: D. VI -10-11; A. 10. Grows to about 2 inches.
Previous Scientific Names: *Gobius citrinus, Gobiodon erythrophaios, Gobiodon hypselopterus, Pseudogobiodon citrinus.*

The Lemon Goby may not remain yellow but could change back and forth from a brownish-yellow or greenish-yellow to the bright yellow color. The black spot near the pectoral and the bright blue lines on the head remain fairly permanently.

These small gobies are generally found among the branches of corals and are easily captured by picking the coral up out of the water and shaking it into a net. This might take some doing as the goby wedges itself tightly into the crevices with its fins and does not shake loose easily. Be sure to replace the coral to its original spot after the gobies are netted.

Although not visible in the photo, this goby has a flattened body.

378.00

Photo by Dr. Herbert R. Axelrod.

Gomphosus varius Lacépède

COMMON NAME: Longface, Beakfish.
RANGE: Widespread throughout tropical Indo-Pacific, Hawaii to South Africa.
MERISTIC CHARACTERISTICS: D. VIII, 13; A. III, 11; 26–30 scales in the lateral line. Grows to about 10 inches.

There are two colorations on this popular aquarium fish; the males turn green when adult and the females are brown.

These are very agile, colorful fish that seem to do very well in the marine aquarium. Their heads are elongated, much like the other labrids, but more so with *varius*. It seems that in the aquarium, the longface likes to poke into small crevices for his food. They are very active and make interesting tankmates to nearly every kind of marine fish.

They must have some vegetation in their diets or they slowly starve. Freeze dried foods are readily taken, especially brine shrimp, but they relish freeze-dried Tubifex with Chlorella algae imbedded in it. They feed heavily on canned Norwegian brine shrimp, as do most marine fishes.

Photo by Dr. Herbert R. Axelrod.

Gramma loreto Poey

COMMON NAME: Fairy Basslet, Royal Gramma.
RANGE: Bermuda, West Indies, Caribbean.
MERISTIC CHARACTERISTICS: D. XII, 10; P. I, 5; grows to about 3 inches.

This is one of the prized aquarium fishes which is usually sold under the now unacceptable name of "Royal Gramma."

A real hider which often poses upside down with its belly against the top of an overhang or floating piece.

Easily cared for and easily obtained. Feeds readily on canned Norwegian brine shrimp or the usual freeze dried foods.

Gramma melacara Böhlke and Randall

COMMON NAME: Blackcap Basslet.
PHOTOGRAPH BY: Dr. John Randall of a 2.2 inch specimen from Grand
Bahamas.
RANGE: Bahamas and British Honduras.
MERISTIC CHARACTERISTICS: D. XIII, 9; P. 17–18. Grows to 4 inches.

Randall reports that this is the most common fish to be found on
steeply inclined reef fronts of the Bahamas at depths greater than 150 feet.
Has never been kept in the aquarium but assumedly it will soon be
available and probably has the same needs as the other grammas.

381.00

Grammistes sexlineatus (Thunberg)

COMMON NAME: Golden Striped Grouper.
PHOTOGRAPH BY: Gene Wolfsheimer.
RANGE: Tropical Indo-Pacific.
PREVIOUS SCIENTIFIC NAMES: *Perca sexlineata, Grammistes orinetalis, Bodianus sexlineatus, Sciaena vittata, Perca triacantha, Perca pentacantha, Grammistes orientalis.*
MERISTIC CHARACTERISTICS: D. VI–VII, I, 13–15; A. 10; lateral line scales 63–72. Grows to about 10 inches.

   G. sexlineatus is very attractive and readily adapts to aquarium surroundings. In nature they are found back in holes and may be nocturnal feeders. They have voracious appetites and are capable of gulping down relatively large fish. Nature has provided this species with built-in protection from predators in the form of a bitter toxic slime which covers the entire body. You might think of them as being the "skunks" of the reef. On Eniwetok a large Turkey Fish (*Pterois volitans*) was observed to stalk a small *Grammistes* and finally succeed in catching it with a mighty gulp of its cavernous mouth. However, a taste of the slime was enough and the Grouper was immediately spit out. The Turkey Fish everted its mouth, shook its head, and behaved as though it had been sucking on a lemon. The slightly ruffled *Grammistes* went about its merry way! Interestingly enough, it seems as though they are their own worst enemies. Large Golden Stripers will feed on smaller ones.

Gymnothorax meleagris (Shaw and Nodder)

COMMON NAME: White-spotted Moray Eel.
PHOTOGRAPH BY: Rodney Jonklaas.
RANGE: Widespread on the reefs of the Indian and Pacific Oceans.
PREVIOUS SCIENTIFIC NAMES: *Muraena mileagris, Gymonthorax leucostictus, Thyrsoidea chlorastigma, Thyrsoida mileagris.*
MERISTIC CHARACTERISTICS: Reaches a length of about 3.5 feet long.

G. meleagris is a wide-ranging species which is identifiable by the many small white dots which completely cover the body. Specimens under 12-inches make excellent aquarium specimens and surprisingly get along quite well with other species in the tank. Feed your White-spotted Moray plently of chopped frozen fish. Place the fish on the end of a piece of wire or net handle and dangle it in front of the fish until it snaps the food up with its powerful jaws. Be sure to provide rock shelter.

383.00

Gymnothorax tesselata Richardson*

COMMON NAME: Leopard Moray.
RANGE: Tropical Indo-Pacific.
PREVIOUS SCIENTIFIC NAMES: *Gymnothorax favagineus, Muraena ising-teena, Muraena tesselata, Muraena python, Thyrsoidae isinglenna.*
MERISTIC CHARACTERISTICS: Grows to about 4 feet.

The Leopard Moray is one of the more attractive members of this large family and makes an excellent aquarium pet. They live a long time in captivity if properly fed and are generally not quarrelsome towards other fishes. Fresh frozen smelt, available at most supermarkets, is an ideal food which should be dangled in front of the eel's mouth on the end of a stick or wire. Keep your tank covered, as they are notorious for slithering out onto the floor!

* Now called *Gymnothorax favagineus.*

Gymnothorax undulatus (Lacepede)

COMMON NAME: Moray Eel.
PHOTOGRAPH BY: Douglas Faulkner.
RANGE: Tropical Indo-Pacific and Red Sea.
PREVIOUS SCIENTIFIC NAMES: *Muraenophis stellata, Muraenophis undulata, Muraena fimbriata, Muraena bullata, Muraena cancellata Thyrsoidea cancellata, Gymnothorax isinglunoides.*
MERISTIC CHARACTERISTICS: Grows to about 5 feet.

The scientific name of this species is based on the pattern of undulating lines on the body. This species has sharp teeth and should not be handled. Provide lots of rock shelter and feed pieces of fish and shrimp.

Haemulon chrysargyreum Gunther

Common Name: Smallmouth Grunt.
Photograph By: Dr. John Randall.
Range: Tropical western Atlantic.
Previous Scientific Names: *Brachygenys chrysargyreum, Brachygenys taeniata.*
Meristic Characteristics: D. XII, 13; A. III, 9 or 10; lateral line scales 49-51. Grows to nearly 10 inches.

This is one of the over 20 species of grunts which occur in the tropical western Atlantic. Small aggregations of this fish are often seen during the day in the shelter of reefs. At night they disperse and feed individually over the adjacent flats. The young eat planktonic organisms which they catch above the bottom. The adults feed on this plankton also, supplemented with bottom-dwelling invertebrates. These fish make a peculiar noise by grinding the pharyngeal teeth together, hence the common name. Live brine shrimp is a favorite food in captivity.

Haemulon flavolineatum (Desmarest)

Common Name: French Grunt.
Range: Tropical western Atlantic.
Previous Scientific Names: *Diabasis flavolineatus, Haemulon hetero-don, Haemulon xanthopteron.*
Meristic Characteristics: D. XII, 14 or 15; A. III, 7 or 8; lateral line scales 47-50. Grows to one foot.

    This is the most common grunt species found on shallow reefs of southern Florida and the West Indies. They have the habit of forming dense aggregations during the day and are a magnificent sight to behold. Many of the members of this family are considered good eating.

387.00

Halichoeres biocellatus L. P. Schultz

RANGE: Bikini, Eniwetok, Rongelap, Lomuilal Island and Johnston Island. Probably more widespread.

PREVIOUS SCIENTIFIC NAMES: None. A relatively new species described by Dr. Leonard P. Schultz in 1960 from specimens he, Brock and Herald collected.

MERISTIC CHARACTERISTICS: D. IX, 12; A. III, 12; P. ii, 11; 20 + 2 + 5 pores in the lateral line, with two rows above the lateral line and 9 below it to the anal pore.

This newcomer is very easy to recognize by the two eye spots in the soft dorsal fin. The "eye spot" in Latin is "ocellus" with the possessive form being "ocellatus." The "bi" makes it two, thus *"biocellatus"* means "with two eye spots."

This fish has shown up fairly regularly in shipments from exporters in the Pacific because the fish seems to be easy to catch and easier to keep alive. It rarely gets larger than 4 inches, but most of the specimens imported are under 3 inches. There seems to be very slight color differences between small specimens about 1 inch long and the larger specimens.

These labrids do well on canned Norwegian brine shrimp, freeze-dried Tubifex and brine shrimp.

388.00

Halichoeres centiquadrus (Lacépède)

RANGE: Widespread throughout the tropical Indo-Pacific to Africa.
PREVIOUS SCIENTIFIC NAMES: *Julis hortulanus* or *Platyglossus hortulanus*.
MERISTIC CHARACTERISTICS: D. IX, 10–11; A. III, 11–12; 26–28 scales
in the lateral line. Grows to about 12 inches.

Most labrids grow too large and eat too much for their maintenance in
the average home marine aquarium. This is one of those species which is
so colorful, that even though people "know better" they always bring
one or two home.

There isn't much that can be said in their favor, except that they are
very colorful, even when fully grown. They do have a handsome set of
teeth which they will use should they be disturbed. They are not for the
amateur when they get larger, and my experience with only one specimen
led me to shy away from them as aquarium inhabitants thereafter.

They eat every kind of fish food, but they are especially partial to
freeze-dried Tubifex with Chlorella.

Halichoeres margaritaceus (Cuvier and Valenciennes)

RANGE: Widespread throughout the East Indies to South Africa.

PREVIOUS SCIENTIFIC NAMES: *Platyglossus pseudominiatus, P. opercularis.*

MERISTIC CHARACTERISTICS: D. IX, 11; A. III, 11; 20 + 2 + 5 pores in the lateral line. A small species rarely exceeding 4 inches. The pectoral rays are usually ii, 11.

This is a very popular labrid and is often seen in the aquariums of more sophisticated collectors. There is quite a bit of difference in coloration between the sexes. The females have a light green background color with dark areas on the scales being black to dark brown. The female's dorsal is barred with reddish tan. There is a black spot in the soft dorsal surrounded by white.

According to L. P. Schultz, he found mature eggs in females about 2 inches long.

390.00

Halichoeres radiatus (Linnaeus)

COMMON NAME: Pudding Wife.

RANGE: Bermuda and North Carolina to Brazil, including the southern Gulf of Mexico.

PHOTOGRAPH BY: Dr. Herbert R. Axelrod

PREVIOUS SCIENTIFIC NAMES: *Labrus brasiliensis, Julis crotaphus, Julis cyanostigma, Julis opalima, Julis patatus, Julis principis, Chlorichthys brasiliensis, platyglossus, cyanostigma, Platyglossus principis, Platyglossus radiatus, Platyglossus.*

MERISTIC CHARACTERISTICS: D. IX, 11; A. III, 12; P. 13. Grows to 18 inches.

As is true of many of the other wrasse species, the juvenile and adult color patterns of this fish are quite different. The juveniles display 5 pale blue bands on the back and a prominent black spot on the front part of the soft dorsal fin. The adult fish lack the bars and dorsal spot and tend to have plain brownish or greenish bodies. The more colorful juveniles are more often kept in aquaria than the unspectacular adults.

In nature this species feeds upon a variety of invertebrate materials supplemented with a small amount of algae. However, they are primarily carnivores, and the algae which is found in the stomachs of dissected specimens may have been eaten accidentally while picking small crustaceans and mollusks off the bottom. Live brine shrimp is an excellent food for this species.

391.00

Hemigymnus fasciatus (Bloch)

Common Name: Banded Wrasse.
Photograph By: Dr. Herbert R. Axelrod.
Range: Tropical Indo-Pacific.
Previous Scientific Names: *Labrus fasciatus, Labrus fuliginosus, Sparus zonephorus, Tautoga fasciata, Hemigymnus leucomus, Thalliurus fasciatus.*
Meristic Characteristics: D. IX, 11; A. III, 11; lateral line scales 29.
Grows to at least 4 feet.

Here's a wrasse species which is exquisitely marked. The basic color pattern is dark purple with white vertical bands. The head is light green with a series of reddish streaks lined with blue. Besides being attractive it is also hardy and thrives in captivity. It's especially fond of chopped shrimp and clam meat, but will not refuse other items and may eventually take dry flake food.

Hemigymnus melapterus (Bloch)

COMMON NAME: Half and Half Wrasse.

RANGE: Tropical Indo-Pacific.

PREVIOUS SCIENTIFIC NAMES: *Labrus melapterus, Tautoga melapterus, Tautoga dimidiatus, Thalliurus melapterus.*

MERISTIC CHARACTERISTICS: D. IX, 10–11; A. III, 11; lateral line scales 28. Grows to about one foot.

Only the young of this species are suited for the aquarium. The adults, besides being drably colored, are much too large for the average tank. The juveniles are handsome fish which exhibit three primary colors. The anterior portion of the body is light gray, the posterior is velvety black, and the tail is bright orange. A good many of the wrasses, if not most of them, are noted for their habit of burying themselves in the sand at night. However, it appears that this Wrasse is an exception and prefers to "nest" among coral branches. The color bleaches out considerably at night and when the fish is frightened.

This Wrasse is solitary in habit and is commonly seen feeding upon small invertebrates in areas of luxurious coral growths.

They are generally good feeders in captivity and will eat a variety of items. Stomach contents reveal a natural diet of gastropods, crustaceans and small amounts of algae.

393.00

Hemipteronotus martinicensis (Cuvier and Valenciennes)

COMMON NAME: Straight-tail Razor Fish.

RANGE: Yucatan and West Indies.

PREVIOUS SCIENTIFIC NAMES: *Xyrichthys martinicensis, Xyrichthys vitta, Novacula martinicensis, Novaculichthys martinicensis.*

MERISTIC CHARACTERISTICS: D. IX, 12; A. III, 12; lateral line 5–6 pored scales in posterior section. Grows to about 6 inches.

The fishes of the genus *Hemipteronotus* are among the hardest fishes to capture alive. Their blunt razor-edged forehead and compressed body enable them to efficiently bury in the sand head first at the approach of a diver. Rather than bury straight down, they apparently travel horizontally under the surface, and it is impossible to tell where they have disappeared to. This species, like all other members of the genus, is equipped with a ferocious set of needle-like teeth which can deliver a nasty bite to their owner if handled carelessly.

This is one of the prettier species of Atlantic razor fishes.

Hemipteronotus novacula (Linnaeus)

COMMON NAME: Pearly Razor Fish.
PHOTOGRAPH BY: Dr. John Randall and Klaus Paysan.
RANGE: Both sides of the tropical Atlantic.
PREVIOUS SCIENTIFIC NAMES: *Coryphaena novacula, Coryphaena psittacus, Coryphaena lineata, Xyrichtyhs uniocellatus, Xyrichthys vitta, Xyrichthys rosipes.*
MERISTIC CHARACTERISTICS: D. IX, 12; A. III, 12; lateral line 5 or 6 scales in the posterior section. Grows to about 9 inches.

The classification of the Atlantic razor fishes was in a badly confused state until very recently. It was thought there were somewhere between 10 and 20 species in the tropical Atlantic, but as a result of a study by Dr. John Randall, it has been found that there are only 5 species which show a wide variety of colors, according to sex and growth stage. *Hemipteronotus* (or *Xyrichthys* as it was formerly called) *psittacus* from the western Atlantic and *H. novacula* from the eastern Atlantic were discovered to be one and the same. In addition, *Xyrichthys uniocellatus* from Brazilian waters is just a geographical color variant of the widespread *novacula.*

Provide the aquarium with plenty of sand, since this species likes to bury itself. Feed them brine shrimp (live, canned or frozen), freeze-dried tubifex and chopped fresh fish and shrimp.

Hemipteronotus novacula (Linnaeus) is an expert at diving into the sand when danger threatens. Here an individual is coming up out of the sand apparently after the danger has passed. Photo by Klaus Paysan.

396.00

Hemipteronotus taeniourus (Lacepede)

COMMON NAME: Saragussum Razor Fish.

PHOTOGRAPH BY: Earl Kennedy.

RANGE: Tropical Indo-Pacific.

PREVIOUS SCIENTIFIC NAMES: *Labrus taeniourus, Labrus hemisphaerium, Julis vanikorensis, Xyrichthys taeniurus, Xyrichthys svanicolensis, Novacula cephalotaenia, Novacula taeniurus.*

MERISTIC CHARACTERISTICS: D. IX, 12 (13); A. III, 13 (14); 25 lateral line scales. Attains a length of about 10–11 inches.

   H. taeniourus is a camouflage expert which can literally disappear into a background of sargassum, which they often do when pursued by a collector. They rock back and forth in perfect synchronization with the wave-swept sea weeds, and only an experienced eye can distinguish them. It's an exceptional aquarium fish which is both colorful and hardy.

   Provide a thick layer of sand, since this species buries itself at night. Freeze-dried foods and frozen and live brine shrimp are recommended.

397.00

Heniochus acuminatus (Linnaeus)

COMMON NAME: Poor Man's Moorish Idol.
RANGE: Widespread throughout the tropical Indo-Pacific to Africa.
PREVIOUS SCIENTIFIC NAMES: *Heniochus macrolepidotus*.
MERISTIC CHARACTERISTICS: D. XI–XII, 23–28; A. III, 15–19; about 45
scales in the lateral line. Fourth dorsal spine greatly elongated. Grows
to about 10 inches.

This is one of the most commonly seen "rarities" in the marine
aquarium. Though looking much like the Moorish Idol, *Zanclus canescens*, because of the resemblance of the elongated dorsal fin, there is
quite a difference in personality.

While *Zanclus* is difficult to feed, *Heniochus* is simple to feed. As a
matter of fact, *Heniochus* are so gluttonous that they often become tame
enough to feed from your fingers!

Larger specimens from 6 to 10 inches are the best as they take acclimatization much more readily than the smaller specimens. They eat Norwegian canned brine shrimp, freeze-dried Tubifex Worms with Chlorella,
freeze-dried brine shrimp and most other freeze-dried foods.

398.00

Heniochus intermedius Steindachner

COMMON NAME: Red Sea Banner Fish.

RANGE: Red Sea.

PREVIOUS SCIENTIFIC NAMES: *Heniochus acuminatus* (in part).

MERISTIC CHARACTERISTICS: D. XI–XII, 24–27; A. III, 16–19; 44–46 vertical scale rows from upper edge of gill opening to base of caudal fin. Grows to about 9 inches.

Warren Burgess of the University of Hawaii is presently investigating the status of this species, which is very close to *H. acuminatus* of the Indian and Pacific Oceans. It may be ultimately decided that *intermedius* is a mere variety or subspecies of the wide-ranging *acuminatus*. Care and feeding of the species is the same as that of the other banner fish species.

Heniochus permutatus Cuvier*

COMMON NAME: Poor Man's Moorish Idol.
RANGE: Bikini, Rongerik, Guam, Eniwetok and probably more wide-spread.
MERISTIC CHARACTERISTICS: D. XII, 21–22; A. III, 18; P. I, i, 13–14; 49–55 scales in lengthwise series. Elongated fourth dorsal spine. Grows to about 8 inches.

This Poor Man's Moorish Idol is much more rare than the most common *H. acuminatus*. It is easily distinguished from *acuminatus* by the extra dark brown transverse band which runs from the scaly base of the dorsal to the caudal. It is more difficult to keep than the *acuminatus*, probably because its habitat is much deeper water. It thrives on canned Norwegian brine shrimp and after a few weeks in captivity it becomes fairly tame.

* Now called *Heniochus chrysostomus*.

400.00

Heniochus varius (Cuvier)

COMMON NAME: Humphead Banner Fish.

RANGE: Indian Ocean, Indo-Australian Archipelago, Micronesia, Melanesia, Polynesia and Philippine Islands.

PREVIOUS SCIENTIFIC NAMES: *Taurichthys varius*, *Taurichthys viridis*, *Diphreutes varius*, *Heniochus pleurotaenia*.

MERISTIC CHARACTERISTICS: D. XI, 22–25; A. III, 17–18; about 52–55 vertical scale rows.

    Juveniles of *H. varius* lack the hump on the forehead which is the characteristic feature of the adult from which the popular name is derived. It can be distinguished from the common *H. acuminatus* by the color pattern and absence of the long trailing dorsal filament. Juveniles look very much like the adults.

A closely related species, *H. pleurotaenia*, can be found in the Indian Ocean. It looks very much like *H. varius* but has an extra white patch in the middle of the body. Unless shipments from Sri Lanka and the African coast increase your probably will not see *H. pleurotaenia* but will only get *H. varius*.

Heniochus varius is fairly common in the Pacific and is often imported to the United States. It should be placed in a large aquarium and fed with small amounts of a variety of foods but frequently. It is usually timid and should not be placed with aggressive fishes like damsels.

Heniochus pleurotaenia from the Indian Ocean. Photo by Klaus Paysan.

Hippocampus brevirostris Cuvier

COMMON NAME: Short-snouted Sea Horse.
PHOTOGRAPH BY: Hilmar Hansen.
RANGE: Mediterranean Sea and eastern Atlantic.
PREVIOUS SCIENTIFIC NAMES: Not available.
MERISTIC CHARACTERISTICS: About 41 segments, D. 17–18. Grows to 8 inches.

This short-snouted species is popular among European aquarists, since it is native to their waters. Live brine shrimp makes an excellent sea horse food, and freshly hatched shrimp are suitable for young specimens. Take caution against feeding unhatched eggs, however, since they are indigestible and may cause fatal intestinal injury. Baby guppies or mollies are sometimes used for feeding the adults. Sea horses have been known to survive in captivity for over 2 years!

403.00

Hippocampus guttulatus Cuvier

COMMON NAME: Mediterranean Sea Horse.
PHOTOGRAPH BY: Hilmar Hansen.
RANGE: Eastern Atlantic and Mediterranean Sea.
PREVIOUS SCIENTIFIC NAMES: Not available.
MERISTIC CHARACTERISTICS: D. 19–21; approximately 43 tail and body
  segments. May reach a length of 8 inches.

Sea horses are one of nature's strangest curiosities. The eggs, after
having been fertilized in a fascinating courtship embrace, are deposited
by the female into a brood pouch on the abdomen of the male. The
lucky female is then free of the mother's burden of childbirth, which now
rests squarely on the shoulders of the male. He incubates the eggs in
his pouch for a period which varies from 1½–2 months, depending on
the species. At the end of this period the young are expelled 10–30 at a
time over a period of several days. The number of young generally
varies from 250–600, this number also dependent of the species involved.
Mildred Bellomy's *Encyclopedia of Sea Horses* (TFH 1969) is a com-
prehensive work for those who would like a complete guide to sea
horse care.   405.00

Hippocampus hippocampus (Linnaeus)

Common Name: Sea Horse.
Photograph By: W.M. Stephens.
Range: Coasts of southern Europe, north to England.
Previous Scientific Names: *Syngnathus hippocampus.*
Meristic Characteristics: D. 20. Grows to about 7-8 inches.

Keeping a tankful of sea horses is an education in itself. They are fascinating creatures which will quickly endear themselves to you. To successfully maintain this species (or any of the sea horses for that matter) you must provide: places for grasping (such as coral, plastic rods, etc.), an adequate food supply and peaceful neighbors. Aggressive tankmates will gobble all the food intended for the slow-moving sea horses, hence they will generally do better in a tank of their own.

Hippocampus erectus Perry

Common Name: Northern Sea Horse.
Photograph By: Marineland, Florida.
Range: Tropical western Atlantic.
Previous Scientific Names: *Hippocampus heptagonus, Hippocampus laevicaudatus.*
Meristic Characteristics: D. 19; Rings 12, 32 to 35. Grows to 10 inches.

    This is the northern species of the sea horses, one which can sometimes be collected by aquarists living in the coastal Middle Atlantic states. However, in the more northern part of its range the population numbers may vary drastically, common one year and almost nonexistent the next. Since this is a large species it requires great amounts of live food. Adult brine shrimp and baby guppies are ideal items and a standing supply of these should be kept in separate aquaria.

407.00

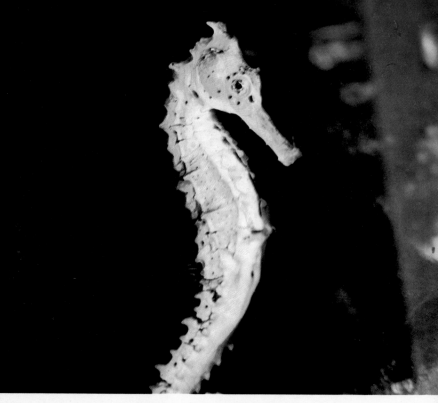

Hippocampus kuda (Bleeker)

COMMON NAME: Oceanic Seahorse.

PHOTOGRAPH BY: Marcuse.

RANGE: Tropical costs of the Indian and Pacific Oceans as far east as the Hawaiian Islands and north to Japan.

PREVIOUS SCIENTIFIC NAMES: *Hippocampus moluccensis, Hippocampus taeniopterus, Hippocampus polytaenia, Hippocampus comes, Hippocampus melanospilos, Hippocampus rhynchomacer, Hippocampus guttulatus, Hippocampus kelloggi, Hippocampus hilonis.*

MERISTIC CHARACTERISTICS: D. 16–18; A. 4; about 36 rings on the body. May reach one foot in length.

This species is widespread throughout the vast Indo-Pacific area and may sometimes be found far out to sea. It is the common species of the Hawaiian Islands, but for some strange reason it is almost never found in the shallow inshore waters there. It can be captured at night, several miles out to sea, by suspending a bright light 2 or 3 feet below the surface. These creatures are attracted by the light and will slowly float up to it on the surface, where they are easily dipped up in a net. The specimens caught in this manner are generally under 4 inches in length. However, the same species has been reported to grow up to 1 foot in the Indo-Australian Archipelago!

Histrio histrio (Linnaeus)

COMMON NAME: Sargassum Fish.

PHOTOGRAPH BY: Dr. Herbert R. Axelrod.

RANGE: Circumtropical, that is, it occurs world-wide in the warm seas of the Atlantic, Pacific and Indian Oceans.

PREVIOUS SCIENTIFIC NAMES: *Lophius histrio, Lophius raninus, Lophius cocinsinensis, Lophius gibbus, Chironectes laevigatus, Lophius histrio marmoratus, Lophius geographicus, Lophius histrio pictus, Chironectes pictus, Chironectes tumidus.*

MERISTIC CHARACTERISTICS: The bizarre sargassum weed-like appearance is sufficient for recognizing this unusual fish. Attains a length of about 9 inches.

The Sargassum Fish has to be rated as one of nature's most perfect creations in the art of camouflage. An inhabitant of floating tangles of sargassum weed, this fish blends in most effectively with its environment, where it sits passively by the hour waiting patiently for a fish to swim by within striking range of its cavernous mouth. It has an amazing appetite and will devour a fish nearly equal to its own size. When a fish happens to swim by within three inches or so of the mouth, these fish dart forward with lightning-fast speed which belies their normal habit of sitting nearly motionless for hours in one spot! Collectors sometimes capture this fish by scooping up large quantities of sargassum weed and then meticulously searching through it for fish.

Histrio is truly a "world traveler" in the sense that it has been carried to all the warm seas of the globe aboard its floating sargassum weed "ships." Naturally, live fish are the ideal food for keeping this species in good health.

409.00

Holacanthus arcuatus (Gray)*

Common Name: Black-banded Angelfish.
Range: Hawaiian Islands.
Meristic Characteristics: D. XIII, 18; A. III, 18; about 48 vertical
scale rows. Grows to about 7 inches.

This angelfish species is most commonly found at depths below 50 feet. As is true of many of the other angelfishes and butterflyfishes, they are frequently seen in pairs. It's one of the slowest-moving and seemingly most dimwitted members of the family. Large adults are easily caught with a single dipnet. They are very easy to corner in a blind "alley" in the coral from which they can be coaxed into the net by hand. The buyer of deep-water fishes such as this seldom appreciates the effort which the collector must make to bring them to the dealer in good shape. If this species is brought to the surface too quickly the entire abdominal cavity may swell with expanding gases, resulting in the death of the fish. It is necessary for the collector to spend as long as an hour slowly decompressing his catch to avoid these complications. A common decompression method consists of placing the collected fish in a plastic bag which is tied to a weighted line running to the boat. After the dive is completed the line is brought up ever so slowly.

This species needs a lot of room since small specimens are seldom available. Feedings of live brine shrimp, chopped fish, shrimp and occasional offerings of lettuce are the staple fare, but these fish have a reputation for sometimes being poor eaters.

* Now called *Apolemichthys arcuatus*.

410.00

Holacanthus ciliaris (Linnaeus)

COMMON NAME: Queen Angelfish.

RANGE: Tropical western Atlantic, including the southern Gulf of Mexico and Gulf coast of Florida.

PREVIOUS SCIENTIFIC NAMES: *Chaetodon ciliaris, Chaetodon squamulosus, Chaetodon parrae, Holocanthus cornutus, Holocanthus formosus, Pomacanthus ciliaris, Angelichthys ciliaris.*

MERISTIC CHARACTERISTICS: D. XIV, 19–21; A. III, 20 or 21; P. 19; Lateral line scales 45–49. Grows to 16–18 inches.

The Angelfishes are noted for having different juvenile and adult color phases, and the Queen Angel is no exception. The young fish has a series of blue bars on the body and a dark band which runs through the eye. The adult fish lacks both of these characters. This beautiful fish, which is common about the shallows and reefs of the Florida Keys, is especially interesting from the standpoint that it is one of the few marine fishes which have been known to form hybrids. More specifically, Dr. Henry Feddern has shown that the formerly recognized species, *Holacanthus townsendi*, is merely a hybrid form which resulted from the interbreeding of the Queen Angel (*H. ciliaris*) and the Blue Angel *(H. isabelita)*!

411.00

A juvenile *Holacanthus ciliaris* (Linnaeus). Note the differences between this fish and the *H. isabelita* individual of about the same size on p. 413.00. Photo by Dr. Herbert R. Axelrod.

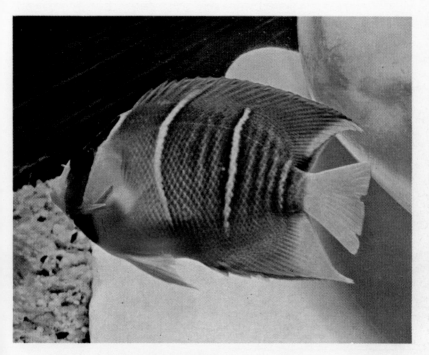

Holacanthus isabelita Jordan and Rutter

COMMON NAME: Blue Angelfish.

PHOTOGRAPH BY: Dr. Herbert R. Axelrod.

RANGE: Bermuda, southern Florida, Gulf of Mexico and the Bahamas.

PREVIOUS SCIENTIFIC NAMES: *Holacanthus ciliaris, Pomacanthus ciliaris, Angelichthys isabelita.*

MERISTIC CHARACTERISTICS: D. XIV, 19–20; A. III, 19–20: lateral-line scales 45–49.

This species is close in appearance to the Queen Angel (*Holacanthus ciliaris*). The juveniles of the two species can be distinguished by observing the second (not including those on the head) light bar on the body. In *H. isabelita* this bar is straight while in the Queen Angel it is curved. The adult Blue Angel lacks the forehead spot which the adult Queen has. Dr. Henry Feddern has discovered that these two species (Queen and Blue Angel) may freely interbreed, resulting in hybrid forms which are intermediate in color.

Feeding is the same as prescribed for *Holacanthus ciliaris*.

413.00

Holacanthus tricolor (Bloch)

COMMON NAME: Rock Beauty.
PHOTOGRAPH BY: Hilmar Hansen.
RANGE: Tropical Western Atlantic, as far north as Georgia and Bermuda.
PREVIOUS SCIENTIFIC NAMES: *Chaetodon tricolor*, *Genicanthus tricolor*,
Pomacanthus tricolor.
MERISTIC CHARACTERISTICS: D. XIV, 17–19; A. III, 18–20; lateral line
scales about 43 to 46. Reaches a length of about one foot.

The Rock Beauty is one of the more popular aquarium fishes found in
U.S. pet shops. It is not as high priced as the closely related pygmy
angelfishes, most of which are imported from the Indian and Western
Pacific Oceans. However, it is every bit as beautiful as these higher
priced imports. The young fish are almost entirely yellow with a blue-
edged black spot on the upper part of the body, very similar to the
coloration of juvenile Lemonpeels (*Centropyge flavissimus*) from the
tropical South Pacific. The size of the black spot increases as the fish
grows larger, until nearly the entire body is covered by it. The head,
breast and caudal fin remains a bright yellow color. Ample shelter should
be provided' in the aquarium for this species, especially when first
introduced since they are usually a bit on the spooky side. Rock Beauties
require algal material in their diet, and it is advisable that a growth of
green algae be allowed to grow on the rear wall of the tank. Brine
shrimp and chopped fish will also be accepted.

Holacanthus trimaculatus Cuvier*

COMMON NAME: Three-spot Angelfish.
RANGE: Tropical Indo-Pacific.
PREVIOUS SCIENTIFIC NAMES: None.
MERISTIC CHARACTERISTICS: D. XIII or XIV, 17–18; A. III, 18; about
45–48 scale rows. Grows to about 10 inches.

There are approximately 30 species of Angelfishes (sub-family Pomacanthidae) and the Three-spot is among the most beautiful. The common name is derived from the black spot on the forehead and the spot just behind the head on both sides. The broad black border on the anal fin is also a helpful character in identifying the species.

It's best to keep only one of this species in a tank, since fighting may occur, resulting in serious injury or death to its fellows. Live brine shrimp is recommended as a "starter" food, which after a few days, may be supplemented with freeze-dried brine shrimp and tubifex. Occasional feedings of lettuce may also be accepted, but be sure to remove all uneaten food to avoid fouling.

* Now called *Apolemichthys trimaculatus.*

415.00

Holocentrus ascensionis (Osbeck)

COMMON NAME: Longjaw Squirrelfish.

PHOTOGRAPH BY: Dr. John Randall of a 10.5-inch specimen from the
Virgin Islands.

RANGE: New York to Bermuda to Brazil including most islands in the
tropical and eastern Atlantic.

MERISTIC CHARACTERISTICS: D. XI, 14–16; A. IV, 10; P. 15–17; 46–51
scales in the lateral line. Grows to about 14 inches.

This is one of the abnormal species of Holocentrinae. It has an elongated air bladder which reaches all the way to the cranium.

Their big eyes indicate they are nocturnal by nature and small specimens kept in aquariums seem to prefer dimly lit tanks. The spine on their
gill cover is poisonous and this fish shouldn't be handled.

416.00

Photo by Dr. Gerald Allen.

Holocentrus rufus (Walbaum)

COMMON NAME: Squirrelfish.

RANGE: Bermuda, Florida and throughout the Caribbean.

MERISTIC CHARACTERISTICS: D. IX, 14–16; A. IV, 9–11; P. 15–17 scales in the lateral line.

Only in *H. ascensionis* and *rufus* of all the Holocentrids does the air bladder reach the skull. In other species the tubular air bladder runs only the entire length of the body cavity.

A truly coral species which is rarely found away from coral reefs but is very plentiful around reefs in its range.

Not a very practical aquarium fish, but found in larger aquariums from time to time.

They feed mainly on crustaceans, so canned Norwegian brine shrimp or freeze-dried brine shrimp are recommended.

Holotrachys lima (Cuvier and Valenciennes)

COMMON NAME: Prickly Squirrelfish.

RANGE: Wide ranging in the Indo-Pacific Oceans, from Hawaii to Madagascar.

PREVIOUS SCIENTIFIC NAMES: *Myripristis lima, Myripristis humilis.*

MERISTIC CHARACTERISTICS: D. XII, i, 13; A. IV, 11; 39 tubed lateral line scales. Reaches a length of 6–7 inches.

As its common name suggests, this fish has very prickly scales, which distinguishes it from the other members of the squirrelfish family. They are generally found in depths exceeding 40 feet and are cavern dwellers like the rest of the members of this family. Feedings of chopped fish and frozen brine shrimp may be accepted, but a variety of live foods are the preferred items. Provide shelter in the form of rocks arranged into small caves.

Hypoplectrus guttavarius (Poey)

Common Name: Shy Hamlet.
Range: Florida Keys and West Indies.
Previous Scientific Names: *Plectropoma guttavarium, Plectropoma melanorhina.*
Meristics Characteristics: D. X, 14-16; A. III, 7; lateral line scales 48-53. Grows to about 5 inches.

   This is another species of hamlet which is rare in occurrence. It is interesting to point out that many of the members of this genus are hermaphroditic, both male and female sex organs being present within one individual. Of course, only one sex functions at a time, and self-fertilization is not possible. This is a handy arrangement which helps to insure the perpetuation of the species on localities where their numbers are few.

Hypoplectrus gummigutta (Poey)

COMMON NAME: Golden Hamlet.
RANGE: Caribbean Sea.
PREVIOUS SCIENTIFIC NAMES: *Plectropoma gummigutta*.
MERISTIC CHARACTERISTICS: D. X, 15; A. III, 8. Grows to 5 inches.

You will be lucky indeed if you happen to acquire one of these gorgeous beauties. It's a rare species which has occasionally been collected by scientists. The brilliant yellow coloration and blue streaks on the face are reminiscent of the coloring of the Lemonpeel (*Centropyge flavissimus*). This is a carnivorous fish which feeds mainly on fishes and crustaceans. It is a member of the grouper family.

420.00

Hypoplectrus puella (Cuvier and Valenciennes)

COMMON NAME: Barred Hamlet.
RANGE: West Indies, Bermuda, Florida Keys and Gulf coast of Florida.
MERISTIC CHARACTERISTICS: D. X, 14–16; A. III, 7; P. 13–14. Reaches to
6 inches in size in Florida; 5 inches in Antilles.

This is the most common hamlet in the West Indies. They are small
fish and act like saltwater cichlids. They have large mouths and do a job
on small fishes if they can be ingested whole.

Young fishes have two black spots on the base of the tail, one on top
of the other. Though this species hasn't as yet been spawned in an
aquarium, it probably will be spawned fairly soon.

Hypoplectrus unicolor (Walbaum)

COMMON NAME: Butter Hamlet.
RANGE: Florida and the West Indies.
MERISTIC CHARACTERISTICS: Same as *H. puella.*

All hamlets have about the same basic body shape and about the same meristic characteristics. They are essentially differentiated by their color and the excellent color photographs make the task of recognizing these characteristics a simple matter indeed.

Inimicus didactylum (Pallas)

COMMON NAME: Popeyed Sea Goblin.

PHOTOGRAPH BY: Hilmar Hansen.

RANGE: Andaman Islands and Malay Archipelago.

PREVIOUS SCIENTIFIC NAMES: *Scorpaena didactylum, Pelor didactylum.*

MERISTIC CHARACTERISTICS: D. III, XIII–XV, 8–9; A. 11–12; P. 10+ii.
Attains a length of 7–8 inches.

Inimicus didactylum has an appearance which lives up to its common name. The upraised bulbous eyes and first three spines isolated from the rest of the dorsal fin are sufficient characters for recognizing this poorly known species.

This fish is a cavern dweller and should be provided with plenty of shelter in the form of rocks. Although there is little information available on the care of this species, it would probably do best on feedings of live fish and crustaceans, at least initially. It is a member of the scorpion fish family and a relative of the lion fishes; therefore the dorsal spines, although probably not as dangerous as those of the *Pterois, Dendrochirus* and *Scorpaena* species, should be respected and handled with caution.

423.00

Kuhlia taeniura (Cuvier and Valenciennes)

COMMON NAME: Reef Trout or Aholehole.

RANGE: Indo-Australian Archipelago and coral reefs of the south and central Pacific.

PREVIOUS SCIENTIFIC NAMES: *Dules taeniurus.*

MERISTIC CHARACTERISTICS: D. X, 9–11; A. III, 10–11; 53–54 scale rows from upper edge of gill opening to base of caudal fin. Attains a length of 10–12 inches.

The kuhliids, of which there are approximately half a dozen species, are an ideal fish for the beginning marine aquarist. They are hardy, almost beyond belief. One individual has been known to survive for several months in a gallon jar with no change of water and feedings of dry flake food. Dr. Earl Herald, Director of the Steinhart Aquarium states that he has kept Aholeholes alive for over 10 years!

In Hawaii, the closely related *K. sandvicensis* is among the most common inhabitants of rocky tidepools; because of its abundance and comparatively drab appearance, it is usually overlooked by collectors. However, the Aholehole has a beauty of its own, and several one-inch specimens will make a handsome addition to any tank. They will accept a wide variety of foods including fresh and frozen brine shrimp, mosquito larvae and a variety of dry foods.

Labrichthys unilineata Guichenot

COMMON NAME: Biglipped Wrasse; One-line Wrasse.

RANGE: Indo-Pacific from Samoa to the coast of Africa. Apparently absent from the Red Sea.

PREVIOUS SCIENTIFIC NAMES: *Cossyphus unilineatus, Labrichthys cyanotaenia, Thysanocheilus ornatus,* and *Chaerojulis castaneus.*

MERISTIC CHARACTERISTICS: D. IX, 11 (rarely 12); A. III, 10 (rarely 11); pectoral fin 14 or 15; lateral line scales 26. Grows to a length of about 5 inches.

Juvenile *Labrichthys unilineatus* are differently colored than the adults. Young individuals are dark brown with bluish reflections with a prominent bluish white stripe from the snout to near the tip of the tail and another bluish white stripe from the lower lip to near the end of the anal fin base. The major stripe is responsible for the scientific name *unilineatus* = one line.

Individuals have been seen on reefs among the living corals, particularly *Acropora* spp., at depths of a few feet to 50 feet or more. They were observed apparently feeding on the live corals much like many species of butterflyfishes. It is suspected that they may also be part-time cleaners as many wrasses are, if only in their juvenile stages, but they have not been observed in the act of cleaning.

Labroides dimidiatus Cuvier and Valenciennes

RANGE: Throughout the tropical Indo-Pacific to South Africa.
PREVIOUS SCIENTIFIC NAMES: *Fissilabrus dimidiatus, Labroides paradiseus.*
MERISTIC CHARACTERISTICS: D. IX, 10–11; A. III, 10; 50–53 scales in the
lateral line. Grows to about 4 inches.

This is one of the really subtle beauties of the coral reef. Easy to keep,
fairly easy to come by, this beauty changes color at will from a light pink,
through straw yellow to dark blue. Its body has movements like flowing
rubber as it weaves through crevices and tunnels in coral reefs or rocky
tide pools.

It has been observed as a "cleaner" fish poking into the mouth and
gill covers of larger fishes, assumedly eating annoying parasites. In
captivity it thrives on canned Norwegian brine shrimp, as well as the
usual freeze-dried foods. It is especially fond of freeze-dried brine shrimp.

Labroides dimidiatus cleaning a *Centropyge loriculus.*

A young *Labroides dimidiatus* at its cleaning station on the reef. Fish come here to have their parasites removed. Photo by Dr. H.R. Axelrod.

427.00

Photo by Dr. Patrick L. Colin.

Labroides rubrolabiatus Randall

RANGE: Society Islands and Tuamotu Archipelago.
MERISTIC CHARACTERISTICS: D. IX, 10–11; A. III, 10–11; P. ii, 11. Grows to slightly over 2 inches.

According to Dr. John Randall, who revised the genus *Labroides*, the juveniles of all *Labroides* appear to have the same basic black coloration, with a broad band of color along the back which extends and narrows onto the head. On *dimidiatus* and *rubrolabiatus* this band is brilliant deep blue; on *bicolor* it is bright yellow; on *phthirophagus*, it is bright purple.

While there is no record of this species having been kept in an aquarium, it is assumed to require the same care and feeding as *dimidiatus*.

428.00

Photo by Dr. Patrick L. Colin.

Lachnolaimus maximus (Walbaum)

COMMON NAME: Hog Fish.

RANGE: Gulf of Mexico and Caribbean Sea.

PREVIOUS SCIENTIFIC NAMES: *Labrus maximus, Lachnolaimus suillus, Lachnolaimus aigula, Lachnolaimus dux, Lachnolaimus caninus, Lachnolaimus psittacus, Lachnolaimus flacatus.*

MERISTIC CHARACTERISTICS: D. XIV, 11; A. III, 10; lateral line scales 32–34. Attains a length of about 3 feet.

The color of this Atlantic species is variable, but usually mottled red with a black spot at the rear base of the dorsal fin. The body is very tall when compared to the other members of the wrasse family. It is considered as an excellent food fish.

In nature it feeds primarily on mollusks, crabs, sea urchins and barnacles.

Photo by Yasuda and Hiyama.

Lactoria cornuta (Linnaeus)

COMMON NAME: Long-horned Cowfish.
RANGE: Tropical Indo-Pacific.
PREVIOUS SCIENTIFIC NAMES: *Ostracion cornutus*.
MERISTIC CHARACTERISTICS: D. 9; A. 9; carapace 5 ridged. May grow
to 20 inches.

The cowfish is truly one of nature's oddballs. The bizarre shape of
the head and protruding horns gives rise to the common name. It's an
excellent fish for the beginner and is not a fussy eater. For those aquarists
longing for a challenge, there is a possibility of spawning this fish in large
aquaria. The females lay eggs which are about 1 mm. in diameter. They
are positively buoyant and float immediately to the surface. Hatching
takes place in 4 or 5 days. Aquarists living in tropical areas where the
cowfish occurs can collect their own eggs by towing a fine mesh plankton net. The eggs are easy to see. They are comparatively large and heavily
pigmented. Barbara Palko and William Richards of the Bureau of Commercial Fisheries lab. in Miami, Florida, have described a method for
hatching the eggs and rearing the young. They recommend keeping the
eggs in an aquarium equipped with only an air stone and without filter
or gravel. A fluorescent or incadescent light should be placed over the
tank. A bloom of green algae should be promoted, as this is an excellent

Lactoria cornuta (Linnaeus), slightly older than the one on page 430.00, have shorter carapace spines. Photo by Gerhard Marcuse.

food source. It is also necessary to periodically provide plankton which has been collected in the same manner as the eggs. An abundance of microscopic food is absolutely essential for successful rearing. The larvae grow fast and are soon able to take newly hatched brine shrimp, which should be maintained in high concentration in the cowfish rearing tank.

431.00

Lepadogaster gouani Lacepede

COMMON NAME: Cling Fish.
PHOTOGRAPH BY: Hilmar Hansen.
RANGE: Mediterranean Sea.
PREVIOUS SCIENTIFIC NAMES: *Lepidogaster acutus.*
MERISTIC CHARACTERISTICS: Not available.

  These odd little creatures are found in tide pools, where they cling tightly to the rocks with their pelvic sucking disks. The disk is derived from folds of skin and underlying muscles, rather than being a modification of the pelvic fin, as seen in the gobies. The skin is naked (no scales) and there is no spinous dorsal fin. This is the best known of several Mediterranean species of cling fishes.

  Offer feedings of freeze-dried brine shrimp, daphnia and tubifex with chlorella algae. Provide smooth rocks which they can cling to.

Liopropoma carmabi (Randall)

COMMON NAME: Candy Basslet.
PHOTOGRAPH BY: Dr. John Randall of a 1.6-inch specimen from Curaçao.
RANGE: Curaçao, Bonaire, Puerto Rico, Barbados and the Bahamas.
MERISTIC CHARACTERISTICS: Grows to about 2 inches.

  This pretty fish closely resembles the swissguard and if the two aren't observed simultaneously they surely will be misidentified by the average hobbyist. They make interesting additions to the marine community aquarium.

433.00

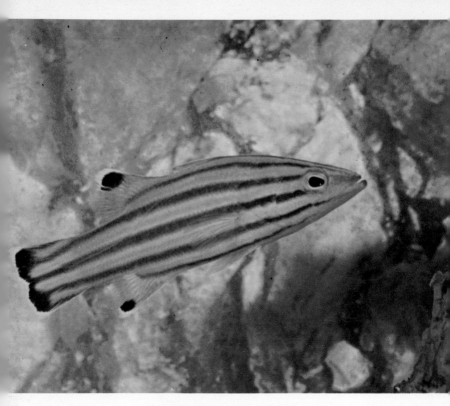

Liopropoma rubre Poey

COMMON NAME: Swissguard Basslet.
RANGE: Florida, Yucatan, Venezuela and the West Indies.
MERISTIC CHARACTERISTICS: Reaches slightly over $3\frac{1}{4}$ inches.

About the easiest (but most illegal) way of catching these beauties is to wrap a net about a small coral head and yank it out of the water. After carefully shaking the head, a few Swissguards will usually fall out. They are nice in the aquarium but they hide so much you rarely see them. They become tame, however, and will come out into the open when they are fed as soon as they gain confidence.

They thrive on canned Norwegian brine shrimp.

434.00

Lo vulpinus (Schlegel and Müller)

COMMON NAME: Lo.

RANGE: Samoa, Solomons, Palau, Bikini, East Indies, Probably more widely distributed.

PREVIOUS SCIENTIFIC NAMES: *Amphacanthus vulpinis, Teuthis vulpinis.*

MERISTIC CHARACTERISTICS: D. XIII, 10; A. VII, 9; V. I, 3, I, P. I, i, 14.

The name "*Lo*" is the vernacular name given to all the Siganidae in the Samoas, and this particular specimen has been placed into a separate genus based upon its short, tubular snout. Modern authors (Woods) prefer to ignore Seale's generic classification and place *vulpinis* into the genus *Siganus*, but the snout is so atypical of the rest of the genus that I prefer the genus *Lo*. Very old specimens of *Siganus pullus* have a slightly produced snout, but nowhere nearly as pronounced as in *Lo*.

This is a coral species and prefers large holes in the coral into which it can dash at the slightest hint of danger. It becomes fairly calm in large aquaria.

Be careful in handling this fish! Its spines are poisonous, and if your hand is pierced you will experience a painful infection.

435.00

Lutjanus kasmira (Forskal)

COMMON NAME: Blue-striped Snapper.

RANGE: Philippines, China, Japan, Polynesia (except Hawaii), Micronesia, Melanesia, Indo-Australian Archipelago and Indian Ocean.

PREVIOUS SCIENTIFIC NAMES: Numerous, a few of which are *Sciaena kasmira, Holocentrus quinquelinearis, Holocentrus bengalensis, Diacope decemlineata, Mesoprion pomacanthus, Lutjanus quinquelinearis, Evoplites kasmira.*

MERISTIC CHARACTERISTICS: D. X–XI, 13–16; A. III, 8 or 9; lateral line with 53–78 scales. Grows to a length of 12 inches.

The Blue-Striped Snapper is a common inhabitant of Indo-Pacific coral reefs. They are usually seen in schools which may number up to several hundred individuals. What a spectacular sight these fish make as they literally swarm around a skin diver who happens to cross their paths. They are often seen in company with the Red Snapper (*Lutjanus bohar*).

This species feeds upon fish and crustaceans, as do the majority of the other snapper species, and should be fed accordingly when kept in captivity.

436.00

Lutjanus sanguineus (Cuvier) *

COMMON NAME: Blood-red Snapper.
PHOTOGRAPH BY: Hilmar Hansen.
RANGE: Tropical Indo-Pacific.
PREVIOUS SCIENTIFIC NAMES: *Diacope sanguinea, Mesoprion angularis, Loxolutjanus erythropterus, Lutjanus erythropterus.*
MERISTIC CHARACTERISTICS: D. XI, 13–15; A. III, 9–10; lateral line 55–65. Grows to about 3 feet.

The common name of this fish is derived from the Latin name *sanguineus*, which refers to the bright purplish-red color of the body stripes and fins. The young are much more brilliant in color, the adults being a uniform reddish or brownish and usually lacking the stripes on the body. The broad oblique band which runs through the eye and onto the dorsal fin is distinctive for both adults and juveniles.

This species is especially fond of live foods.

* Now called *Lutjanus erythropterus.*

Lutjanus sebae (Cuvier and Valenciennes)

COMMON NAME: Red Emperor.

PHOTOGRAPH BY: Earl Kennedy

RANGE: Philippines, New Caledonia, inshore reefs of the Indo-Australian Archipelago.

PREVIOUS SCIENTIFIC NAMES: *Diacope sebae, Diacope siamensis, Mesoprion sebae, Cenyoroge sebae.*

MERISTIC CHARACTERISTICS: D. XI, 15–16; A. III, 10–11. 48–57 lateral line scales. Grows to a length of 12 inches.

Small specimens of the Red Emperor are excellent aquarium animals. They are fairly hardy and don't require a great deal of attention. In the Indo-Australian Archipelago region it is caught by local fishermen by hook and line and with the use of wire fish traps. However, it is not considered a good food fish.

L. sebae does best in the aquarium when fed on a diet of live food. Earthworms, brine shrimp and tubifex worms are acceptable items.

Lutjanus vaigiensis (Quoy and Gaimard)★

COMMON NAME: Black-tailed Snapper.

PHOTOGRAPH BY: Dr. John Randall of a specimen 10.5 inches from Eniwetok.

RANGE: Reefs of the Indo-Australian Archipelago, Philippines, Micronesia, Melanesia, Polynesia (except Hawaii) and Indian Ocean.

PREVIOUS SCIENTIFIC NAMES: *Diacope vaigiensis, Diacope marginata, Diacope immaculata, Diacope xanthopus, Diacope axillaris, Diacope flavipes, Diacope analis, Diacope aurantiaca.*

MERISTIC CHARACTERISTICS: D. X, 13–14; A. III, 8 or 9; lateral line with 47–50 scales. Attains a length of about 18 inches.

Black-tailed Snappers are seldom seen for sale, but the young are quite handsome and make desirable aquarium fish. If possible purchase several and keep them together, since schooling is the preferred habit. They thrive when fed live fish and brine shrimp, as these foods closely approximate their native diet. Chopped fish and shrimp are also acceptable food items. Tanks of over 50 gallons capacity are recommended for keeping snappers healthy and happy.

★Now known as *Lutjanus fulvus.*

439.00

Lythrypnus dalli (Gilbert)

COMMON NAME: Catalina Goby.
PHOTOGRAPH BY: Gene Wolfsheimer.
RANGE: Catalina Island, California.
PREVIOUS SCIENTIFIC NAMES: Not available.
MERISTIC CHARACTERISTICS: D. VI, 17; A. 14. Grows to $1\frac{1}{4}$ inches.

Californians have a fish from their own "backyard" which rivals any costly tropical beauty as far as looks are concerned. The Catalina Goby must be seen to be appreciated. The blue bars on a bright red background are best appreciated when displayed under ultraviolet light. This species is found on Catalina Island, which lies about 25 miles offshore from Los Angeles. They are inhabitants of rocky tide pools and depths of down to 300 feet!

The recommended foods for this fish are canned Norwegian brine shrimp and freeze-dried tubifex with chlorella algae.

Macropharyngodon meleagris (Cuvier and Valenciennes)*

COMMON NAME: Spotted Wrasse.
PHOTOGRAPH BY: Dr. John Randall of a 4.6-inch specimen from Eniwetok.
RANGE: Indo-Australian Archipelago, Philippine Islands, Ryukyu Islands, Micronesia and Polynesia.
PREVIOUS SCIENTIFIC NAMES: *Macropharyngodon pardalis.*
MERISTIC CHARACTERISTICS: D. IX, 11; A. III, 11; about 27 lateral line scales.

A common dweller of south and central Pacific coral reefs, the Spotted Wrasse is a fish which readily acclimates to aquarium surroundings. Don't be surprised if your pet suddenly disappears in the evening, for the wrasses are well known for the habit of burying themselves for the night.

This species should be offered a typical wrasse diet of live and frozen brine shrimp, finely chopped fish and clam meat supplemented with occasional feedings of dry flake food.

*The photo on this page is of *Halichoeres marginatus*, not *Macropharyngodon meleagris.*

441.00

Macropharyngodon pardalis (Kner)*

COMMON NAME: Leopard Wrasse.
RANGE: Indo-Australian Archipelago and Tropical South Pacific.
PREVIOUS SCIENTIFIC NAMES: *Leptojulis pardalis, Platyglossus nigromaculatus, Halichoeres nigropunctatus.*
MERISTIC CHARACTERISTICS: D. IX, 11; A. III, 11; about 27 lateral line scales.

This beauty is rarely seen in marine aquarium shops. However, it is very common on many central Pacific atolls, where it is found over living coral on the leeward ocean reefs. It is also found on lagoon reefs in water as shallow as 3–5 feet.

This species relishes feedings of live brine shrimp, mosquito larvae and chopped fish. Let's hope the Leopard Wrasse will be imported in greater quantity in the future!

*Now recognized as the female of *Macropharyngodon meleagris.*

442.00

Photo by K.H. Choo.

Malacanthus latovittatus (Lacepede)

COMMON NAME: Blue Whiting.
RANGE: Tropical Indo-Pacific.
PREVIOUS SCIENTIFIC NAMES: *Labrus latovittatus*.
MERISTIC CHARACTERISTICS: D. 47–51; A. 39–41; lateral line scales 130.
Reaches a length of 15 inches.

The Malacanthids are interesting fishes which are found in sandy areas. They live in burrows on the bottom, often under rocks or wreckage. This species is extremely attractive with its light blue coat and black median bar. Offer feedings of live and frozen brine shrimp supplemented with freeze-dried tubifex and frozen smelt.

A juvenile *Chaetodon trifascialis* with the broad black posterior band. This diminishes in size with age. Photo by Earl Kennedy.

A subadult *Chaetodon trifascialis*. Note the diminished posterior black band. Photo by Paul Allen.

Megaprotodon strigangulus (Gmelin)*

Common Name: Triangulate Butterfly Fish.

Range: Wide-spread from the Red Sea to island areas of Micronesia, Melanesia and Polynesia, including Hawaii and Johnston Atoll.

Previous Scientific Names: *Chaetodon strigangulus, Chaetodon trifascialis, Chaetodon triangularis, Chaetodon bifascialis, Chaetodon leachii, Megaprotodon bifascialis, Eteira triangularis, Sarothrodus strigangulus, Tetragonopterus strigangulus.*

Meristic Characteristics: D. XIV, 15-17; A. IV, 15-16; about 23-25 vertical scale rows. Grows to 6 inches.

This common inhabitant of Indo-Pacific reefs is usually seen swimming among growths of table coral (*Acropora*). They are often caught with the aid of wire fish traps, but are nearly impossible to take with the standard dipnets used by many collectors. The species literally abounds at Johnston Atoll, which lies some 600 miles south of the Hawaiian chain, but until recently it was unknown from Hawaiian waters proper. One morning several years ago, Lester Zukeran of the Hawaii Institue of Marine Biology pulled up his fish traps which were set in the shallow water of Kaneohe Bay on the island of Oahu. Much to his surprise there were several *Megaprotodon* among his catch, the first such record from the Hawaiian Islands! Lester has long been a

* Now called *Chaetodon trifascialis* Quoy and Gaimard.

445.00

supplier to large U.S. mainland public aquaria. However, these rare specimens were preserved and turned over to scientific collectors.

Unfortunately, this species is hard to keep alive for more than a few months. At this time a suitable substitute for their natural diet of living coral polyps has not yet been found. Perhaps an experimental-minded aquarist will come up with the solution to this problem.

Photo by Fujio Yasuda from Living Fishes of Japanese Coastal Waters.

Meiacanthus atrodorsalis (Gunther)

Common Name: Forktail Blenny.
Range: Tropical western Pacific.
Previous Scientific Names: *Petroscirtes atrodorsalis*.
Meristic Characteristics: D. IV, 26-27; A. II, 16-17; P. 14-15. Reaches a length of 4 inches.

The Meiacanthids are a group of Blennies which inhabit Indo-Pacific coral reefs. There are several brightly colored species in the genus. Unlike many of the Blenny species, which are strictly bottom dwellers, they are often seen swimming well off the bottom. They make admirable aquarium fish and will accept a variety of live and freeze-dried foods.

446.00

Meiacanthus mossambicus Smith

Common Name: Yellow-tailed Blenny.
Photograph By: Hilmar Hansen.
Range: East African coast.
Previous Scientific Names: None.
Meristic Characteristics: D. IV-V, 25-26; A. II, 14-16; P. 16.

      This species, which was described by Dr. J.L.B. Smith in 1959, is very close to *M. atrodorsalis* from the Pacific. However, the late Dr. Smith considered it to be distinct on the basis of fewer anal rays. At present it is known only from the East African coast. They are good aquarium fish and thrive on a diet of finely chopped fish and shrimp, live brine shrimp and freeze-dried tubifex with chlorella algae.

447.00

Meiacanthus oualanensis (Gunther)*

Common Name: Canary Blenny.
Photograph By: Hilmar Hansen.
Range: Tropical Indo-Pacific.
Previous Scientific Names: *Petroscirtes oualensis.*
Meristic Characteristics: D. V, 26; A. II, 14-16. Attains a length of
about 5 inches.

This is by far the most spectacular of the *Meiacanthus* species.
The bright yellow color is very distinctive, although another species,
Meiacanthus atrodorsalis, has the posterior portion of the body yellow.
The behavior and feeding of this fish is the same as that described for
the other Meiacanthids.

* Now called *Meiacanthus atrodorsalis oualanensis.*

Melichthys ringens (Osbeck)*

Common Name: Black-finned Trigger Fish.
Photograph by: Hilmar Hansen.
Range: Tropical Indo-Pacific.
Previous Scientific Names: *Balistes ringens, Balistes buniva.*
Meristic Characteristics: D. III, 31-33; A. 28-30. Reaches about 20
  inches.

It's obvious from the accompanying photos that the color of this
species is variable. The body hue sometimes fades in captivity. Don't
let the small mouth of this species fool you. Trigger Fishes have power-

* Now called *Melichthys indicus* Randall and Klausewitz.

This individual of *Melichthys indicus* is much lighter in color than the one on p. 449.00 but the patterns are almost identical. Photo by Klaus Paysan.

ful jaws and are adept at catching and eating relatively large invertebrates such as crabs and sea urchins. The larger ones can also take part of your finger if they mistake it for food or are put on the defense. Take care in adding *M. ringens* to the community tank as they are apt to be overly aggressive. They are particulárly bad tank mates for small Butterflies and Angels.

Melichthys vidua (Solander)

Common Name: Pink-tail Trigger Fish.

Range: Throughout the vast Indo-Pacific area including the China Coast, Ryukyu Islands and Hawaii.

Previous Scientific Name: *Balistes vidua.*

Meristic Characteristics: D. III-30; A. 28; about 63 scale rows from rear of head to base of caudal fin. Grows to 12 inches.

The most attractive of several species of Trigger Fishes, the Pink-tail is a welcome addition to the aquarium and soon develops into a regular "personality" fish. At feeding time it will immediately recognize its keeper and promptly bob up and down at the surface, wistfully begging for food. You can feed them by hand, but keep your fingertips a safe distance away from your pet's teeth. The Trigger Fishes are equipped with sharp teeth and a bone-crushing set of jaws which have been known to take a healthy chunk out of an unsuspecting person's hand on more than one occasion.

In nature the Pink-tail feeds upon algae, crabs and clams; a seafood diet which closely parallels these items is recommended in captivity.

451.00

Microcanthus strigatus (Cuvier and Valenciennes)

COMMON NAME: Stripey.
RANGE: Hawaii, Japan, China, Philippines and Queensland.
PREVIOUS SCIENTIFIC NAMES: *Chaetodon strigatus, Microcanthus hawaiiensis.*
MERISTIC CHARACTERISTICS: D. XI, 16–17; A. IV, 13–14; about 55–60
lateral line scales.

The Stripey is an excellent fish for the community tank. They are
hardy and accept a wide variety of foods. In Hawaii, the young are
abundant in certain rocky tidepool areas from February to April. When
they first appear in the pools they average about one-half-inch in length
and grow to a size of about 2 inches in 4 months. These are an ideal
size for the average marine tank.

Stripeys will eat nearly everything that is offered including freeze-
dried daphnia, tubifex, fairy shrimp, live brine shrimp, guppy fry and
assorted dry flake foods. Chlorella algae is a good supplementary item.

452.00

Microspathodon chrysurus (Cuvier and Valenciennes)

COMMON NAME: Atlantic Yellow-tail Damselfish.

PHOTOGRAPH BY: Dr. Herbert R. Axelrod.

RANGE: West Indies.

PREVIOUS SCIENTIFIC NAMES: *Glyphidodon chrysurus, Pomacentrus denegatus.*

MERISTIC CHARACTERISTICS: D. XI, 15; A. II, 13. Attains a length of 7–8 inches.

The young are highly attractive with their dark blue coat and light blue spots. The adults tend to lose the spots and are uniformly dark brown with a bright yellow tail. Because of the juvenile's sparkling color pattern they are sometimes called "jewelfish." According to Dr. John Randall, the young are common on coral reefs, where they are usually seen among the branches of yellow stinging coral. They feed upon coral polyps, fine algae and certain small invertebrates.

Give them a well balanced aquarium diet consisting of brine shrimp, tubifex, dry flake food and chlorella algae.

453.00

Mirolabrichthys tuka Herre   Photo by Dr. Gerald R. Allen.

COMMON NAME: Purple Queen.
RANGE: Indo-Australian Archipelago and Tropical Western Pacific.
PREVIOUS SCIENTIFIC NAMES: *Entonanthias pascalus*.
MERISTIC CHARACTERISTICS: D. IX–XI (usually X), 14–16; A. III, 7;
lateral line scales 45–48. Grows to 5 inches.

The Purple Queen is a fish which is virtually unknown to the aquarium
field. I'm sure if collectors can come up with a steady supply of these
eye-catching beauties they will fast become one of the most popular of
aquarium fishes. They are indescribably beautiful, and although there
is no captivity data on them at this time, they should prove to be reasonably hardy. It's a school fish which is generally found in water over
thirty feet deep. At Eniwetok, small specimens (2–3 inches) form aggregations of up to 50 fish at the entrances of caverns in the coral reef.

Since this fish is a newcomer to the aquarium, experiment with a wide
variety of food items until certain preferences are observed.

454.00

Photo by K.H. Choo.   **Monocentrus japonicus** (Houttuyn)

COMMON NAME: Pinecone Fish.
RANGE: Tropical Indo-Pacific.
PREVIOUS SCIENTIFIC NAMES: *Gasterosteus japonicus.*
MERISTIC CHARACTERISTICS: D. V or VI, 11–12; A. I or II, 8–9 lateral;
line scales 15. Grows to 5 inches.

Here's a real oddity which gets its common name from the scaly
appearance of the body. Chances are you won't find this one at your
neighborhood pet shop, since it is rare and usually found deep (over
100 feet). One of the few places you can see the Pinecone Fish on display
is at the Steinhart Aquarium in San Francisco, where they have successfully kept a pair for over two years now! The fish were a gift from the
Crown Prince of Japan, who is an ichthyologist of reputation as well.

455.00

Photo by Hiroshi Azuma.

Monodactylus sebae (Cuvier)

COMMON NAME: Moonfish.
RANGE: West Africa in tropical waters usually close to fresh-water rivers.
PREVIOUS SCIENTIFIC NAMES: *Psettus sebae, Psethus sebae.*
MERISTIC CHARACTERISTICS: D. VIII, I; 32–36; A. III, 37. Lateral line
scales 50. Grows to 7 inches.

The Moonfish is slightly reminiscent of *Platax orbicularis,* one of the
bat fish species. The body is rounded and greatly compressed with three
dark bars. They occur around the mouths of rivers and may wander
far upstream into water which is almost entirely fresh. They do well in
captivity in either fresh water or salt water. For food, they prefer frozen
brine shrimp, but will take freeze-dried foods readily.

Mulloidichthys martinicus (Cuvier and Valenciennes)

COMMON NAME: Yellow Goatfish.
RANGE: Tropical western Atlantic.
PREVIOUS SCIENTIFIC NAMES: *Upeneus martinicus, Upeneus balteatus, Upeneus flavovittatus, Mulloides flavovittatus.*
MERISTIC CHARACTERISTICS: D. VII–I, 8; P. 15–17; lateral line scales 34–39. Recorded to 15.5 inches.

Here's a fish which is better known as a table delicacy than an aquarium pet, but the young are sometimes kept in captivity. The long "whiskers" of the goatfish are used to detect food particles on the bottom. In nature, the preferred food items are small fishes, polychaete worms, crustaceans and gastropods. Try to provide a diet which is similar.

457.00

Mycteroperca interstitialis (Poey)

COMMON NAME: Yellowmouth Grouper.
PHOTOGRAPH BY: Dr. John Randall of a 12.7 inch specimen from the
   Virgin Islands.
RANGE: Tropical western Atlantic.
MERISTIC CHARACTERISTICS: D. XI, 16–18; A. III, 11–12; the largest
   known is 27 inches.

The Yellowmouth is probably one of those fish which is a female when
young and gradually some change into males. Not too much is known
about their sexual habits since they have never been bred in captivity
and without actual testing, it is rather difficult to prove that a functional
female which once laid eggs changed into a functional male which fertilized eggs. There are random reports of certain specimens bearing eggs
and having male organs as well.

Mycteroperca rubra (Bloch)

COMMON NAME: Comb Grouper.

PHOTOGRAPH BY: Dr. John Randall of a 6.9 inch specimen from the Virgin Islands.

RANGE: Eastern Atlantic from the Mediterranean to Angola and from the Caribbean to Brazil.

MERISTIC CHARACTERISTICS: D. XI, 15–17; A. III, 10–12; reaches about 30 inches.

This is one of the most common groupers because it is readily available to European, African, South American and North American collectors. It is a large fish which becomes very tame if small specimens are hand fed with freeze-dried Tubifex worms or some other delicacy.

They grow rather quickly and require large tanks with very efficient filtering systems.

Mycteroperca venenosa (Linnaeus)

COMMON NAME: Yellowfin Grouper.
PHOTOGRAPH BY: Dr. John Randall of an 8.8-inch specimen from the Virgin Islands.
RANGE: Tropical western Atlantic.
MERISTIC CHARACTERISTICS: D. XI, 15–16; A. III, 11; reaches 3 feet in length.

With a name that refers to poison and a maximum size of 3 feet, you wouldn't expect to see many of these in aquaria. But you do because small specimens are easily kept in large tanks and as they get larger they become tamer until they are the pets of the aquarium . . . and who is going to destroy a two-pound pet on his way to 20 pounds?

Public aquaria are the places in which these large groupers are found after the unlucky aquarist has had to "donate" a growing specimen.

Groupers as a whole are great for eating because they are missing their intramuscular bones. That's probably why they are sluggish and found resting most of the time close to "home." Home is a cave amongst the coral.

Myrichthys oculatus (Kaup)

COMMON NAME: Gold-spotted Snake Eel.
RANGE: Bermuda to Brazil in the western Atlantic and the islands of the tropical eastern Atlantic.
PREVIOUS SCIENTIFIC NAMES: *Pisodonophis oculatus, Ophisurus latimaculatus, Ophichthys pardalis.*
MERISTIC CHARACTERISTICS: Not available. Reaches a length of about 3 feet.

461.00

This Gold-spotted Snake Eel has found a home in an old helmet shell. Photo by Gerhard Marcuse.

The snake eels are very interesting fishes. One of their distinguishing features is the hard pointed tail with no fin around the tip. This helps them to burrow into the sand amazingly fast or to find even the smallest hole in a net or corner of a tank through which they can escape. In nature the Gold-spotted Snake Eel is fairly common and has been observed in turtle grass beds in relatively shallow water (most in less than 4 feet of water).

The teeth are blunt, most being molariform or granular, an adaptation for feeding on their favorite food—crabs. They do fairly well in captivity with a proper diet and no escape holes. Provide them with a good layer of sand and some nooks and crannies where they can hide. The characteristic gold spots edged in dark brown may in some young specimens be a solid brown in the lower series. The gold centers will appear in these as the eel grows.

Myripristis jacobus Cuvier and Valenciennes

COMMON NAME: Blackbar Soldierfish.
PHOTOGRAPH BY: Dr. John Randall of a 5.2 inch specimen from the
Virgin Islands.
RANGE: Northern Florida to Brazil; Trinidad to all the islands of the
eastern and central Atlantic.
MERISTIC CHARACTERISTICS: D. X + I, 14; A. IV, 13; P. 15; 34–36 scales
in the lateral line. Grows to about 9 inches.

The obvious black bar just to the rear of the gill opening is the basis for
the name. Why our great leaders call this fish a "soldier fish" and not a
"squirrelfish" is illogical; because this fish is in another sub-family they
split it out of the "squirrelfish" even though it looks like one to the casual
observer. This author, while he is disciplined enough to follow the
consensus of systematists, objects to the random use of illogical popular
names for rather well known fishes.

463.00

Myripristis kuntee (Cuvier and Valenciennes)

COMMON NAME: Blacktip Soldierfish.
RANGE: Tropical Indo-Pacific.
PREVIOUS SCIENTIFIC NAMES: *Myripristis botche, Myripristis adustus.*
MERISTIC CHARACTERISTICS: D. X, I, 16; A. IV, 13. Lateral line scales 27.
Grows to about 10 inches.

The fishes of the genus *Myripristis* have long been a headache to taxonomists. There are about 15 species, most of which look very much alike. Recently, Dr. David Greenfield has worked out the classification of this puzzling group, and his results will be published soon. Helpful characters which are used to separate many of the species are the number of lateral line scales and the extent of the dark marking on the rear portion of the gill flap.

This is a nocturnal species which does best when fed a variety of live foods. Brine shrimp and guppy fry are particularly good.

464.00

Myripristis murdjan

COMMON NAME: Bigeye Squirrel Fish, Mempachi.
RANGE: Tropical Indo-Pacific.
PREVIOUS SCIENTIFIC NAMES: *Sciaena murdjan, Perca murdjan, Myripristis adustus, Myripristis botche.*
MERISTIC CHARACTERISTICS: D. X–I, 14–16; A. IV, 12–13; lateral line scales 28–30.

The Bigeye Squirrels are curious looking creatures with their huge dark eyes and bright red bodies. These eyes enable this fish to see amazingly well at night and in the dark crevices where they spend their daytime hours. The mempachi spends most of the night searching for such food items as small crabs, shrimp and occasional juvenile fish. They retire to their holes just before dawn.

Keep the natural behavior of this species in mind when it is kept in an aquarium and they will prove to be hardy. Large feedings of frozen and live brine shrimp, supplemented with live fish fry, earthworms and tubifex are recommended food items. Rock shelter is a necessity.

465.00

Myripristis pralinus (Cuvier and Valenciennes). Red Soldier Fish. Photo by Dr. Herbert R. Axelrod.

Myripristis pralinus (Cuvier and Valenciennes)

Common Name: Red Soldier Fish.
Range: Tropical Indo-Pacific.
Previous Scientific Names: *Myripristis sanguineus, Myripristis mooreanus, Myripristis kuim, Myripristis bleekeri.*
Meristic Characteristics: D. X, 15-17; A. IV, 12-15; lateral line scales 36-40. Attains a length of about 7 inches.

Here is one of the more attractive and popular members of the Squirrelfish family. In their native habitat, these fish are found by day in caves and crevices of the shallow reef and for this reason they should be provided with ample retreat space when kept in captivity. A pile of good-sized rocks fashioned into a cave or series of caves and grottoes will help make these creatures feel right at home. These fish are nocturnal; that is, they are active primarily at night, and feedings should be administered in the evening or early morning. They are voracious eaters and do best when given a diet of live foods. Such items as brine shrimp and guppy fry are acceptable.

467.00

Naso brevirostris (Valenciennes)

COMMON NAME: Short-nosed Unicorn Tang.
RANGE: Tropical Indo-Pacific.
PREVIOUS SCIENTIFIC NAMES: *Naseus brevirostris.*
MERISTIC CHARACTERISTICS: D. VI, 27–29; A. II, 28–30. Attains a length
of at least 18 inches.

The juveniles of this species lack the typical unicorn growth of the
adult, but there are traces of it at a fairly small size. The adults are rather
uniformly gray colored, but the juveniles tend to be darker and covered
with irregular white blotches. These young make fine aquarium specimens.

Dr. Robert Jones of the University of Guam is a leading authority on
the feeding habits of the Unicorn Tang and has evidence of a most
unusual sequence of feeding habits in this species. It seems that the
young are typical bottom-feeding surgeonfishes which subsist primarily
on algae. However, when they reach a certain size they become plankton
feeders. In other words they feed in mid-water, well up off the bottom.
Provide the young with plenty of algae when kept in captivity.

468.00

Naso lituratus (Bloch and Schneider)

COMMON NAME: Smoothhead Unicorn Fish.

PHOTOGRAPH BY: Gerhard Marcuse.

RANGE: Wide-ranging on the reefs of the Indo-Pacific, from the Hawaiian Islands to East Africa and the Red Sea.

PREVIOUS SCIENTIFIC NAMES: *Acanthurus lituratus, Aspisurus elegans, Naseus lituratus, Harpurus lituratus, Monoceros lituratus, Callicanthus lituratus, Monoceros garreti.*

MERISTIC CHARACTERISTICS: D. VI, 28–30; A. II, 28–30. **Grows to approximately 18 inches.**

469.00

Naso lituratus is the most attractive member of its genus. Most of the unicorn fishes (at least the adults), as their name denotes, are characterized by the presence of a unicorn-like projection on the forehead. However, even the very large adults of this species are lacking this protuberance. The larger the size it attains, the more prolonged are the trailing filaments on the upper and lower corners of the caudal fin.

In Hawaii, young specimens are moderately common during the late spring and summer months. They can be captured fairly easily since they are prone to enter small one-way holes or seek refuge under isolated rocks. It is only necessary that the collector surround the entrance of the hole with a dipnet or plastic bag while at the same time poking into the crevice with a short stick or piece of wire. The fish will generally dart out into the captor's net. Small specimens (under 3 inches) show a mottled pattern on the back and generally lack the brighter colors of the adults.

As is true with many of the surgeonfish species, feeding may prove to be a problem. Brine shrimp (frozen) may be accepted and must be supplemented with some green material. Ideally, the aquarium which contains unicorn fish should be placed near a window where there is enough light to promote a healthy growth of algae on the back wall of the tank. The fish will graze on the algae, and there is no better natural food.

A juvenile *Naso lituratus* (Bloch and Schneider) showing the characteristic spotted pattern. Photo by Dr. Herbert R. Axelrod in Hawaii.

470.00

Ocyurus chrysurus (Bloch)

COMMON NAME: Yellowtail Snapper.

PHOTOGRAPH BY: W. A. Starck, II of a 6.3-inch specimen from Florida Keys.

RANGE: Bermuda and Massachusetts to Brazil; also recorded from the Cape Verde Islands.

PREVIOUS SCIENTIFIC NAMES: *Acara pitamba, Sparus chrysurus, Anthias rabirubia, Sparus semiluna, Mesoprion aurovittatus, Ocyurus rijgersmaie.*

MERISTIC CHARACTERISTICS: D. X, 12–14 (usually 13); A. III, 8 or 9 (rarely 8); lateral line scales 46–49.

The Yellowtail is an attractive snapper species which can be identified by the bright yellow line which runs along the side of the body. It is frequently seen high off the bottom where it feeds on plankton; however, crustaceans and small fishes are also taken off the bottom. In the West Indies it is highly esteemed as a fish food and may reach 5 pounds in weight.

Odonus niger Rüppell

COMMON NAME: Black Triggerfish.

PHOTOGRAPH BY: Klaus Paysan.

RANGE: Tropical Indo-Pacific and Red Sea.

PREVIOUS SCIENTIFIC NAMES: *Xenodon niger, Erythrodon niger, Pyrodon niger, Balistes erythrodon, Zenodon caeruleolorum.*

MERISTIC CHARACTERISTICS: D. III, 32–36; A. 28–31; lateral line scales 17–20. Grows to about 8 inches.

The Black Triggerfish is a handsome species with a record of being an excellent aquarium fish. However, as is true of all the species belonging to this family, they must not be housed in the same tank with shy, non-aggressive fishes.

The triggerfishes get their common name by virtue of the peculiar interlocking dorsal spines. At night or when pursued by a collector, they retreat to a snug crevice or among the branches of coral and literally "lock" themselves in place with their trigger-like dorsal spine mechanism. The erect "locked-in" first dorsal spine can be released by the wise collector by simply reaching in (that is, if the crevice is large enough) and depressing the second spine, which unlocks the mechanism.

Ophioblennius atlanticus (Cuvier and Valenciennes)

COMMON NAME: Atlantic Blenny.
RANGE: Tropical Western Atlantic and Gulf of Mexico.
PREVIOUS SCIENTIFIC NAMES: *Emblemaria atlantica.*
MERISTIC CHARACTERISTICS: D. 35; A. 24; P. 15. Grows to 2–4 inches.

The blennies are common inhabitants of warm seas around the globe. They are typically fond of rocky habitats and may be seen scurrying about in short dashes during the daylight hours. Many species lay their eggs in rocky crevices, and these are cared for and guarded by the male.

Feedings of freeze-dried fairy shrimp, tubifex, frozen and live brine shrimp and chlorella algae are recommended.

Photo by Dr. Herbert R. Axelrod.

Opistognathus aurifrons (Jordan and Thompson)

COMMON NAME: Yellowhead Jawfish.
RANGE: Florida Keys and West Indies.
MERISTIC CHARACTERISTICS: D. XI, 15–17; A. III, 14–16; P. 19–21; 81–94
 scales rows posterior to the opercular flap. Grows to about 4 inches.

The Yellowhead is a popular aquarium fish and has been kept for many years by aquarists. It almost always builds itself a burrow if the sand in the aquarium is deep enough and there are small rocks available with which it can fortify the sides. The holes are usually straight down and the fish enter them tail first.

This is the most attractive of the eleven species of jawfishes known from the western Atlantic. Their unusual behavior of hovering vertically over their sandy burrows makes than an interesting attraction in the aquarium. The males, of some of the species at least, are known to incubate the eggs in their mouth.

They are carnivorous and especially fond of live brine shrimp. They may be induced to take freeze-dried foods after they become acclimated. Provide plenty of fine sand and small pebbles so they can build a burrow.

474.00

Ostracion cubicus Linnaeus

COMMON NAME: Spotted Cube.
RANGE: Tropical Indo-Pacific.
PREVIOUS SCIENTIFIC NAMES: *Ostracion tuberculatus.*
MERISTIC CHARACTERISTICS: D. 9; A. 9; P. 10 or 11. Reaches a length of 8–9 inches.

O. cubicus is one of the more attractive box fish species. The young are bright yellow with black polka dots. This fish, once acclimated, becomes very tame and will beg for your attention. A 5-inch specimen kept in an aquarium at Eniwetok Island would bob up and down just at the surface and spit a stream of water until its keeper brought food. Some fish may be smarter than you think! In nature *O. cubicus* is a bottom feeder which lives primarily on sand-dwelling polychaete worms, gastropods and small crustaceans. In the aquaruim, feed them fresh frozen chopped fish, shrimp and clams supplemented with tubifex and chlorella algae.

Ostracion meleagris (Shaw)

COMMON NAME: Spotted Box Fish.

RANGE: Indian Ocean, Indo-Australian Archipelago, Philippines, Melanesia, Micronesia and Polynesia (Hawaii included).

PREVIOUS SCIENTIFIC NAMES: *Ostracion lentiginosus, Ostracion punctatus, Ostracion sebae, Ostracion bombifrons, Ostraction camurus, Ostracion oahuensis.*

MERISTIC CHARACTERISTICS: D. 9; A. 9; P. 10. Grows to 5 or 6 inches.

Another fish which displays male-female color differences is the Spotted Box Fish. The male, which is pictured, is beautifully decorated with orange spots on the sides, while the female is uniformly covered with smaller white dots on a black background.

It has been discovered that the box fishes exude a toxic mucus when they are alarmed, and this secretion can kill everything in the aquaria in a matter of minutes. Some collectors say that after a box fish has given off its slime, it takes a period of time to regenerate more. They expose the fish to stress by holding it out of the water for a minute or two and then rinse off the discharged mucus thoroughly before placing the fish into the collecting bucket. It is recommended that box fishes be kept isolated until they are feeding well and appear happy. Then they should be carefully transferred to a community tank and watched closely at first. There are exceptions to every rule, and sometimes a freshly caught or newly purchased box fish can be introduced without fatal results, but it is better to be safe than sorry!

476.00

Oxycirrhites typus Bleeker

COMMON NAME: Long-nose Hawkfish.

RANGE: Broadly distributed over the vast Indo-Pacific region from the western coast of Mexico to the eastern coast of Africa.

PREVIOUS SCIENTIFIC NAMES: *Oxycirrhites morrisi, Oxycirrhites seftion.*

MERISTIC CHARACTERISTICS: D. X, 13; A. III, 7; lateral line scales 51-53. Attains a length of 3 to 4 inches.

Every once in a while a species (or genus) with a greatly elongated snout is encountered in a family of normal-snouted fishes. This has appeared in the butterflyfishes (*Forcipiger, Chelmon*), the wrasses (*Gomphosus*), the filefishes (*Oxymonacanthus longirostris*), etc., and can be seen here in this hawkfish. In most cases, and this seems to be no exception, the long snout is a feeding adaptation allowing the fish to reach food that short-snouted fishes cannot.

Oxycirrhites typus inhabits deeper waters, the depth range being estimated at between 50 and 300 feet, where one encounters black coral. Even so, this fish is regularly, though not commonly, available at marine aquarium stores. Live brine shrimp at first, then a variety of frozen foods, seems to be sufficient.

Oxymonacanthus longirostris (Bloch and Schneider)

COMMON NAME: Longnosed Filefish.
RANGE: Indo-Australian Archipelago, Micronesia, Melanesia, Polynesia (except Hawaii).
PREVIOUS SCIENTIFIC NAMES: *Balistes hispidus* var. *longirostris, Monacanthus longirostris, Monacanthus chrysospilos.*
MERISTIC CHARACTERISTICS: D. II—31–32; A. 29–30; P. 11. Grows to 4 inches.

The Longnosed Filefish is immediately recognizable by virtue of its striking pattern. It is found in shallow waters, usually swimming among the branches of staghorn coral or between layers of table coral. These fish are wary and hard to catch without the use of chemicals (now often used by collectors to anesthetize their prey).

Oxymonacanthus longirostris is perhaps the most beautiful of all the filefishes, but may prove to be one of the more difficult species to maintain in captivity. Feeding is a problem, since in its native habitat it feasts upon the polyps of living coral. However, with a little experimentation, the aquarist may find an acceptable substitute. These fish seem to feel more at home when there are several of them in the same tank. Dead staghorn coral should be provided, as it is ideal for them to "wedge" into during the night.

478.00

Paracanthurus hepatus (Linnaeus)

COMMON NAME: Blue Surgeon.

RANGE: from East Africa to the Philippines and Ryukyu Islands (also recently collected in the Line Islands in the Central Pacific).

PREVIOUS SCIENTIFIC NAMES: *Teuthis hepatus, Acanthurus hepatus, Acanthurus theuthis, Acanthurus triangulus, Colocopus lambdurus, Paracanthurus lambdurus, Paracanthurus theuthis.*

MERISTIC CHARACTERISTICS: D. IX, 19–20; A. III, 18–19; P. 16. Reaches a length of 6–7 inches.

This beauty has to be considered the king of the surgeonfishes. They look like something out of an abstract painter's sketchbook. The contrast of black and blue is a sight to behold. It has been claimed that there is no bluer fish in the world, but we'll let you be the judge. One of the most wondrous sights in nature is to view a large school of *P. hepatus* swarming over a multicolored coral reef. It's almost unreal!

Give these fish plenty of room, since the 3–4-inch sizes are the ones most commonly imported; 2 or 3 per 30-gallon tank is about right. The tank should be well lighted for at least part of the day, and a healthy growth of algae on the back wall will help round out the diet. Freeze-dried products which contain chlorella algae are also excellent.

479.00

Paracentropogon longispinis (Cuvier)

COMMON NAME: Wispy Scorpion Fish.
PHOTOGRAPH BY: Karl Knaack.
RANGE: Mauritius, India, China and East Indies.
PREVIOUS SCIENTIFIC NAMES: *Apistus longispinus, Tetraroge longispinis.*
MERISTIC CHARACTERISTICS: D. XIII–XV, 6–8; A. III, 4 or 5; lateral
line tubes 20. Attains about 3 inches.

There are two helpful characters for recognizing this species. One is
the strongly indented spinous dorsal fin and the other is the white spot
on the middle of the body. These creatures are regarded as rare, but
due to their excellent camouflage, may be more common than is generally thought. It's a member of the scorpion fish family and chances
are the dorsal spines are venomous, so handle carefully. Their small
size makes them an excellent prospect for the marine tank. Live foods
are recommended.

480.00

Parachaetodon ocellatus (Bloch)

COMMON NAME: Ocellate Butterflyfish.
PHOTOGRAPH BY: Earl Kennedy in Manila, Philippine Islands.
RANGE: Tropical Indo-Pacific.
PREVIOUS SCIENTIFIC NAMES: *Platax ocellatus, Chaetodon oligacanthus, Sarothrodus oligacanthus, Tetragonopterus oligacanthus.*
MERISTIC CHARACTERISTICS: D. VI, 28–30; A. III, 19–20; 40 to 45 scale rows in the lateral line.

Mr. Earl Kennedy, one of the world's outstanding marine fish collectors, is solely responsible for bringing this magnificent beauty to the attention of aquarists.

Kennedy told the author (HRA) that the fish is relatively simple to maintain and ships well if properly acclimated. Kennedy keeps his marine specimens in large aquaria, outdoors, slightly shaded from the strong sun.

The fish do well on canned Norwegian brine shrimp, freeze-dried brine shrimp and tubifex worms. They enjoy playing about the coral and seem to inhabit the lower parts of the aquarium.

The fish illustrated here have the same meristic characteristics as *P. ocellatus*, but the literature describes *ocellatus* as having four vertical black bands. The bands in this species are brown. I have never seen a black-banded fish similar to this one.

Paracirrhites arcatus (Cuvier and Valenciennes)

COMMON NAME: Arc-eyed Hawkfish.

RANGE: Celebes, New Guinea, Indian Ocean, Melanesia, Micronesia and Polynesia, including Hawaii.

PREVIOUS SCIENTIFIC NAMES: *Cirrhites arcatus, Cirrhites amblycephalus, Amblycirrhites arcatus, Amblycirrhites amblycephalus, Paracirrhites amblycephalus.*

MERISTIC CHARACTERISTICS: D. X, 11–12; A. III, 6; lateral line with 48 scales. Grows to 5 inches.

The hawkfishes get their name from their habit of perching on coral heads or rocky outcrops in the manner of their avian counterparts. The pectoral fins are modified for hanging onto rocks and act as supports when they are sitting on the bottom. Small fish and crabs are the preferred food items in the native habitat, and these fish swoop down on their prey with lightning-fast rapidity. Several rocks or pieces of dried coral will help your hawkfish pet feel right at home. Live foods are best, but frozen shrimp and chopped fish may be substituted.

482.00

Paracirrhites typee Randall

COMMON NAME: Typee Hawkfish.
PHOTOGRAPH BY: Dr. John Randall of a 3-inch specimen from Tahiti.
RANGE: Society and Marquesas Islands.
PREVIOUS SCIENTIFIC NAMES: None.
MERISTIC CHARACTERISTICS: D. X, 11; A. III, 6; lateral line scales 49.

    Until recently this species was known only from the originally collected specimen (known as the holotype) taken back in 1838 by a French expedition to the Marquesas. Dr. John Randall collected and photographed this perfect specimen in Tahiti. This extremely rare species is similar in habit to the other hawkfish species. It enjoys occasional feedings of live food, especially small guppies.

483.00

Paraluteres prionurus (Bleeker)

COMMON NAME: Valentini Mimic.
RANGE: Japan, Indo-Australian Archipelago, Micronesia.
PREVIOUS SCIENTIFIC NAMES: *Alutarius prionurus, Monacanthus prionurus.*
MERISTIC CHARACTERISTICS: D. I, 25–28; A. 24; P. 11–12. Grows to 4–5 inches.

The young are very attractive, their color pattern being much more vivid than that of the adults. This fish is likely to be confused with the sharp-nosed puffer species *Canthigaster valentini*, to which it shows a remarkable resemblance. However, it possesses a single dorsal spine and is actually a member of the filefish family.

The young make fine aquarium fish and should be fed a diet consisting of live brine shrimp, finely chopped smelt (or other fish), and freeze-dried tubifex.

484.00

Parapercis schauinslandi (Steindachner)

COMMON NAME: Red Grub Fish.
PHOTOGRAPH BY: Dr. John Randall of a 3-inch specimen from Hawaii.
RANGE: Hawaiian Islands.
PREVIOUS SCIENTIFIC NAMES: *Parapercis pterostigma, Osurus schauinslandi.*
MERISTIC CHARACTERISTICS: D. V, 21; A. 18. Grows to about 7 inches.

This endemic Hawaiian species is usually found at depths below 100 feet. Their large mouth and canine teeth enable them to eat small fishes and crustaceans which they capture in 2–3 foot lightning-swift darts. They prefer sandy bottoms, but are occasionally seen under rock ledges.
Live foods are recommended in captivity.

485.00

Parupeneus pleurostigma (Bennett)

COMMON NAME: Blackspot Goatfish.

RANGE: Tropical Indo-Pacific.

PREVIOUS SCIENTIFIC NAMES: *Upeneus pleurostigma, Upeneus brandesii, Mullus pleurostigma.*

MERISTIC CHARACTERISTICS: D. VIII–I, 8; A. I, 6; lateral line scales 28–30. Grows to about 15 inches.

Parupeneus pleurostigma gets its common name from the large dark blotch situated just below the posterior part of the spinous dorsal fin. It is highly esteemed as a food fish, and young specimens make an admirable aquarium addition. At night the color pattern changes considerably and becomes a blotchy combination of red and white. At this time they sit quietly on the bottom and are easy to catch in a net or spear by torchlight. Give feedings of live brine shrimp and guppy fry supplemented with chopped fresh frozen sea foods.

486.00

Pempheris oualensis (Cuvier and Valenciennes)

COMMON NAME: Silver Sweeper.

PHOTOGRAPH BY: Dr. John Randall of a specimen 8.0 inches from Tahiti.

RANGE: Widespread in the Indo-Pacific area, is common on shallow reefs of Micronesia and Polynesia.

PREVIOUS SCIENTIFIC NAMES: *Pempheris otaitensis, Pempheris taitensis.*

MERISTIC CHARACTERISTICS: D. VI, 9; A. III, 38–42; 62–68 scales in lateral line. Grows to about 12 inches.

The juveniles of this species make handsome aquarium fish, being somewhat reminiscent of the freshwater hatchet fishes. This fish is best kept in schools, since this is how they are found in their natural environment. They are commonly found schooling near the surface around shallow piers and wrecks when encountered in their Indo-Pacific domain.

Sweepers are not often seen in captivity and little is known about their feeding requirements. Since they occur at the surface, they may feed on falling insects. However, brine shrimp and flake food may prove to be acceptable substitutes.

487.00

Pempheris schomburgki Muller and Troschel

COMMON NAME: Copper Sweeper.
RANGE: Tropical western Atlantic.
PREVIOUS SCIENTIFIC NAMES: None.
MERISTIC CHARACTERISTICS: D. V, 8 or 9; A. III, 32–35; lateral line
  scales 52–60. Attains 6 inches.

The Copper Sweeper receives its name from the general coppery reflections off the body when it receives the proper lighting. It is also recognized by the dark band along the base of the anal fin. This fish is often seen,
when young, in small schools around the reef, and it may be best to keep
several of them together in a tank. Their natural food is zooplankton
(especially the larval stages of invertebrates) which is picked from the
water column at night. Live brine shrimp proves to be an excellent
substitute. During the day the Copper Sweeper is most usually found in
caves, so such shelters should be provided for these fish. Make sure to
keep the light dim.

Pervagor spilosoma (Lay and Bennett)

COMMON NAME: Fantailed Filefish.
RANGE: Hawaiian Islands and Johnston Atoll.
PREVIOUS SCIENTIFIC NAMES: *Monacanthus spilosoma, Stephanolepis spilosomus, Stephanolepis pricei.*
MERISTIC CHARACTERISTICS: D. I—38; A. 35–36; movable pubic spine present. Grows to a length of 5 inches.

The Fantailed Filefish is a Hawaiian import which is both attractive and at the same time not too costly. The inshore population numbers of this species appear to fluctuate drastically from one year to the next around the main islands of the Hawaiian chain. During the late spring of certain years, young 2-inch specimens are everywhere, abundant in water as shallow as 2 feet! However, in other years the young are seldom seen. This is a mystery which remains unsolved by ichthyologists. It may be the result of critical changes in the physical environment while the young fish are still pelagic, which is the period after hatching during which the larvae are at the mercy of ocean currents to carry them to a suitable inshore area where they can transform into juveniles and take up a bottom-dwelling existence. Evidence of harmful physical factors was witnessed recently in the form of literally thousands of young Fantailed

489.00

In a defensive or aggressive posture, all fins are erected and the dorsal spine locked in place. Photo by Gene Wolfsheimer.

Filefish floating dead on the surface off the island of Kauai. Perhaps a sudden change of water temperature in the form of a cold current sweeping down from the north was responsible for this mass mortality.

Not a great deal is known about the natural food habits of this species, but specimens kept in the aquarium will accept feedings of live and frozen brine shrimp and dry flake food.

Pervagor melanocephalus (Bleeker)

COMMON NAME: Red-tail Filefish.
RANGE: Throughout the Indo-Pacific.
PREVIOUS SCIENTIFIC NAMES: *Monacanthus melanocephalus, Monacanthus janthinosoma,* and *Monacanthus aspricaudus.*
MERISTIC CHARACTERISTICS: D. I, 30-34; A. 26-30; pectoral fin 12-13. Attains a length of about 6 inches.

The Red-tail Filefish is common throughout its range, usually in the weedy areas around coral. It is variable in color pattern, particularly in the caudal fin and in the presence of the spot or blotch behind and below the eye. This has led some workers to divide this species up into subspecies. The red tail is similar to that of *Pervagor spilosoma* but the body pattern is so different there should be no problem distinguishing between them.

Provide plenty of shelter for this species as it tends to be a bit shy, at least at first. It will accept most varieties of marine aquarium fish food.

491.00

Petrometopon cruentatum (Lacepede)

COMMON NAME: Graysby.

RANGE: Tropical western Atlantic.

PREVIOUS SCIENTIFIC NAMES: *Sparus cruentatus, Saranus apiarius, Serranus coronatus, Petrometopon apiarius, Bodianus cruentatus, Epinephelus guttatus.*

MERISTIC CHARACTERISTICS: D. XI, 14; A. III, 8; P. 16. Grows to about 12 inches.

This is a friendly grouper which has been caught in Texas waters. It does well in large tanks and probably changes sex from female to male as it gets older. Very easy to spear, as it seems almost unafraid of divers. Don't keep this species with smaller fish or they will soon be devoured. Feedings of chopped fish, shrimp and clam meat are advised.

492.00

Platax batavianus Cuvier and Valenciennes

COMMON NAME: Batavia Bat Fish.
RANGE: Indo-Australian Archipelago and Indian Ocean.
PREVIOUS SCIENTIFIC NAMES: *Platax arthriticus.*
MERISTIC CHARACTERISTICS: D. VII, 29–32; A. III, 22–23. Grows to
about 12 inches.

The bat fishes present a problem to fish taxonomists. There are
several species which undergo considerable change in appearance as
they grow from juvenile to adult. Often the juvenile carries one scientific
name while the mature form has another. Hopefully some ichthyologist
will soon work with this beautiful group and unscramble the name
problem. *P. batavianus* may prove to be the adult form of some already
described species.

493.00

Platax orbicularis. Photo by Dr. Herbert R. Axelrod.

Platax orbicularis (Forskal)

COMMON NAME: Orbiculate Bat Fish.

PHOTOGRAPH BY: Klaus Paysan.

RANGE: Widespread from the Red Sea and Indian Ocean, throughout the Indo-Australian Archipelago, north to the Philippines, coasts of China and southern Japan and Central and South Pacific Islands.

PREVIOUS SCIENTIFIC NAMES: *Chaetodon orbicularis, Chaetodon vespertilio, Chaetodon pentacanthus, Platax vespertilio, Platax raynaldi, Platax ehrenbergi, Platax blochi, Platax guttulatus.*

MERISTIC CHARACTERISTICS: D. V, 34–38; A. III, 26–28. Scales small. Grows to a length of about 20 inches.

495.00

The Orbiculate Bat Fish is an aquarium prize which will give its owner endless hours of enjoyment. Here is a real "personality" fish which will, in a very short time, become as tame as your household dog or cat. It will actually rise to the surface to have its nose petted! The bat fish relishes feedings of chopped fresh frozen fish and will eat out of your fingers until its belly is bulging. This species is extremely hardy and if properly cared for will grow at an amazing rate. A 2-inch specimen may be kept alone in a 10 gallon tank, but will soon outgrow it and progressively larger tanks must be provided. As is true for many marine species, the larger the tank you can provide, the better off your bat fish will be. Adult fish (exceeding 10 inches) should be kept in tanks of over 100 gallons capacity.

This spectacular species gets its common and scientific name from the body shape of the adult. The young are markedly sickle-shaped and become gradually round as they increase in size. Perhaps "Sickle Fish" would be a better name for the bat fishes (genus *Platax*), since another group of weird bottom-dwelling fishes (the Oligocephalidae) are commonly called bat fishes also.

A young Batfish, **Platax orbicularis**. Photo by Earl Kennedy.

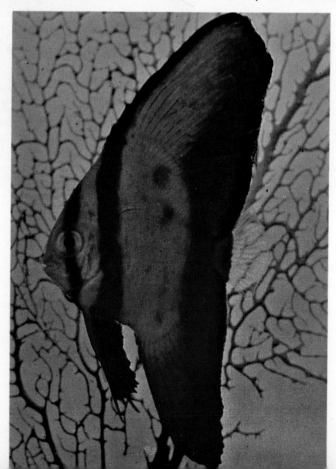

Photo by A. van den Nieuwenhuizen.

Platax pinnatus (Linnaeus)

COMMON NAME: Red-rimmed Bat Fish.

RANGE: Throughout the entire Indo-Pacific region exclusive of the Hawaiian Islands.

PREVIOUS SCIENTIFIC NAMES: *Chaetodon pinnatus, Platax gampret, Platax expansus, Chaetodon setosus.*

MERISTIC CHARACTERISTICS: D. V-VI (usually V), 36-40; A. III, 26-29; about 50 scales in a longitudinal line. Grows to a length of 14 inches or more.

This is the most beautiful species of a very spectacular family of fishes. There are few aquatic creatures which exhibit such grace in form and movement as the exotic bat fishes. While they command rather high prices, they are certainly worth the money. *P. pinnatus* appears to be not as hardy as *P. orbicularis*, and it is advised that the inexperienced aquarist confine himself to the latter species. For some reason *pinnatus* is often reluctant to start feeding in captivity; more than one amateur aquarist has watched his expensive bat fish wither away and eventually die.

One of the most fantastic of sights is to view a school of these fish in their native habitat. They prefer shallow areas close to shore, especially where mangrove trees overhang. The fish will often be seen swimming among the submerged branches of these trees; they sometimes attempt to play dead by either floating on the surface on their sides or drifting on the bottom from side to side with the current. In both instances it takes an experienced eye to distinguish their form from that of a dead leaf. Nature has been kind to the bat fish and provided it with excellent protective mimicry which helps it to elude would-be predators.

Platax pinnatus adult with typical silvery body and dark anterior bands.

Platax pinnatus

PHOTOGRAPH BY: Earl Kenned

Platax teira (Forskal)

COMMON NAME: Long-finned Bat Fish.
RANGE: Tropical Indo-Pacific.
PREVIOUS SCIENTIFIC NAMES: *Chaetodon teira*.
MERISTIC CHARACTERISTICS: D. V, 30–30; A. III, 23–24; lateral line
    60–65. Attains a length of 24 inches.

Juvenile bat fishes are known for their extravagant finnage, but this
species has really gone to extremes. Not only are the dorsal and anal fins
elongated, but the pelvic fins are as well, a character that as the fish gets
older helps differentiate this species from the others. As the Long-finned
Bat Fish grows the fins decrease in length proportionally so that it
becomes more similar in shape to the other species of the same age. The
colors of the juveniles are also lost, and the adults of all the species
become generally silvery with blackish bands through the eye, across the
body behind the head, and sometimes across the posterior part of the
body.

If *Platax pinnatus* is considered the most difficult bat fish to keep and
P. orbicularis the easiest, *P. teira* is right smack in the middle. This can
also be said of the price of these fishes, *P. teira* being midway between the
more expensive *P. pinnatus* and the relatively inexpensive *P. orbicularis*.

It is best to start with a large tank, for the bat fishes are fast growers and
reach a large size even in an aquarium. The juveniles also may be only 2
inches long or so, but such a fish might be 6 inches high and thus require
more swimming space compared to another 2-inch fish. Be sure to avoid
tankmates that are fin nippers because the bat fishes' fins make tempting
targets. The butterflyfishes and angelfishes are good fishes to keep with
the bat fishes since they require similar care and have approximately
similar diets in home aquaria. A varied diet including several types of
frozen fleshy foods along with a substantial amount of vegetable food is
recommended.

Platax teira (Forskal) has very elongate dorsal, anal and pelvic fins
when young. Photo by Earl Kennedy.

500.00

Plectorhynchus albovittatus (Ruppell)*

COMMON NAME: Yellow-lined Sweetlips.

PHOTOGRAPH BY: Klaus Paysan.

RANGE: Red Sea, Coast of India, Indo-Australian Archipelago, and Philippine Islands.

PREVIOUS SCIENTIFIC NAMES: *Diagramma albovittatum, Diagramma blochii, Plectorhinchus lineatus.*

MERISTIC CHARACTERISTICS: D. XIII, 18–19; A. III, 7–8; about 73 lateral line scales. Reaches a size of 8 inches.

This species is very similar in appearance to the Oriental Sweetlips (*P. orientalis*). Care and feeding are the same as for *orientalis*.

* Now called *Gaterin albovittatus.*

Plectorhynchus chaetodonoides (Lacepede)*

Common Name: Clown Sweetlips.
Range: Red Sea, Indian Ocean, Indo-Australian Archipelago, Philippines and Caroline Islands.
Previous Scientific Names: *Plectorhynchus papuensis, Lutjanus chaetodonoides, Diagramma plectorhynchus, Diagramma pardalis.*
Meristic Characteristics: D. XI or XII, 18; A. III, 8; lateral line scales 58-65. Grows to 3 feet.

Plectorhynchus chaetodonoides is one of the more spectacular fishes commonly imported from Singapore and the Philippine Islands. The striking contrast of large white dots on a purplish background makes this one of the more desirable aquarium fishes. These fish are inhabitants of shallow reef areas where the bottom is covered with much coral and rubble which affords ample shelter. Unfortunately, the adults are not nearly so colorful and tend to lose the large white spots which make the young so attractive.

Be sure and provide this species with plenty of shelter in the form of coral and rocks. Feedings should consist of live brine shrimp and finely chopped fish or lean beef.

* Now called *Gaterin chaetodonoides*.

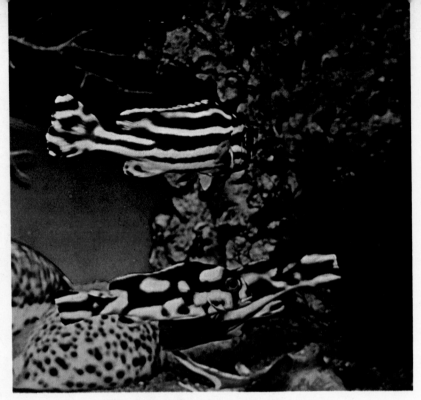

Plectorhynchus orientalis (Bloch)*

COMMON NAME: Oriental Sweetlips.

PHOTOGRAPH BY: Klaus Paysan.

RANGE: Philippine Islands, Indo-Australian Archipelago and Indian Ocean.

PREVIOUS SCIENTIFIC NAMES: *Anthias orientalis, Lutjanus aurantius, Serranus orientalis, Diagramma pica, Diagramma orientale, Diagramma sibbaldi.*

MERISTIC CHARACTERISTICS: D. XIII–XIV, 17; A. III, 8; about 80 scales in the lateral line. Reaches a length of about 6 inches.

The several species of sweetlips (genus *Plectorhynchus*) are closely allied to the snapper family. They are fairly hardy and generally make good aquarium pets. This species is one of the more spectacular members of the genus as far as color and markings are concerned.

Offer your sweetlips a wide assortment of live and frozen foods including shrimp, chopped fish, clams and earthworms. Provide ample shelter and keep them together in pairs if possible, since they appear to feel more at ease in captivity when they are provided with neighbors of their own kind.

* Now called *Gaterin orientalis.*

504.00

Plectropomus maculatus (Bloch)★

COMMON NAME: Saddleback Grouper.

RANGE: Red Sea, Indian Ocean, Indo-Australian Archipelago Islands of, Central and South Pacific.

PREVIOUS SCIENTIFIC NAMES: *Bodianus maculatus, Labrus laevis, Bodianus cyclostomus, Bodianus melanoleucus, Holocentrus leopardus, Plectropoma punctatum.*

MERISTIC CHARACTERISTICS: D. VII–VIII, 11–12; A. III, 8; lateral line has 80–110 scales. Grows to about 4 feet.

Only the young of this species make good aquarium fish, and even these must be kept with larger fish. They are predators known for their healthy appetites!

This fish is interesting from the standpoint that it belongs to a group of fishes which are sometimes responsible for ciguatera poisoning, which results from eating the toxic flesh of entrails of individuals which harbor the poison. Just how the fish become poisonous is a question which continues to baffle scientists. It has been theorized that these fish become toxic by eating smaller herbivores (plant eaters) who themselves pick up the poison by grazing on new growths of certain blue-green algae. Ciguatera is a poison which attacks the nervous system; symptoms range from a slight stomach ache to severe paralysis and eventual death. Inhabitants of areas where this poisoning is common are encouraged to feed a small portion of doubtful fish to the family cat before eating a large portion themselves. If the flesh is toxic, symptoms usually develop within a few hours. Fortunately ciguatera is confined to tropical reefs, and fish from the colder areas are free of it.

★The fish pictured is now known as *Plectropomus melanoleucus.*

505.00

Plectrypops retrospinis (Guichenot)

COMMON NAME: Cardinal Soldier Fish.

PHOTOGRAPH BY: Dr. John Randall of a 3.9-inch specimen from the Virgin Islands.

RANGE: Caribbean Sea.

PREVIOUS SCIENTIFIC NAMES: *Holocentrum retrospinio, Holocentrum prospinosum.*

MERISTIC CHARACTERISTICS: D. XII, 14; IV, 11; P. 16–17; 32–35 scales in the lateral line. Grows to about 5 inches.

This is the king of Atlantic Squirrelfishes as far as the aquarist is concerned. It is bright, bright red and stays small.

While not very common, enough specimens are available that anyone can collect one, or buy one should they so prefer. The squirrelfishes are not, as a rule, found in stock with all wholesalers, since they are much less "romantic" than the Pacific coral fishes, especially the butterfly and anemone fishes. But try a few of these if you have the chance and you'll find some very interesting habits.

For the working man, this is a great fish. They usually hide all day and come out at night.

Plesiops caeruleolineatus Ruppell

COMMON NAME: Crimson-tipped Long-fin (The Australian name is used here).

RANGE: Tropical Indo-Pacific.

PREVIOUS SCIENTIFIC NAMES: *Plesiops corallicola, Plesiops melas, Plesiops oxycephalus.*

MERISTIC CHARACTERISTICS: D. X–XII, 6–8; A. III, 8; 23–27 scales in lateral series. Grows to 6 inches.

This particular species is of relatively little interest to the aquarist. Its colors are plain and its behavior is on the shy side. *P. caeruleolineatus* is an inhabitant of rocky ledges or holes in the coral reef, where it feeds principally on small crustaceans.

507.00

Plotosus anguillaris (Bloch)

COMMON NAME: Salt Water Cat Fish.
PHOTOGRAPHED BY: Klaus Paysan.
RANGE: Tropical Indo-Pacific.
PREVIOUS SCIENTIFIC NAMES: *Plotosus lineatus, Plotosus arab, Plotosus papuensis.*
MERISTIC CHARACTERISTICS: D. I, 4–5+80–100; A. 70–77. Attains a length of 30 inches.

Juvenile Salt Water Cats are extremely handsome, but beware when handling this species. The dorsal and pectoral fin spines are capable of inflicting serious and very painful wounds. This species is a bottom spawner which lays its eggs in rocky crevices in shallow water.

Feedings of freeze-dried tubifex, earthworms and shrimp as well as a variety of other foods will be accepted by the Salt Water Cat Fish.

Pomacanthus annularis (Bloch)

COMMON NAME: Blue King Angelfish.

RANGE: Indo-Australian Archipelago and coasts of India and Ceylon.

PREVIOUS SCIENTIFIC NAMES: *Chaetodon annularis, Holacanthus annularis, Holacanthus septentrionalis, Chaetodon verticosus, Holacanthus pseudannularis, Acanthochaetodon annularis.*

MERISTIC CHARACTERISTISC: D. XIII, 21–22; A. III, 20–21; lateral scale rows about 70. Grows to about 2 feet.

This is one of the hardier species of Angelfishes and also one of the most attractive. Rodney Jonklaas of Ceylon reports they often frequent turbid inshore waters where visibility is scarcely more than a few feet. The young are present in these waters at the beginning of the year (the Ceylonese summer), but are usually not very numerous. They are easy to catch, but the adults require exceptional collecting skill, at least during the daylight hours. They are best caught on dark moonless nights, at which time they retire to rocky crevices and remain in an inactive state, similar to what we know as sleep. They are blinded by a bright light and are easily scooped up with a net.

509.00

Pomacanthus arcuatus (Linneaus)

COMMON NAME: Gray Angelfish.

RANGE: West Indies, north to New Jersey, south to Bahia.

PREVIOUS SCIENTIFIC NAMES: *Chaetodon arcuatus, Chaetodon aureus, Chaetodon lutescens, Chaetodon littoricola, Pomacanthus balteatus, Pomacanthus cingulatus, Pomacanthus quinquecinctus, Pomacanthus aureus.*

MERISTIC CHARACTERISTICS: D. IX, 31–33; A. III, 23–25. Has been reported to reach a length of 2 feet.

The Gray Angel is similar in appearance to the French Angel, but the adult Gray is lighter in color. The young of these two species are almost identical but can be separated by the following characteristics: in the French Angel the median yellow band on the forehead stops at the base of the upper lip, and the black spot in the middle of the tail is large and nearly round, while the Gray Angel has a forehead bar which crosses the mouth and ends on the chin and a yellow tail fin with a vertically elongate black spot in the middle. The young of both these species are spectacular showpieces!

The care and feeding parallels that of the French Angel.

510.00

Pomacanthus imperator (Bloch)

COMMON NAME: Emperor Angelfish.

RANGE: Red Sea, Indian Ocean, Indo-Australian Archipelago, China, Japan, Melanesia, Micronesia and Polynesia (except Hawaii).

PREVIOUS SCIENTIFIC NAMES: *Chaetodon imperator, Holocanthus imperator, Holocanthus geometricus, Holocanthus nicobariensis, Acanthochaetodon nicobariensis, Holocanthus marianas, Holocanthus bishopi.*

MERISTIC CHARACTERISTICS: D. XIV, 19–21; A. III, 18–21; about 90 vertical scale rows. Grows to at least one foot.

The Emperor Angel is deserving of its title, for this prize has one of the most striking color patterns of all the angelfishes. The juveniles were formerly considered to be another species, *Holocanthus nicobariensis,* but it has been shown that a remarkable transformation in color pattern takes place from juvenile to adult. The young are generally dark blue with a series of concentric white rings, while the adults are marked with about 28 horizontal lines which are a rich golden color.

Emperor Angels are either found in pairs or are solitary in habit. They are often seen near the entrance of caves and ledges which they dart into when alarmed. When disturbed they are able to produce a strange clicking sound which can be heard clearly underwater.

511.00

Pomacanthus paru (Bloch)

COMMON NAME: French Angelfish.
PHOTOGRAPH BY: Dr. John Randall of a juvenile and adult specimen from the Virgin Islands.
RANGE: Tropical Atlantic.
PREVIOUS SCIENTIFIC NAMES: *Chaetodon paru, Chaetodon arcuatus*.
MERISTIC CHARACTERISTICS: D. X, 29–31; A. III, 22–24; about 85–90 scale rows above lateral line. Grows to 16 inches.

The French Angel is a popular beauty which is commonly collected in Florida waters. The young, which are most desirable to aquarists, are colored differently from the adults. The body is jet black with a series of circular bright yellow bands. The adults are entirely blackish, with the edges of the scales yellow. They are inhabitants of shallow coral reefs and are often seen living near large growths of sponges which form part of their diet.

These fish fight among themselves, and one per tank is recommended. Brine shrimp, dry flake food, chopped fish and shrimp, chopped earthworms and finely chopped lettuce and spinach are recommended for a balanced diet.

Juvenile angelfishes of this size (about 2 inches) are ideal for marine aquaria. Note that the stripes are yellow in contrast to those of the Emperor and Koran angelfish juveniles which are white and more numerous. Photo by Douglas Faulkner.

The yellow bars of the French Angelfish, **Pomacanthus paru**, disappear as the fish grows. Photo by Dr. Herbert R. Axelrod.

514.00

Pomacanthus semicirculatus (Cuvier and Valenciennes)

COMMON NAME: Semicircle Angelfish.

PHOTOGRAPH BY: Hilmar Hansen.

RANGE: Red Sea, Indian Ocean, Indo-Australian Archipelago, Philippines, China, Okinawa and Melanesia.

PREVIOUS SCIENTIFIC NAMES: *Holocanthus semicirculatus, Holacanthus alternans, Holacanthus coeruleus, Holacanthus micropelpis, Holacanthus iburu, Holacanthus caerulescens, Acanthochaetodon semicirculatus, Acanthochaetodon alternans, Holacanthus ignatius.*

MERISTIC CHARACTERISTICS: D. XIII, 21–23; A. III, 20–21; about 75 vertical scale rows. About 16 inches is maximum length for this species.

515.00

The Koran angelfish juveniles are among the more readily accessible angelfishes for the marine aquarium. They are also very popular with aquarists. Photo by K.H. Choo.

Here's another angelfish which undergoes a fantastic color change as it grows into an adult. The young are marked with about 10 semicircular bands, while the adult lacks bands and is much less spectacular in appearance. The adult is yellowish anteriorly, gray or brownish posteriorly, with the sides mottled with dark spots. The pectoral fins are yellowish and the pelvics are blue. Large specimens require plenty of room and may prove difficult to feed in the aquarium since this species is primarily a sponge eater in nature. Best bet is to feed a wide variety of live, frozen, and dried foods until certain preferences are noted.

Pomacentrus coelestis Jordan & Starks

Common Name: Blue Damsel Fish.
Range: Tropical Indo-Pacific.
Previous Scientific Names: *Pomacentrus pulcherrimus.*
Meristic Characteristics: D. XIII, 14 or 15; A. II, 15 or 16; vertical
  scale rows 26-30. Grows to a length of 3 inches.

This species is a gorgeous display item with its electric blue body
and yellowish anal and caudal fins. It is moderately common on tropical Pacific atolls, frequenting shallow rubble areas. They are attractive enough in the aquarium, but make a fantastic sight when observed in their natural habitat. The play of sunlight on the body almost
makes them glow. They are generally found in groups which vary in
number from perhaps 10-50 individuals. It's a territorial fish and may
prove to be on the quarrelsome side when kept in captivity, particularly towards smaller members of its own species. A hardy fish which eats
nearly anything.

517.00

Pomacentrus coeruleus Quoy and Gaimard*

COMMON NAME: Blue Devil.
PHOTOGRAPH BY: Dr. Herbert R. Axelrod.
RANGE: Tropical Indo-Pacific.
PREVIOUS SCIENTIFIC NAMES: None.
MERISTIC CHARACTERISTICS: D. XI–XIII, 13 or 14; A. II, 14 or 15. Tubes
in lateral line 16 or 17. Attains a length of about 4 inches.

This is the right choice if you want to add a touch of blue to your
tank. Several of these brightly colored fish make a gorgeous display.
They are small and although they may engage in squabbles with themselves they are generally peaceful towards other species in the aquarium.
They will do best if the aquarium is heavily landscaped with rocks and
coral, as this will closely approximate their natural habitat. It's not a
fussy eater and will accept dry flake preparations, freeze-dried brine
shrimp and chopped fish.

* Now called *Abudefduf cyanea* (Quoy and Gaimard).

Pomacentrus vaiuli Jordan and Seale

COMMON NAME: Ocellate Damselfish.
RANGE: Tropical Indo-Pacific.
PREVIOUS SCIENTIFIC NAMES: None
MERISTIC CHARACTERISTICS: D. XIII, 15; A. II, 14–16; transverse scale rows 25–28. Grows to 4 inches.

Hardiness is the byword among the many species of damsels and this little beauty is no exception. It is one of the more abundant fishes to be found inshore on tropical Pacific atolls. It is primarily a browsing plant feeder, but takes small fishes and invertebrates which occur in the branching coral heads where it resides.

Freeze-dried brine shrimp, tubifex and daphnia are excellent foods which will keep your damsel healthy, but be sure to add chlorella algae as a supplement.

Premnas biaculeatus (Bloch)

COMMON NAME: Spine-cheeked Anemone Fish.

RANGE: Coasts of India, Philippines, Mauritius, Madagascar, and coral reefs of the Indo-Australian Archipelago.

PREVIOUS SCIENTIFIC NAMES: *Chaetodon biaculeatus, Lutjanos trifasciatus, Scorpaena aculeata, Holocentrus sonnerat, Holacanthus biaculeatus, Premnas trifasciatus, Premnas leucodesmus, Premnas semicinctus, Premnas unicolor, Sargus ensifer, Premnas epigrammata.*

MERISTIC CHARACTERISTICS: D. X, 17–18; A. II, 14–15; 47–55 scales in the lateral line. Attains a length of 6 inches.

The Spine-Cheeked Anemone Fish can be differentiated from the rest of the anemone fishes (genus *Amphiprion*) by the presence of one or two well developed spines below the eye. The larger of these spines may extend as far back as the posterior border of the white headbar. However, as far as behavior and feeding habits are concerned, they are nearly identical to the other anemone fish species. In nature these beauties are always found in the company of a large sea anemone, but they may thrive without an anemone in the aquarium once they are induced to feed and become accustomed to their surroundings. It is advised that large adults be kept alone, as fighting and severe fin nipping may often take place. If a mating pair can be found, an exception to this rule can be made.

Premnas is one of the several marine species which might possibly be induced to spawn by the advanced aquarist, providing the requirements for proper nutrition and comfortable physical surroundings are satisfied. Nearly forty years ago Dr. J. Verwey reported on several spawnings of this species in several large aquaria at his lab in Java. His tanks were provided with a continuous supply of fresh seawater which he pumped up from the nearby ocean, and he kept the fish in company with their native sea anemones. The male and female fish cleaned a nest site near the base of the anemone, where upwards of a thousand small (3.5 mm.) capsule-shaped eggs were laid directly upon the bare rock, and meticulously cared for by the male. The eggs hatch in 6–7 days. Adult and juvenile *P. biaculeatus* are fond of feedings of live and frozen brine shrimp, different varieties of chopped fish and dry flake food.

Premnas biaculeatus, like species of *Amphiprion*, are always found in the presence of sea anemones. Photo by Dr. Gerald R. Allen.

Priacanthus arenatus Cuvier and Valenciennes

COMMON NAME: Bigeye.

PHOTOGRAPH BY: Dr. John Randall of a 10.6-inch specimen from the Virgin Islands.

RANGE: Tropical Atlantic, south to Brazil, occasionally northward in the Gulf Stream to Newport and Woods Hole.

PREVIOUS SCIENTIFIC NAMES: *Priacanthus fulgens, Priacanthus catalufa, Priacanthus macropthalmus.*

MERISTIC CHARACTERISTICS: D. X, 13–15; A. III, 14–16; 61–73 scales in the lateral line.

The juvenile Bigeye is one of the easiest of fishes to collect. They seem to be almost totally oblivious of a diver and can be netted during the day with ease. However, at night these fishes are active and it is a different story.

It is best to keep Bigeyes in larger aquaria and provide them with plenty of rocks in the forms of caves, since this is their preferred habitat. Feed large quantities of live foods such as mosquitoe larvae, brine shrimp, and livebearer fry.

Priacanthus cruentatus (Lacepede)

COMMON NAME: Glasseye, Aweoweo (Hawaiian).
RANGE: Circumtropical in Caribbean-Atlantic; Pacific and Indian Oceans.
PREVIOUS SCIENTIFIC NAMES: *Labrus cruentatus, Priacanthus cepedianus.*
MERISTIC CHARACTERISTICS: D. X, 13; A. III, 14; 54–63 lateral line scales.
 Grows to about 1 foot.

The color of this species varies according to the time of day and its surroundings. For instance, they may appear bright red in a dark cave or will bleach out considerably when swimming over white sandy bottom. This is one of about 15 tropical inshore species which is found world wide. In Hawaii *P. cruentatus* is widely sought after by spear fishermen since the flesh of this fish is excellent eating.

They make interesting specimens when they are small and should be fed live foods such as brine shrimp and small fish. They are basically nocturnal, but will feed at all times.

523.00

Prognathodes aculeatus (Poey)*

COMMON NAME: Longsnout Butterflyfish.
RANGE: Southern Florida and the West Indies.
PREVIOUS SCIENTIFIC NAMES: *Chelmon aculeatus, Chelmon pelta.*
MERISTIC CHARACTERISTICS: D. XIII, 18–19; A. III, 14–16; P. 13–15;
22–28 scales in the lateral line.

While I have gone along with the scientifically accepted name "longsnout" for this species, I do it with hesitation, for it certainly is not very long snouted when compared with the longsnouts of the Indo-Pacific genera *Forcipiger* and *Chelmon*, which are also butterflyfishes.

These Caribbean beauties are rare in the aquarium, for they seldom venture into shallow reef waters, preferring to stay at depths over 100 feet. It feeds on the tentacles of tubeworms, the tubefeet of sea urchins and small crustaceans, as well as fish eggs. In captivity they take freeze-dried brine shrimp, daphnia and canned Norwegian brine shrimp. They are difficult fish to keep alive, as they often refuse to feed. Only consider buying acclimated specimens which are robust and healthy.

* Now called *Chaetodon aculeatus.*

524.00

Promicrops lanceolatus (Bloch)

COMMON NAME: Giant Spotted Grouper.
PHOTOGRAPH BY: Hilmar Hansen.
RANGE: Tropical Indo-Pacific.
PREVIOUS SCIENTIFIC NAMES: *Holocentrus lanceolatus, Serranus lanceolatus, Serranus geographicus, Serranus horridus, Batrachus gigas.*
MERISTIC CHARACTERISTICS: D. XI, 14–15; A. III, 8; lateral line scales 95.
Grows to as long as 10 feet!

Needless to say, only the young are suited to keeping in the home aquarium. The adults reach a length of 10 feet and may approach 1,000 pounds in weight! The young are colorful and hardy, but don't keep small fish in the same tank unless they are purposely placed there for food, since this fish has an insatiable appetite. They are territorial and will usually take over a pile of rocks or corner of the tank. In nature, the adults are fond of large caverns in the coral reef which they guard zealously, even against a diver.

525.00

Pseudobalistes fuscus (Bloch and Schneider)

COMMON NAME: Blue-lined Triggerfish.
PHOTOGRAPH BY: H. Hansen.
RANGE: Red Sea and tropical Indo-Pacific.
PREVIOUS SCIENTIFIC NAMES: *Balistes fascus, Balistes chrysospilos, Balistes reticulatus, Xantichthys fuscus.*
MERISTIC CHARACTERISITICS: D. III, 25; A. 23; P. 13. Grows to 8 inches.

The demand for this gaily colored fish far exceeds the supply. There are only a couple of species of Triggerfishes which have a more stunning color pattern. *P. fuscus* is an inhabitant of shallow reef waters, and the young never stray far from a safe hole into which they can retreat when faced with danger. Like many fishes, they have the capability of producing distinct sounds. These are produced by the jaws and resonated by the swim bladder, which results in a grunting type noise.

Freeze-dried brine shrimp and tubifex supplemented with live brine shrimp and an occasional feeding of chopped fish are excellent sources of nutrition for this species.

526.00

Pseudocheilinus evanidus Jordan and Evermann

COMMON NAME: Scarlet Wrasse.
RANGE: Tropical Indo-Pacific.
PREVIOUS SCIENTIFIC NAMES: None.
MERISTIC CHARACTERISTICS: D. IX, 11; A. III, 9; about 23 scales in the
lateral line. Reaches a length of about 5 inches.

The wrasses of the genus *Pseudocheilinus* are known for their beautiful
color patterns and this species is no exception. It can be distinguished
from the other species by its lack of broad stripes. *P. evanidus* is similar
in habit to the 3 other species, being found in areas of live coral. Feed this
beauty a variety of live, dry flake and freeze-dried foods.

527.00

Pseudocheilinus hexataenia (Bleeker)

COMMON NAME: Six-lined Wrasse.

RANGE: Tropical south and central Pacific.

PREVIOUS SCIENTIFIC NAMES: *Cheilinus hexataenia, Pseudocheilinus psittaculus, Cossyphus echis.*

MERISTIC CHARACTERISTICS: D. IX, 12; A. III, 9; lateral line with 25–29 scales. Reaches about 4 inches in length.

This fantastically-colored species is common on tropical Pacific atolls. It occurs solitarily among the branches of live coral. They feed primarily on small invertebrates which live on the bottom adjacent to the coral patches. They have also been seen around the bases of large anemones and may benefit by the protection which these stinging invertebrates afford them against predators. However, they do not enter the tentacles of the anemone like the fishes of the genus *Amphiprion.*

Live brine shrimp most closely approximate their native food of small invertebrates, but they should be given a variety of dry flake and freeze-dried foods as well.

528.00

Pseudocheilinus octotaenia Jenkins

COMMON NAME: Eight-lined Wrasse.
RANGE: Tropical Indo-Pacific.
PREVIOUS SCIENTIFIC NAMES: *Pseudocheilinus margaretae.*
MERISTIC CHARACTERISTICS: D. IX, 11; A. III, 9; 23 pores in the lateral line. Grows to 5 inches.

This Wrasse has more horizontal lines on the body than the other three species of *Pseudocheilinus.* They are quite shy in nature, and a diver can only get a quick glimpse of this bright little fish before it ducks back in the coral.

Since it is an eater of small crustaceans in nature, live brine shrimp makes a good substitute in captivity.

Pseudocheilinus tetrataenia Schultz

COMMON NAME: Three-lined Wrasse.

PHOTOGRAPH BY: Dr. John Randall of a specimen 1.6 inches from Eniwetok.

RANGE: Tropical central Pacific including Hawaii.

PREVIOUS SCIENTIFIC NAMES: None.

MERISTIC CHARACTERISTICS: D. IX, 11; A. III, 20; 23–25 pores in lateral line. Grows to a length of 3 or 4 inches.

Another handsome species of *Pseudocheilinius* which, because of its small size when mature, makes an ideal aquarium fish. At present it is known only from the Marshall Islands and Hawaii, but further collecting should broaden the range of this species.

Feed as prescribed for the other members of the genus.

530.00

Ptereleotris microlepis (Bleeker)

COMMON NAME: Blue Gudgeon.
PHOTOGRAPH BY: Dr. John Randall of a 2.5-inch specimen from Moorea.
RANGE: Tropical Indo-Pacific.
PREVIOUS SCIENTIFIC NAMES: *Eleotis microlepis, Eleotris elongata, Ptereleotris playfairi.*
MERISTIC CHARACTERISTICS: D. VI–I, 27; A. I, 27; lateral line scales
more than 100. Grows to 6 inches.

This species is a bottom dweller which lives in sandy burrows. They never stray far from the mouth of their den and beat a hasty retreat, entering head first, at the approach of intruders. They are among the hardest of fish to catch. The chemical anesthetic quinaldine is just about the only way to collect them, and sometimes this doesn't work if they fall "asleep" deep inside the burrow.

The price of this fish is likely to be high when it is available, due to the difficulty encountered in their capture. They make extremely handsome aquarium fish.

Ptereleotris splendidum*

COMMON NAME: Fire Fish.
RANGE: Tropical Indo-Pacific.
PREVIOUS SCIENTIFIC NAMES: *Nemateleotris magnificus*.
MERISTIC CHARACTERISTICS: D. VI–I, 28; A. I, 24; lateral line 118.
  Attains a length of 3–4 inches.

The current and previous scientific names give an accurate description
of this fish. It is indeed splendid and magnificent. Here's another one of
those beauties which has not yet been imported in any great quantity,
probably because of the difficulty involved in catching them. The light
pink anterior and blazing red posterior, not to mention the delicate
elongated dorsal filament, set it apart from all other fishes. They are
extremely popular in Far Eastern aquaria and hopefully will become more
available in the near future.

  Provide a thick layer of fine sand and plenty of rocks. *P. splendidum*
lives in sandy burrows which it constructs. Offer live brine shrimp at
first, followed in a couple of days with chopped fish and shrimp, supplemented with freeze-dried tubifex and canned Norwegian brine shrimp.

* Now called *Nemateleotris magnificus* Fowler.

532.00

Ptereleotris tricolor Smith

Common Name: Scissortail.
Range: Tropical Indo-Pacific.
Previous Scientific Names: None.
Meristic Characteristics: D. VI-I, 25; A. I, 24-25; P. 22-23. Attains a
   length of nearly 6 inches.

   The genus *Ptereleotris* has usually been placed in the family Eleo-
tridae (sleepers) because the pelvic fins are separate, not fused as in the
typical Gobiidae (gobies). However, evidence now points to *Ptereleotris* actually being a true goby which has lost the sucking disk. This
species is a burrow dweller, and specimens are sometimes found in
pairs. Unlike many others of the members of the family they are free-
swimming and are usually seen hovering off the bottom, a short distance from their holes.

Pterois antennata (Bloch)

COMMON NAME: Spotfin Lion Fish.
PHOTOGRAPH BY: Hilmar Hansen.
RANGE: Indian Ocean, Philippines, China Sea, Melanesia, Micronesia and Polynesia (except Hawaii).
PREVIOUS SCIENTIFIC NAME: *Scorpaena antennata*.
MERISTIC CHARACTERISTICS: D. XII, 10–12; A. III, 6–7, 50–55 scales rows from upper edge of gill opening to base of caudal fin. Attains a length of 7–8 inches.

The Spotfin Lion Fish usually commands a lower price than its cousin *Pterois volitans*, but it is almost as attractive, especially the juveniles whose pectoral filaments are even more exaggerated than those of the adults. A word of caution is necessary about the dorsal spines of this species, as they are as poisonous as those described for *P. volitans*.

534.00

The Spotfin is often quite common on shallow reefs of the Indo-Pacific and is usually found perched upside down on the ceiling and walls of coral grottoes. They are commonly encountered in pairs and sometimes in the company of *Pterois radiata*, a closely related species. They are generally quite shy and retreat rapidly when poked at with a stick or net handle. However, on occasion they may become provoked and actually strike out with their venomous dorsal spines in rattlesnake fashion. On one occasion in the Western Caroline Islands a provoked Spotfin struck out at a wooden net handle in the manner described above and actually penetrated the wood so deeply that it could not dislodge itself and was hopelessly caught. This is not the recommended method for capturing these beasts!

Pterois radiata Cuvier and Valenciennes

COMMON NAME: Whitefin Lion Fish.
RANGE: Tropical Indo-Pacific and Red Sea.
PREVIOUS SCIENTIFIC NAMES: *Pterois cincta.*
MERISTIC CHARACTERISTICS: D. XII, 10–12; III, 6 or 7; scale rows 50–54. Grows to 10 inches.

Another of the gorgeous *Pterois* species, *P. radiata* is an eye-catcher. The character which will help you immediately recognize this species is the broad horizontal bar at the base of the tail. Another helpful character is the plain white pectoral ray filaments, which in small specimens may be longer than the body. Needless to say, these fish have few natural enemies, but strangely enough, larger specimens may turn cannibal and consume their brethren! This species is native to dark caverns and is often found in aggregations. They are normally nocturnal, but will revert to daytime activities in the aquarium.

Pterois sphex (Jordan and Evermann)

COMMON NAME: Hawaiian Lion Fish.
PHOTOGRAPH BY: Dr. Herbert R. Axelrod.
RANGE: Hawaiian Islands.
PREVIOUS SCIENTIFIC NAMES: None.
MERISTIC CHARACTERISTICS: D. XIII, 11; A. III, 7; P. 16; vertical scale
rows 56. Grows to 9–10 inches.

This species is similar in appearance to *Pterois antennata*. The best
way to tell if the fish you have is *Pterois sphex* is to find out where it
comes from. If it's from Hawaii, you can be sure it's *sphex*, since that's
the only species of *Pterois* which occurs there. It's a relatively uncommon
species in the Islands, occurring usually below 20 feet. It appears to be
an annual spawner with the tiny (1 inch) young making their appearance
in May and June. They grow to a length of 5 inches during the first
year and are soon reproductively mature.

537.00

Pterois volitans   Photo by Dr. Herbert R. Axelrod.

Pterois volitans (Linnaeus)

COMMON NAME: Turkey Fish, Lion Fish, Scorpion Fish, Butterfly Cod.
RANGE: Widespread in the Indian, South and Central Pacific Oceans.
PREVIOUS SCIENTIFIC NAMES: *Gasterosteus volitans*, *Scorpaena volitans*, *Scorpaena miles*, *Pterois miles*, *Pterois muricata*.
MERISTIC CHARACTERISTICS: D. XIII, 10–11; A. III, 7; 90–100 scale rows, scales small. Grows to 15 inches.

Just as the lion is considered the king of land-bound beasts, the Lion Fish surely deserves the title of king of aquatic beasts. There are approximately six or seven species of lion fishes, or turkey fishes as they are sometimes called, but all must take a back seat to the elegant *Pterois volitans*, which is among the most bizarre and at the same time most graceful of all the sea's creatures. *P. volitans* is distinguishable from the other members of the genus *Pterois* by the feathery appearance of its pectoral fins, the free rays of which are wider than those of the other two species (*P. radiata* and *P. antennata*) which are most commonly encountered in aquarium shops. Also, *P. volitans* has over twice as many alternating brown and white bands on the body as these other two species.

While the cost of this species is likely to be high, specimens are well worth the money and are truly one of the "personality" fishes. However, handle these beauties with care, since the dorsal spines have hollow tips loaded with a nerve toxin which under certain conditions has been known to violently injure or even kill unsuspecting natives who blundered into the spines. As friendly as these fishes may become, never make the mistake of bringing the hand in close proximity to the dorsal spines. Always handle a turkey fish with a net and remove it from your tank before attempting to clean the tank. In the event that a person is pricked by these sharp spines, the injured member should be immediately soaked in *hot* water and a physician called. It has been found that the hot water treatment is effective in denaturing the toxin and drastically reducing the amount of pain which would normally be experienced.

In nature turkey fishes feed primarily on live crabs, supplemented with small fishes. They thrive in the aquarium when fed small live fish, but they may be trained to accept pieces of dead fish. In Hawaii, a popular food item which is available for these fishes is the common freshwater shrimp or "opai" which is abundant in many streams and reaches a size of 1 to $1\frac{1}{2}$ inches. Extremely small *P. volitans* specimens should not be kept with their larger brothers, as this species has been known to turn cannibal in the company of small juveniles.

Pygoplites diacanthus (Boddaert)

COMMON NAME: Royal Empress Angelfish.

RANGE: Reefs of the Indo-Pacific.

PREVIOUS SCIENTIFIC NAMES: *Chaetodon diacanthus, Chaetodon boddaerti, Chaetodon dux, Chaetodon fasciatus, Holacanthus dux, Holacanthus diacanthus, Centropyge diacantha.*

MERISTIC CHARACTERISTICS: D. XIV, 17–19; A. III, 17–19; 45–50 scale rows in lengthwise series from upper edge of gill opening to base of caudal rays. Grows to 7 inches.

The Royal Empress Angel is truly a regal beauty! Unfortunately, most of the specimens available to aquarists are too large for the average-sized tank. Small specimens (under 3 inches total length) are every bit as attractive as the adult and are characterized by having a large black

540.00

Juvenile *Pygoplites diacanthus* look very much like the adult but do have an ocellated spot in the dorsal fin. Photo by Dr. Herbert R. Axelrod.

spot on the soft dorsal fin. The reason that the young fish are seldom available is because of their shy and retiring habit of living far back in dark crevices and caves of the reef. They are therefore often overlooked by collectors. By contrast the adults are often seen swimming out in the open, sometimes in water as shallow as 3 to 4 feet.

The adults do best in tanks of 100+ gallons capacity. If you are fortunate enough to acquire a juvenile fish it will be comfortable in a 30–50 gallon tank and may be kept in the company of several other small species. Be sure and provide your fish with lots of shelter, since this is essential to its well being. In nature most of the angelfish species are fond of sponges, but in the aquarium they can be induced to take feedings of frozen or live brine shrimp, chopped fish and algal material.

Rhinecanthus aculeatus (Linnaeus)

COMMON NAME: Humu-humu-nuku-nuku-a-puaa (Hawaiian).
RANGE: Tropical Indo-Pacific and western coast of Africa where the water is warm enough.
PREVIOUS SCIENTIFIC NAMES: *Balistapus*, *Balistes aculeatus*.
MERISTIC CHARACTERISTICS: D. III–ii, 23–24; A. i, 21–22; P. i, 12–13. 41–42 scale rows; 8 teeth in upper and 8 teeth in lower jaws. Grows to about one foot.

A very favorite fish in Hawaii and frequently exported. Capable of inflicting a bad bite, so handle with care. Many Pacific peoples claim the meat of this fish is poisonous, probably from eating newly formed algae (based upon a conversation with Dr. John Randall.)

In the aquarium they are nice when small, but they require too much food when they are larger. They eat almost anything, but they do extremely well on freeze-dried tubifex worms and canned Norwegian brine shrimp. A whole shrimp hanging in the aquarium, shell and all, will soon disappear as they devour it.

Photo by K.H. Choo.

Rhinecanthus rectangulus (Bloch and Schneider)

COMMON NAME: Humu-humu-nuku-nuku-a-puaa (Hawaiian).

RANGE: From the east coast of Africa to the islands of the central and South Pacific and coasts of China and Southern Japan.

PREVIOUS SCIENTIFIC NAMES: *Balistes medinilla, Balistes erythopteron, Balistes echarpe, Balistes cinctus.*

MERISTIC CHARACTERISTICS: D. III, 23 or 24; A. 21; 35 scale rows from opercular opening to base of caudal fin.

This fish has an appearance which is almost as unusual as its common name. It is a common shallow water inhabitant of the South Pacific islands, and the juveniles are among the most easy of fishes to catch. They have the habit of retiring to small holes in the bottom when approached by a swimmer. Often these holes are in small rocks, which the collector can easily pick up and place in the collecting bucket. On the protected lagoon reefs of Tahiti, a good collector can catch as many as 15–20 juvenile fish per hour!

Watch this species closely when first introducing them to the aquarium, since they are usually belligerent towards smaller fish of the same and other species. In nature, the Humuhumu, as it is called for short, feeds upon algae and various crustaceans. A diet consisting of live and frozen brine shrimp, chopped fish, earthworms and green algae is excellent fare for this member of the triggerfish family.

543.00

Rhinogobius viridi punctatus (Cuvier and Valenciennes)

COMMON NAME: Spotted Goby.
RANGE: Indian Ocean and Indo-Australian Archipelago.
PREVIOUS SCIENTIFIC NAMES: *Gobius viridi-punctatus.*
MERISTIC CHARACTERISTICS: D. VI, 1–10; A. I, 9 or 8. Grows to about 4
   inches.

The Spotted Goby is a common inhabitant of shallow coral reefs.
It's a hardy fish that does well in captivity, but due to its lack of color, is
seldom seen on the pet market. They are omnivorous and should be fed
a diet which includes algae. Freeze-dried foods which include chlorella
algae are ideal.

Runula rhinorhynchos (Bleeker)*

COMMON NAME: Saber-toothed Blenny.

RANGE: Indo-Australian Archipelago and adjacent areas.

PREVIOUS SCIENTIFIC NAMES: *Petroscirtes rhinorhynchos*.

MERISTIC CHARACTERISTICS: D. 44; A. 32; P. 12. Attains a length of 4–5 inches.

Many swimmers and divers of the tropical South Pacific are familiar with this attractive but badly behaved member of the blenny family. As the common name suggests, these small and harmless appearing fish are equipped with hugh needle-like teeth. They have the habit of nipping at the legs of divers and can be a big nuisance where they are plentiful. Thankfully nature has allowed this fish to reach only a small size and therefore the bite is bothersome, but harmless, although they may draw blood. There are several species in the Indo-Pacific.

Runula subsists in nature by nipping scales and fins off other fishes, and these appear to be the primary food items. Because of this nasty habit, it is recommended that this species be kept in a tank by itself. Offer feedings of brine shrimp and chopped fish.

* Now called *Plagiotremus rhinorhynchos*.

545.00

Photo by M. Goto, *Marine Life Documents.*

Runula tapeinsoma (Bleeker)*

COMMON NAME: Saber-toothed Blenny.
RANGE: Red Sea, Indian Ocean, Indo-Australian Archipelago, Polynesia and Micronesia.
PREVIOUS SCIENTIFIC NAMES: *Petroscirtes tapeinosoma.*
MERISTIC CHARACTERISTICS: D. 45; A. 30; P. 12. Grows to 4 inches.

Here is another of the sabre-toothed blennies well known for its habit of biting swimmers and nipping scales and fins of other fishes. That which was said for *R. rhinorhynchos* applies for this species as well.

* Now called *Plagiotremus tapeinosoma.*

546.00

Sargus vulgaris Geoffroy Saint-Hilaire*

COMMON NAME: Two-banded Bream.
RANGE: Tropical eastern Atlantic. Common in the Mediterranean.
PREVIOUS SCIENTIFIC NAMES: None.
MERISTIC CHARACTERISTICS: D. XI-XII, 13-16; A. III, 12-15. Reaches a
　length of about 12 inches or more.

　The Two-banded Bream is a member of the family Sparidae (porgies,
etc.) and is common in the Mediterranean Sea where it most usually seen
near algae–covered rocks close to sandy areas. The food is chiefly in the
form of invertebrates, such as small worms, crustaceans, etc.
　The eggs and young are pelagic. At a size of about half an inch or so the
larval fish move inshore. By the time they reach a length of just under 2
inches they have acquired the black bands characteristic of the species.

*Now called *Diplodus vulgaris*.

Scarus croicensis Bloch

COMMON NAME: Striped Parrot Fish.

RANGE: Bermuda, southern Florida and Caribbean Sea.

PREVIOUS SCIENTIFIC NAMES: *Erychthys croicensis, Csalliodon lineatu, Scarus alternans, Pseudoscarus lineolatus, Scarus sanctae-crucis.*

MERISTIC CHARACTERISTICS: D. IV, 10; A. II, 9; 32 vertical scale rows on body. Grows to 10 inches.

The adult male has a spectacular color pattern, but is suited to only larger marine aquaria due to its size. Parrot fishes are most interesting creatures which get their common name from the beak-like structure of the teeth which have fused together. This arrangement is ideal for feeding on live coral (skeleton and all) which forms a large part of the diet. In captivity they can be induced to feed on live brine shrimp and tubifex; when they become acclimated they will accept a variety of freeze-dried and dry flake foods.

548.00

Scarus jonesi (Streets)

COMMON NAME: Blue Parrot Fish.
PHOTOGRAPH BY: Dr. John Randall of a 18.5-inch specimen from Tahiti.
RANGE: Tropical islands of the South and Central Pacific.
PREVIOUS SCIENTIFIC NAMES: *Pseudoscarus jonesi, Scarus brighami, Scarus lupus, Callyodon latax.*
MERISTIC CHARACTERISTICS: D. IX, 10; A. III, 9; P. 16. Grows to a length of about 20 inches.

The parrot fishes have a unique way of turning in for the night. They first retire to a crevice and then spin themselves a snug cocoon. Actually the cocoon is a mucous sheath which is secreted by the skin of the fish. At dawn they break out of the mucous envelope and begin a day of foraging. Because of this behavior they are very easy to collect at night and may actually be picked up by hand as long as no sudden jerky movements are made.

S. jonesi thrives on feedings of brine shrimp (live, frozen and freeze-dried) and fresh frozen fish and clam meat.

Male, photo by Michio Goto, Marine Life Documents.

Scarus sexvittatus Ruppell*

COMMON NAME: Parrot Fish.
RANGE: Tropical Indo-Pacific.
PREVIOUS SCIENTIFIC NAMES: *Scarus frenatus, Pseudoscarus frenatus, Pseudoscarus viridis, Callyodon frenatus, Scarus randalli.*
MERISTIC CHARACTERISTICS: D. IX, 10; A. III, 9; about 25 lateral line scales.

Another of the parrot fishes which have vast male and female color differences. The females and juveniles are generally reddish with 6 or 7 dark horizontal lines on the body. The males present a magnificent display of blue and green. It is hard to realize that these fish are the same species! Give feedings of freeze-dried fairy shrimp, tubifex and mosquito larvae supplemented with live brine shrimp.

*Now called *Scarus frenatus.*

Female, photo by Dr. J.E. Randall.

Scarus taeniopterus Desmarest

COMMON NAME: Princess Parrot Fish.

PHOTOGRAPH BY: Dr. John Randall of a 9.4-inch male specimen from Puerto Rico.

RANGE: Bermuda, southern Florida and Caribbean Sea.

PREVIOUS SCIENTIFIC NAMES: *Scarus vetula, Pseudoscarus psittacus, Scarus virginalis, Scarus psittacus, Pseudoscarus taeniopterus.*

MERISTIC CHARACTERISTICS: D. IX, 10; A. II, 9. Reaches a maximum length of about 1 foot.

The Princess Parrot Fish has two color phases. The drab phase displayed by the females consists of three dark brown stripes on a pale background with plain bluish fins. The colorful adult males are primarily blue-green and orange with a broad yellowish stripe beneath the pectoral fin. The dorsal and anal fins are blue with a broad orange band through their middle. The young make fine aquarium fish, but the brightly colored males are generally too large for the average tank.

Scarus venosus Cuvier and Valenciennes ★

COMMON NAME: Coral Parrot Fish.
PHOTOGRAPH BY: Dr. John Randall of a 7.4-inch female from Eniwetok.
RANGE: Tropical western Pacific.
PREVIOUS SCIENTIFIC NAMES: *Pseudoscarus pentazona, Xanothon pentazona.*
MERISTIC CHARACTERISTICS: D. IX, 10; A. III, 9; 22–24 scales in lateral
line. Grows to about 1 foot.

There are approximately 85 species of tropical parrot fishes. This
beauty was captured by Dr. Randall in the lagoon at Eniwetok Atoll. All
the parrot fishes are similar in behavior and food habits. They feed
principally on algae which they scrape off the bottom, at the same time
ingesting coral and rock material. These inorganic substances are ground
up by their efficient pharyngeal apparatus and passed out with the feces.
Because of this habit, they are often one of the principal producers of
sand in certain localities where they are abundant!

★Now called *Scarus schlegeli.*

552.00

Photo by Hans J. Richter.

Scatophagus argus (Bloch)

COMMON NAME: Spotted Scat.
RANGE: East Indies.
PREVIOUS SCIENTIFIC NAMES: *Chaetodon argus, Ephippus argus, Chaetodon atro-maculatis, Scatophagus ornatus, Scatophagus purpurascens, Scatophagus macronotus, Cacodoxus argus.*
MERISTIC CHARACTERISTICS: Grows to 10 inches.

Here's a species which often travels up the mouths of rivers into fresh or brackish water. They are a common sight around the docks of East Indian seaports, grubbing around the bottom in search of any kind of edible garbage they can find. This all adds up to a versatile aquarium fish which can be kept in salt or fresh water and which will eat a wide variety of foods. They will thrive on freeze-dried brine shrimp, chopped fish and occasional offerings of lettuce and spinach.

553.00

Scolopis bilineatus (Bloch).

COMMON NAME: Two-lined Snapper.
RANGE: Tropical Indo-Pacific.
PREVIOUS SCIENTIFIC NAMES: *Anthias bilineatus, Lutjanus ellepitcus, Scolopsides bilineatus, Scolopsis bleekeri.*
MERISTIC CHARACTERISTICS: D. X, 9; A. III, 7; 44–46 scales in lateral line. Grows to about 8 inches.

The two lines, above and below the eye, are distinctive characters. *S. bilineatus* is common where coral growth is luxuriant, usually in depths of at least 6 feet. This is a live food eater (fish and crustacea) which can be converted to an aquarium diet of frozen fish and canned Norwegian brine shrimp.

554.00

Scorpaena brasiliensis Cuvier and Valenciennes

COMMON NAME: Barb Fish.
PHOTOGRAPH BY: Dr. John Randall of a 8-inch specimen from the
Virgin Islands.
RANGE: Virginia to Brazil.
PREVIOUS SCIENTIFIC NAMES: *Scorpaena stearnsi.*
MERISTIC CHARACTERISTICS: D. XII, 9; A. III, 5; P. 18–20; 50–58 lateral
line scales. Grows to about 14 inches.

A very widespread fish which has been observed in waters from the
shallows to more than 300 feet in depth. An inactive fish recommended
for the more advanced marine hobbyist. Prefers small live fishes for food,
but acclimates to freeze-dried tubifex worms and chopped fish.

Scorpaena plumieri Bloch

COMMON NAME: Spotted Scorpion Fish.
PHOTOGRAPH BY: Dr. John Randall of a 6.4-inch specimen from the Virgin Islands.
RANGE: Eastern Pacific and Massachusetts to Rio de Janeiro in the Atlantic Ocean. Also reported from St. Helena and Ascension.
PREVIOUS SCIENTIFIC NAMES: *Scorpaena bufo, Scorpaena rascacio.*
MERISTIC CHARACTERISTICS: D. XII, 9; A. III, 5; P. 18–21; 42–47 lateral line scales. Grows to about $1\frac{1}{2}$ feet.

Small specimens are interesting for the larger marine aquarium. They are not active fish and spend most of their time lying quietly on the bottom. Their spines are probably poisonous, so do not handle them. No deaths have ever been reported from any *Scorpaena* species, but the wound might prove painful.

Live foods are recommended.

556.00

Scorpaena scrofa Linnaeus

COMMON NAME: Whiskery Chin Scorpion Fish.
PHOTOGRAPH BY: Klaus Paysan
RANGE: Mediterranean Sea and Tropical Eastern Atlantic.
PREVIOUS SCIENTIFIC NAMES: None.
MERISTIC CHARACTERISTICS: D. XII, 9; A. III, 15. Attains a length of at
. least 20 inches.

This species gets its common name from the membranous barbels
which hang from the lower jaw, giving the appearance of whiskers.
These sedentary carnivores are peaceful aquarium fish as long as their
tank mates are not too small. Not seen very often in U.S. aquaria, they
are more popular in Europe.

Scorpaena ustulata Lowe

COMMON NAME: Red Scorpion Fish.
PHOTOGRAPH BY: Dr. Karl Probst.
RANGE: Mediterranean Sea.
PREVIOUS SCIENTIFIC NAMES: None.
MERISTIC CHARACTERISTICS: D. XII, 9; A. III, 5; lateral line pores
23–24. Attains a length of 1 foot.

This is one of the more popular scorpion fishes from Europe. It is a
typical member of this large family of carnivores. Its normal habit is to
sit quietly under a rock waiting for dinner in the form of a passing crab
or fish. Live foods are recommended, but it is possible to switch your
scorpion fish to a diet of fresh frozen fish and shrimp.

Scorpaenodes caribbaeus Meek and Hildebrand

COMMON NAME: Reef Scorpion Fish.
PHOTOGRAPH BY: Dr. John Randall of a 2.7-inch specimen from Bimini.
RANGE: Caribbean Sea.
PREVIOUS SCIENTIFIC NAMES: *Not available.*
MERISTIC CHARACTERISTICS: D. XIII, 9; A. III, 5; P. 18–19; 41–42 lateral
   scale rows. Rarely exceeds 5 inches in size.

This is one of the smallest of the scorpion fishes, and even though
it is quite common in its range, it is so well camouflaged that it is rarely
collected. It is found on rocky bottoms which are usually shallow, making
the species difficult to catch by net and all but impossible to collect by
the skin diver. They do appear from time to time at the pet shop. As
with all the other scorpion fish species, live foods such as livebearer fry
and brine shrimp are recommended food items.

Scorpaenodes parvipinnis (Garrett)

COMMON NAME: Short-spined Scorpion Fish.
PHOTOGRAPH BY: Dr. John Randall of a specimen 3.8 inches from Eniwetok.
RANGE: Tropical islands of the South and Central Pacific.
PREVIOUS SCIENTIFIC NAMES: *Scorpaena parvipinnis*.
MERISTIC CHARACTERISTICS: D. XIII, 9; A. III, 5; 23 or 24 pores in the lateral line. Attains a length of 6 inches.

S. parvipinnis is a dweller of rocks and ledges where it sits patiently waiting for a passing meal. Because of their inactivity they are overlooked by most aquarists.

It's best to feed your scorpion fish a diet of live foods including small fishes and brine shrimp.

560.00

Photo by Dr. Patrick L. Colin.

Serranus annularis (Gunther)

COMMON NAME: Orangeback Bass.
RANGE: Bermuda and the West Indies to Brazil.
PREVIOUS SCIENTIFIC NAMES: Not available.
MERISTIC CHARACTERISTICS: D. X, 10–12; P. 13–14; 46–50 lateral line
  scales. Grows to about 3.5 inches.

This is a colorful little bass which is very active and suitable for a
community aquarium in which no sensitive fishes (like butterfly fishes)
are housed. They are prolific feeders and will often eat until their bellies
are bulging.

They are hardy and make an ideal fish for the beginner. Offer live
brine shrimp at first and gradually supplement this diet with a variety
of freeze-dried foods and chopped frozen fish.

561.00

Photo by Dr. Patrick L. Colin.

Serranus baldwini (Evermann and Marsh)

COMMON NAME: Lantern Bass.
RANGE: Southern Florida and the Caribbean.
PREVIOUS SCIENTIFIC NAMES: Not available.
MERISTIC CHARACTERISTICS: D. X, 11–13; P. 13–15; 42–48 scales in the
lateral line. Grows to about 2.5 inches long.

This is a tiny member of a family (Serranidae) which includes
species weighing in excess of 600 pounds! It is a common aquarium
fish, being both inexpensive and hardy.

As with all the basses and groupers, feeding is no problem since
they eat almost all kinds of fish foods which have some unified mass to
them. They don't seem to like pecking at small particles of food.
Freeze-dried tubifex worms suit them quite well.

Serranus cabrilla Cuvier

COMMON NAME: Comber.
PHOTOGRAPH BY: Paysan.
RANGE: Mediterranean Sea.
PREVIOUS SCIENTIFIC NAMES: None.
MERISTIC CHARACTERISTICS: D. X, 14; A. III, 7. Grows to 16–18 inches.

This fish isn't too popular, but is sometimes kept by European aquarists. The 8 vertical brownish bands are distinctive marks which will help to identify the species. Chopped smelt and shrimp are favorite foods in captivity.

Serranus tabacarius (Cuvier and Valenciennes)

COMMON NAME: Tobacco Fish.
RANGE: Bermuda, Southern Florida and the West Indies.
PREVIOUS SCIENTIFIC NAMES: *Prionodes tabacarius, Centropristes tabacarius, Serranus jacome, Haliperca tabacaria, Haliperca jacome.*
MERISTIC CHARACTERISTICS: D. X, 11–12; P. 14–15; 50–52 scales in the lateral line. Grows to about 7 inches.

The yellow color of tobacco is obvious in this fish, and that's how it got its scientific and popular names. It is rarely found in the home aquarium simply because there are so many more colorful fishes.

It is occasionally featured as a rare item at pet shops.

564.00

Serranus tigrinus (Bloch)

COMMON NAME: Harlequin Bass.

RANGE: Bermuda, Florida and throughout the Caribbean.

PREVIOUS SCIENTIFIC NAMES: *Prionodes tigrinus, Holocentrus tigrinus, Serranus praestigiator, Centropristis praestigiator, Haliperca praestigiator.*

MERISTIC CHARACTERISTICS: D. X, 12; P. 14; 48–51 lateral line scales. Grows to 4 inches.

Because of its small size and striking color pattern the Harlequin Bass is a most desirable aquarium specimen. Be sure that neighbor fish in the tank are nearly the same size or larger, since this species is a predator which relishes both small fishes and crustaceans.

Sparisoma chrysopterum (Bloch and Schneider)

COMMON NAME: Redtail Parrot Fish.

PHOTOGRAPH BY: Dr. John Randall of a male specimen 10.5 inches from Puerto Rico.

RANGE: Tropical Western Atlantic.

PREVIOUS SCIENTIFIC NAMES: *Scarus chrysopterus, Scarus chloris, Scarus lateralis.*

MERISTIC CHARACTERISTICS: D. IX, 10; A. II, 9; 30 vertical scale rows on body. Maximum length is 20 inches.

The parrot fishes are well known for their gaudy display of colors. Unfortunately for the aquarist, some of the most brilliant patterns are exhibited only by the fully grown adult males, which are generally too large for the average home aquarium. Such is the case with *S. chrysopterum*, whose juvenile and female colorations are not nearly as exciting.

Parrot fishes, being largely feeders upon live corals, are often a problem to feed in captivity. Live brine shrimp is the best "starter" food and may later be substituted for with chopped frozen fish and canned Norwegian brine shrimp.

Sparisoma viride (Bonnaterre)

COMMON NAME: Stoplight Parrot Fish.

RANGE: Tropical western Atlantic.

PREVIOUS SCIENTIFIC NAMES: *Scarus viride, Scarus melanotis, Scarus catesby, Callyodon psittacus, Scarus catesbaei, Sparisoma abildgaardi.*

MERISTIC CHARACTERISTICS: IX, 10; A. III, 9; 22–24 lateral line scales. Grows to 20 inches.

The females of *S. viride* are brownish above with a bright red belly and fins. Thus the common name of Stoplight Parrot Fish. The males, however, lack the bright red color and are principally green with three diagonal orange bands on the upper part of the head. The fins are blue and yellow, and there is a large yellow spot at the base of the tail. These beautiful fish are common on West Indian coral reefs.

567.00

Sphoeroides testudineus (Bloch)

Common Name: Brown Blow Fish.
Range: Tropical Indo-Pacific.
Previous Scientific Names: *Tetraodon testudineus*.
Meristic Characteristics: D. 10; A. 9; P. 17. Grows to at least 6 inches.

The Brown Blow Fish is not as nicely patterned as some of the other members of the family, but nevertheless it's a hardy fish and makes a good aquarium pet. It will get along fine if fed a diet of finely chopped fish and shrimp, and enjoys an occasional offering of live guppies and brine shrimp.

Spilotichthys pictus (Thunberg)

COMMON NAME: Painted Sweetlips.

RANGE: Widespread in the tropical Indo-Pacific to South Africa.

PREVIOUS SCIENTIFIC NAMES: *Plectorhynchus pictus, Diagramma pictus, Diagramma punctatus.*

MERISTIC CHARACTERISTICS: D. IX–X, 21–25; A. III, 6–7; 90–110 scales. Grows to 18 inches.

The adults of this fish are completely different from the juveniles. No adult would be shipped as an "exotic" fish, as they are just gray, silvery, spotted and uninteresting (except to eat).

The young specimens, 2–3 inches long, are characterized by the broad bands so clearly seen in the accompanying photograph. As the fish gets older the bands break into spots and gradually diminish.

These are active, schooling fish and require a fairly large aquarium. Five specimens in a 50-gallon aquarium would be their minimum space requirement, so obviously they are not for the small aquarist.

They feed upon anything, but prefer canned Norwegian brine shrimp and cooked fairy shrimp.

Stanulus seychellensis Smith

COMMON NAME: Mottled Blenny.
PHOTOGRAPH BY: Dr. John Randall of a 1.4-inch specimen from the Marshall Islands.
RANGE: Tropical Indo-Pacific.
PREVIOUS SCIENTIFIC NAMES: *Fallacirripectes minutus, Fallacirripectes wellsi.*
MERISTIC CHARACTERISTICS: D. 21; A. 13. Grows to 2 inches.

This little beauty is ideal for small aquaria. Several may be kept in a tank as small as 8 gallons. They are shy and should be provided with abundant shelter. This is a species which shows great promise as a potential spawner in captivity.

Give feedings of brine shrimp, finely chopped fish and lean beef, and occasional feedings of chopped lettuce or spinach. Freeze-dried tubifex with chlorella algae is also an excellent food.

Stethojulis bandanensis (Bleeker)

COMMON NAME: Tahitian Red-shouldered Wrasse.
RANGE: Widely distributed in the Pacific from the Indo-Malayan region
to the eastern Pacific islands of Clipperton and Cocos.
PREVIOUS SCIENTIFIC NAME: *Stethojulis rubromacula.*
MERISTIC CHARACTERISTICS: D. IX, 11; A. II, 11-12; about 27 scales in
the lateral line. Grows to a length of about 5 inches.

The Tahitian Red-shouldered Wrasse has two distinct color phases.
The female and juvenile pattern is shown above. The male is quite colorful, with several blue-white lines on the head and body, one extending
from behind the lower part of the gill cover, over the pectoral base and
onto the base of the caudal fin, and another from the eye to and along the
dorsal fin base. Both sexes have the red shoulder spot.

This fish was commonly called *Stethojulis axillaris* until it was
discovered that *S. axillaris* is a synonym of *S. balteata*, a wrasse endemic
to the Hawaiian Islands.

The natural food consists mainly of invertebrates. They will accept
most of the frozen foods currently packaged for marine aquarium fishes.

Photo by James H. O'Neill.

Suttonia lineata Gosline

COMMON NAME: Hawaiian Soap Fish.
PREVIOUS SCIENTIFIC NAMES: None.
MERISTIC CHARACTERISTICS: VI or VII, 23–24; A. III, 20–22; 58–61
vertical scale rows. Attains a length of about 5 inches.

Here's a newcomer to the Hawaiian fauna. It was first discovered by
Dr. William Gosline and described in 1960. Every year one or two new
species is added to the growing list of Hawaiian inshore fishes, and there
are now close to 450 species known from the islands. *S. lineata* is a secretive fish and spends most of its time hiding among the rocks, usually in
depths exceeding thirty feet. They are attractive, but because of their
shy nature are not ideal aquarium fish. Live brine shrimp supplemented
with freeze-dried foods is recommended.

572.00

Synchiropus splendidus (Herre)

COMMON NAME: Mandarin Fish.
RANGE: Indo-Australian Archipelago.
PREVIOUS SCIENTIFIC NAMES: *Callionymus splendidus.*
MERISTIC CHARACTERISTICS: D. IV, 9; A. 8; P. 29. This species grows to
at least 3 inches.

Here is one of the most fantastically colored of all tropical reef
fishes, and that includes some pretty stiff competition! Although once
rare and expensive, this species is now regularly imported. Its beauty
can be had at reasonable prices and it is much in demand.

Little is known about the eating habits of this "gem," so the aquarist should experiment with a wide variety of foods. These fish are
members of the dragonet (Callionymidae) family.

573.00

Photo by Helmut Debelius.

Synodus species★

COMMON NAME: Lizard Fish.

RANGE: Several species of lizard fishes are present in all the tropical seas of the world.

PREVIOUS SCIENTIFIC NAMES: Not available.

MERISTIC CHARACTERISTICS: Not available. Grows to about 1 foot.

The lizard fishes are ferocious creatures which have an amazing appetite. They live on the bottom and their mottled color pattern makes them hard to distinguish from the background. This camouflage is no doubt one of the reasons they are such successful hunters. They strike out at their prey, usually at close range, with blinding speed. However, it is not uncommon to see them streak 30 to 40 feet to seize a small fish in their jaws. This is a fish for those who like to keep the unusual, but is definitely not recommended for the community tank. Live fishes are the best food, but live *Artemia* may be substituted.

★Identified as *Synodus variegatus*.

574.00

Photo by Dr. Gerald Allen.

Taenionotus triacanthus Lacepéde

COMMON NAME: Sailfin Leaf Fish.
RANGE: Tropical Indo-Pacific.
PREVIOUS SCIENTIFIC NAMES: *Taenionotus citrinellus.*
MERISTIC CHARACTERISTICS: D. XII, 11; A. III, 7; 23 tubes in lateral line.
Attains a length of about 4 inches.

This species obtains its common name because the body is very thin
and presents the appearance of a dead leaf as it sits passively on the
bottom, waving to and fro with the current. A wide variety of color
phases are present in this species, and individuals may range from blackish
to yellow in coloration. These fish are usually considered as being rare,
but may be more common than is generally thought. They blend in well
with the bottom; even an experienced collector encounters them only
by chance. Although they are a member of the scorpion fish family,
noted for their poisonous spines, this species is sluggish and can be

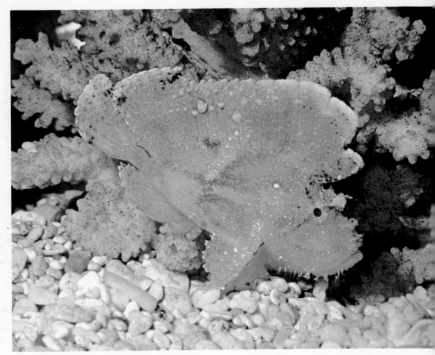

Taenionotus triacanthus Lacepede comes in a great variety of colors from a pale yellow to reds and browns. When frightened they act dead, letting themselves be carried back and forth with the surge of the current, and look like just another piece of floating debris. Photo by Dr. Gerald R. Allen.

handled safely, either in the palm of your hand or by picking it up by the sail-like dorsal fin between your fingers.

Live foods are a must for this species. Brine shrimp is the best food which is available in most pet shops. Even better are the small freshwater and brackish water shrimps which abound in many tropical and semi-tropical areas and reach a length of about an inch. Such a shrimp is the "opai" found in Hawaii.

Teuthis corallinus (Cuvier and Valenciennes)*

COMMON NAME: Spotted Rabbit Fish.
PHOTOGRAPH BY: Pederson.
RANGE: Indian Ocean, Indo-Australian Archipelago, Philippine Islands
and Okinawa.
PREVIOUS SCIENTIFIC NAMES: *Amphacanthus corallinus, Siganus corallinus.*
MERISTIC CHARACTERISTICS: D. XIII, 10; A. VII, 9; about 160–175
lateral line scales.

The rabbit fishes are closely related to the surgeonfishes. Young of
this species form large schools which swarm over the bottom grazing on
growths of algae. Handle this species carefully since the spines are said
to be poisonous and will give a painful wound. Feed chlorella algae and
allow green algae to grow freely on the back wall of the aquarium.

*Now called *Siganus puelloides.*

577.00

Teuthis vermiculatus (Cuvier and Valenciennes)*

COMMON NAME: Vermiculated Rabbit Fish.

PHOTOGRAPH BY: Klaus Paysan.

RANGE: Indian Ocean, Indo-Australian Archipelago, Philippine Islands, Taiwan, Melanesia and Polynesia.

PREVIOUS SCIENTIFIC NAMES: *Amphacanthus vermiculatus, Siganus vermiculatus, Siganus shortlandensis.*

MERISTIC CHARACTERISTICS: D. XIII, 10; A. VII, 9; lateral line with about 125 scales.

The rabbit fishes are very close in appearance to the Surgeon Fishes of the family Acanthuridae. However, they differ in at least one important respect. The surgeons have only the first pelvic ray spiny, while the rabbit fishes have both the first and last ray spinous. Incidentally, these pelvic spines should be respected, as they are said to carry a toxic substance.

* Now called *Siganus vermiculatus.*

578.00

Thalassoma amblycephalus (Bleeker)

Common Name: Rainbow Wrasse.
Range: Tropical Indo-Pacific.
Previous Scientific Names: *Julis amblycephalus.*
Meristic Characteristics: D. VIII, 13; A. III, 10; lateral line scales 26-
27. Grows to 5 inches.

This delicately shaded species is an inhabitant of rubble-strewn reefs throughout the Central Pacific. The males are generally a bit larger and more colorful. They spawn either in pairs or in large aggregations. During aggregate spawning the group mills nervously a short distance off the bottom, suddenly comes together, and dashes for the surface in unison. Just before reaching the surface they abruptly turn for the bottom and at the same instant let fly with a cloud of sperm and eggs. Often a single male will spawn with several females at once. The eggs are positively buoyant and rise to the surface. This species feeds on a wide variety of small invertebrates.

579.00

Thalassoma ballieui (Vaillant and Sauvage)

COMMON NAME: Hinalea Luahine.
PHOTOGRAPH BY: Dr. Herbert R. Axelrod.
RANGE: Hawaiian Islands and Johnston Atoll.
PREVIOUS SCIENTIFIC NAMES: *Julis ballieui, Julis obscura, Julis verticalis, Thalassoma obscurum.*
MERISTIC CHARACTERISTICS: D. VII, 13; A. II, 11; about 30 vertical scale rows from upper edge of gill opening to base of caudal. Reaches a length of 2 feet.

In contrast to many of the other wrasse species, there seems to be little change in color from juvenile to adult. However, the old adults may be slightly blackish. The Hawaiian Islands are unique in that over 30% of the fish found there are found no where else. *T. ballieui* is one such endemic. It occurs over a wide variety of habitats in the Islands and is often notorious as a bait stealer. This is one the of the largest members of the genus *Thalassoma*. They are not fussy eaters and will accept a wide variety of items. Live and frozen brine shrimp are favorites.

Thalassoma bifasciatus (Bloch)

COMMON NAME: Bluehead.

RANGE: Bermuda, southern Florida, southern Gulf of Mexico and Caribbean Sea.

PREVIOUS SCIENTIFIC NAMES: *Labrus bifasciatus* var. *torquatus, Julis detersor, Labrus ornatus, Julis gillianus, Chlorichthys bifasciatus, Julis bifasciata.*

MERISTIC CHARACTERISTICS: D. VIII, 12 or 13; A. III, 10 or 11; about 28 scale rows from upper edge of gill opening to base of caudal fin. Grows to 6 inches.

The actual blue-headed fish are adult males which spawn individually with selected females. Photo by H. Hansen.

Dr. John Randall has commented on the different color phases which this fish goes through in his book *Caribbean Reef Fishes*. Juvenile fish generally have a black mid-lateral stripe with a whitish or yellowish body coloring. On slightly larger fish the mid-stripe may be broken up or nearly absent and the entire fish yellow. Individuals displaying this color phase may be either male or female, and fishes as small as 1.5 inches may be fully mature adults! The largest phase has a blue head, with two wide black bars over and just behind the pectoral fin and green posteriorly. The bluehead phase individuals are always males.

This fish enjoys feedings of live and frozen brine shrimp which may be supplemented with a wide variety of live and dried foods.

Thalassoma lucasanum (Gill)

COMMON NAME: Mexican Rock Wrasse.
RANGE: Gulf of California and Pacific coast of Mexico.
PREVIOUS SCIENTIFIC NAMES: *Julis lucasanus, Chlorichthys lucasanus.*
MERISTIC CHARACTERISTICS: D. VIII, 13; A. III, 12. About 26 scale rows
from upper edge of gill opening to base of caudal fin. Grows to about
5 inches.

This fish gets its common name from the habit of occurring in rocky
tide pools along the Mexican coastline. They are often abundant and
easily caught by hook and line. In nature the rock wrasses feed upon a
variety of crustaceans, of which small crabs and shrimp are usually
preferred. Live brine shrimp makes an excellent food when this species
is kept in captivity.

Thalassoma lunare (Linnaeus)

COMMON NAME: Lyretail Wrasse.
PHOTOGRAPH BY: Gerhard Marcuse.
RANGE: Tropical Indo-Pacific and Red Sea.
PREVIOUS SCIENTIFIC NAMES: *Labrus lunaris, Scarus gallus, Julis porphy-rocephalus.*
MERISTIC CHARACTERISTICS: D. VIII, 13; A. III, 11; lateral line scales 28–29.

The Lyretail Wrasse earns its common name from the darkened outer rays of the caudal fin. In addition it has a dark bar on the pectoral fins. These fish are usually found in areas of abundant coral growth, but never in large numbers. They spawn in typical *Thalassoma* fashion (see section under *Thalassoma amblycephalus*) either in aggregations or in pairs.

They are reasonably good aquarium fish which do best in large aquaria. Fresh frozen fish and chopped lean beef supplemented with occasional feedings of live brine shrimp are excellent fare.

584.00

Thalassoma species (Juvenile)*

COMMON NAME: Wrasse.
PHOTOGRAPH BY: Dr. Hilmar Hansen.
RANGE: Tropical Indo-Pacific.
PREVIOUS SCIENTIFIC NAMES: Not available.
MERISTIC CHARACTERISTICS: Not available.

It's difficult to identify this species just by looking at the picture since the color pattern exhibited here is typical of several species belonging to the genus *Thalassoma*. As the fish grows the pattern will gradually change until the adult coloration is assumed. Only then would it be possible to make a reliable identification. Young wrasses make attractive pets and should be supplied with a rich layer of not too coarse gravel. Many of the species bury themselves at night or when alarmed. Live and frozen brine shrimp are favorite wrasse foods, but this should be supplemented with a variety of other items (tubifex, fish, etc.).

*Young or female color phase of *Thalassoma amblycephalus*.

Upeneus vittatus (Forskal)

COMMON NAME: Banded-tail Goat Fish.
PHOTOGRAPH BY: Dr. John Randall.
RANGE: Tropical Indo-Pacific.
PREVIOUS SCIENTIFIC NAMES: *Mullus vittatus, Mullus bandi, Hypeneus vittatus, Upeneoides vittatus, Upeneoides philippinus.*
MERISTIC CHARACTERISTICS: D. VIII–I, 8; A. I, 7; lateral line scales 35–36. Grows to 15 inches.

There are several species of banded-tails, all of which are very similar in appearance. Their flesh is a highly valued food item in many localities in the South Pacific. These bottom feeders occur in large schools and will venture into shallow water right next to shore. A good cast-net fisherman can catch hundreds in a single day! They are less known as an aquarium fish, but the young do make attractive display items.

In nature, small crustaceans and fish are preferred foods. Live brine shrimp supplemented with chopped fish are ideal substitutes in captivity.

Variola louti (Forskal)

COMMON NAME: Painted Coral Bass or Trout.
RANGE: Very widespread throughout tropical Indo-Pacific.
PREVIOUS SCIENTIFIC NAMES: *Serranus punctulatus, Serranus flavimar-*
ginatus.
MERISTIC CHARACTERISTICS: D. IX, 13–14; A. III, 8; there are 65 tubular
scales. Grows to 30 inches.

The color of this species varies greatly with age as well as between large
specimens (possibly different sexes or even different species). The adults
are easily recognized by the spotted pattern and the lunate tail edged in
yellow. This is a colorful grouper, and small specimens do very well in
captivity. Habits and food are similar to those for species of the genus
Cephalopholis.

587.00

Vanderhorstia ornatissima Smith

COMMON NAME: Ornamented Goby.
PHOTOGRAPH BY: Dr. John Randall.
RANGE: Tropical Indo-Pacific.
PREVIOUS SCIENTIFIC NAMES: None.
MERISTIC CHARACTERISTICS: D. VI-I, 13; A. I, 13; P. 20; vertical scale
   rows 65. Grows to 3–4 inches.

The late Dr. J. L. B. Smith described this species in 1959. The color
is variable and some specimens are actually very colorful. It is a secretive
species which has rarely been captured alive. It was originally known
only from East Africa and the Seychelles, but Dr. Randall collected this
lovely specimen on the island of Moorea in French Polynesia.

Wetmorella ocellata Schultz

COMMON NAME: Arrowhead Wrasse.
RANGE: Tropical South Pacific.
PREVIOUS SCIENTIFIC NAMES: Not available.
MERISTIC CHARACTERISTICS: D. IX or X, 9 or 10; A. III, 8.

This colorful pair of *Wetmorella ocellata* was taken by Dr. Herbert Axelrod on a collecting trip to Marau, Solomon Islands. This labrid can be found among coral heads in depths between 20 to 40 feet. It is rare in the aquarium trade, but hopefully this species will soon become available in large quantities.

589.00

Xanthichthys mento (Jordan & Gilbert)

COMMON NAME: Redtail Triggerfish.

RANGE: Pacific Ocean from Japan to California, including the Hawaiian Islands, Easter Island, and Pitcairn Island.

PREVIOUS SCIENTIFIC NAMES: *Xanthichthys gotonis, Xanthichthys purus,* and *Xanthichthys surcatus.*

MERISTIC CHARACTERISTICS: D. III, 29-32; A. 26-29. There are about 41-50 scale rows along the body. Grows to about 9 or 10 inches in length.

Xanthichthys mento has been confused with, and often united with, a close relative, *Xanthichthys ringens.* However, it has been determined that these are two species with separate distributions rather than only one with a circumtropical distribution. Whereas *X. mento* is found in the Pacific Ocean, *X. ringens* is apparently restricted to the Atlantic. They are distinguishable by color pattern.

The sexes of *X. mento* can also be distinguished on the basis of color pattern. The male is shown in the photo above; the female has yellow replacing the pink of the tail and, oddly enough, pink or reddish replacing the yellow on the edge of the soft dorsal and anal fins.

Large triggerfishes tend to be rather aggressive toward smaller members of their own and other species and should be watched closely when first introduced into the aquarium. Sometimes it may prove best to keep larger specimens in tanks by themselves or at least with species that are well able to take care of themselves.

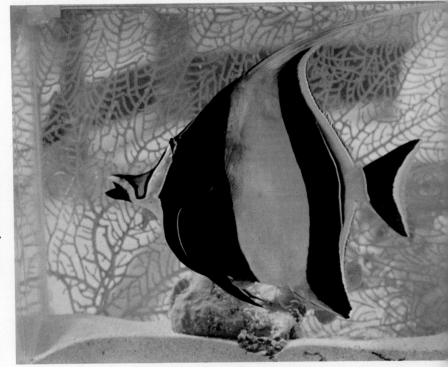

Zanclus canescens (Linnaeus)

COMMON NAME: Moorish Idol, Toby.
RANGE: Widespread in tropical Indo-Pacific, from the Red Sea to Mexico.
PREVIOUS SCIENTIFIC NAMES: *Zanclus cornutus*.
MERISTIC CHARACTERISTICS: D. VII, 38–41; A. III, 32–35. Grows to about
8 inches.

It has long been thought that there were two species of Moorish Idols,
namely *Zanclus cornutus* and *Z. canescens*. These two forms were essentially identical except for the presence of small spines in front of the eye
on *canescens*. However, Dr. Donald Strasburg, in a short article in the
scientific magazine *Copeia*, points out that the spines are shed as the
fish grows larger and are merely a juvenile character. *Zanclus canescens*
is the older name and therefore the valid one for this species.

   This fish is generally acknowledged as one of the hardest of fishes to
keep, since they are often reluctant to feed upon most foods which are
offered. Some success has been obtained with the new freeze-dried
foods, but it hasn't been universal. At any rate, I have successfully kept
them for a year by feeding them Norwegian brine shrimp (canned) as
well as fairy shrimp and freeze-dried tubifex worms with chlorella algae.

Zebrasoma flavescens (Bennett)

COMMON NAME: Yellow Tang.

RANGE: Indian Ocean, Indo-Australian Archipelago, Philippines, Ryukyu Islands, Melanesia, Micronesia and Polynesia.

PREVIOUS SCIENTIFIC NAMES: *Acanthurus flavescens, Acanthurus rhombeus.*

MERISTIC CHARACTERISTICS: D. V, 24–25; A. III, 19–20; P. 15. Grows to a length of 7 inches.

Here's a popular aquarium fish which is commonly imported from Hawaii. It's the brightest-colored member of the surgeonfish family with its shining coat of canary yellow. The Yellow Tang occurs over a wide area of the Indian and Pacific Oceans, but appears to be most common in Hawaii, where it lives on coral reefs usually in depths of over 6 feet. Large specimens are taken in wire fish traps, while the juveniles are easily caught with chemical anesthetics. Kaneohe Bay, on the windward side of Oahu, is an especially good hunting ground for this fish.

Z. flavescens is primarily an algae eater in its native habitat and will thrive in the aquarium if a green mat of algae is allowed to grow on the sides and rear wall of the tank. It will also accept feedings of live and frozen brine shrimp.

Photo by K.H. Choo.

Zebrasoma scopas (Cuvier)

COMMON NAME: Brown Tang.

RANGE: Tropical Indo-Pacific.

PREVIOUS SCIENTIFIC NAMES: *Acanthurus scopas, Acanthurus rhombeus, Acanthurus altivelis, Harpurus scopas, Acanthurus goramensis, Harpurus rhombeus, Zebrasoma rostratum, Zebrasoma supra-alba.*

MERISTIC CHARACTERISTICS: D. V, 23–25; A. III, 19–21. Grows to 6–7 inches.

The Brown Tang adult is close in appearance to the adult of the Yellow Tang in many areas outside Hawaii. However, the young of *Z.*

scopas are colored similar to adults, with perhaps a slight purplish tinge to the body color. These young are much more attractive than the adult and because of their size are better suited for aquarium life.

It has recently been shown that this species is distinct and not a mere color variety of *Zebrasoma flavescens*. Although it is just as plentiful and occurs over a much wider area than the Yellow Tang, it has not achieved the popularity of its bright-colored cousin. In fact *Z. scopas* is rarely seen in pet shops. In spite of this lack of acceptance as an aquarium fish, the juveniles are attractive with their large dorsal and anal fins and slightly purplish coloration.

The care and feeding of this species is identical to that recommended for the Yellow Tang.

Zebrasoma veliferum (Bloch) juveniles with their elongate dorsal and anal fins resemble young batfishes (*Platax*) except for color. Photo by Douglas Faulkner.

Zebrasoma desjardinii Bennett

Common Name: Sailfin Tang.
Photograph By: Gerhard Marcuse.
Range: Red Sea and Indian Ocean.
Previous Scientific Names: *Acanthurus ruppellii*.
Meristic Characteristics: D. IX, 28-33; A. III, 22-26. Grows to a
  length of 12 inches.

The young of this species are extremely handsome and somewhat
reminiscent of the bat fishes of the genus *Platax*, at least as far as body
shape is concerned. It is widespread in occurrence and varies slightly
in color pattern from one locality to another. Red Sea examples show a
pattern of orange dots and lines on the body and fins which specimens
from other areas lack. They are tricky to catch; unless chemical anesthetics are used, they must be captured at night when they are "resting" among the coral.

Feed this species a variety of foods including chlorella algae, canned Norwegian brine shrimp, freeze-dried tubifex worms, and live
brine shrimp.

595.00

Zonogobius semidoliatus (Cuvier and Valenciennes)

COMMON NAME: Regal Goby.
RANGE: Tropical Indo-Pacific and Red Sea.
PREVIOUS SCIENTIFIC NAMES: *Gobius semidoliatus*.
MERISTIC CHARACTERISTICS: D. VI, 1–8 or 9; A. I, 7 or 8. Reaches a
  length of 1 inch.

This small goby is found in rocky or coral reef areas. It has a habit of
swimming upside-down near the roof of a cave or top of a crevice and
may, indeed, carry this behavior into the home aquarium. The male, as is
the case with many sexually dimorphic gobies, has very elongate spines
in the first dorsal fin, so long, in fact, that they reach almost to the caudal
fin base when depressed. The color of an individual in its best color is
said to be wine red with whitish crossbands in the anterior portion. The
fins are paler than the body and all of them except the pelvics are crossed
by many rows of red spots. So far this fish has rarely if ever been seen in
the hobby and little is known about its diet, but it should be expected to
accept live baby brine shrimp readily.

Index

Filefishes, 104.00, 478.00
  Brown, 256.00
  Fantailed, 489.00, 490.00
  Longnosed, 478.00
  Red-Tail, 491.00
  Tail-Light, 257.00
  Whitespotted, 255.00
Fire Fish, 532.00
Fishing Frog, 203.00, 204.00, 205.00, 208.00
Flamefish, 218.00
Flaming Angelfish, 272.00
Flammeo,
  marianus, 373.00
  opercularis, 374.00
  sammara, 375.00
  scythrops, 376.00
Flat-tailed Trigger Fish, 129.00
Flounders
  Painted Coral, 587.00
  Peacock, 249.00
  Tropical, 250.00
Forcipiger flavissimus, 377.00
Forktail Blenny, 446.00
Foureye Butterflyfish, 283.00
Four-striped Cardinal Fish, 222.00
Freckled Cardinalfish, 212.00
French Angelfish, 512.00-514.00
French Grunt, 387.00
Fringed Squirrel, 167.00
Frogfishes (Fishing Frogs), 109.00, 207.00
Garoupa, 360.00, 361.00, 362.00
Gaterin albovittatus, 502.00
  chaetodonoides, 503.00
  orientalis, 504.00
Giant Labrid, 315.00
Giant Spotted Grouper, 525.00
Glasseye, 523.00
Gnathanodon speciosus, 54.00
Goatfishes, 126.00
  Banded-tail, 586.00
  Blackspot, 486.00
  Yellow, 457.00
Gobeidae, 126.00
Gobiodon citrinus, 378.00
Gobiosoma oceanops, 354.00
Goby, 378.00
Goby, Gobies, 126.00, 179.00, 432.00, 533.00, 596.00
  Banded, 179.00
  Catalina, 440.00, 596.00
  (Goby), 378.00
  Neon, 354.00
  Ornamented, 588.00
  Regal, 596.00
  Spotted, 544.00

Golden Angelfish, 271.00
Golden Butterfly, 307.00
Golden Devil, 131.00
Golden Hamlet, 420.00
Golden Striped Grouper, 382.00
Golden-headed Sleeper, 355.00
Gold-spotted Snake Eel, 461.00, 462.00
Gomphosus varius, 379.00
Gramma loreto, 380.00
  melacara, 381.00
Grammistes sexlineatus, 382.00
Gray Angelfish, 510.00
Gray Surgeon, 153.00
Graysby, 492.00
Groupa, 360.00, 361.00, 362.00
Grouper, 280.00
Groupers, 69.00, 173.00, 208.00, 277.00, 358.00, 359.00, 458.00, 460.00
  Black, 275.00
  Boenacki, 277.00
  Comb, 459.00
  Giant Spotted, 525.00
  Golden Striped, 382.00
  Polkadot, 317.00
  Red, 279.00
  Saddleback, 505.00
  Spotted, 276.00
  Yellowfin, 460.00
  Yellowmouth, 458.00
Grunts, 236.00, 386.00, 387.00
  Barred, 236.00
  French, 387.00
  Red-mouth, 236.00
  Smallmouth, 386.00
Gymnothorax favagineus, 384.00
  meleagris, 383.00
  tesselata, 384.00
  undulatus, 385.00
Haemulon chrysargyreum, 386.00
  flavolineatum, 387.00
Half and Half Wrasse, 393.00
Halichoeres biocellatus, 388.00
  centiquadrus, 389.00
  margaritaceus, 390.00
  radiatus, 391.00
Hamlets, 419.00, 422.00
  Barred, 421.00
  Butter, 422.00
  Golden, 420.00
  Mutton, 173.00
  Shy, 419.00
Harlequin Bass, 565.00
Hawaiian Lion Fish, 537.00
Hawaiian Sharp-nosed Puffer, 260.00

603.00

longnose Hawkfish, 477.00
Longnosed Filefish, 478.00
Longsnout Butterflyfish, 524.00
Longspine Squirrelfish, 373.00
Lutjanus fulva, 439.00
  kasmira, 436.00
  sanguineus, 437.00
  sebae, 438.00
  vaigiensis, 439.00
Lyretail Coralfish, 210.00
Lyretail Wrasse, 584.00
Lythrypnus dalli, 440.00
Macropharyngodon meleagris,
  441.00, 442.00
  pardalis, 441.00, 442.00
Malacanthus latovittatus, 443.00
Malamalama, 329.00
Mandarin Fish, 573.00
Marginate Damselfish, 337.00
Mediterranean Sea Horse, 405.00
Mediterranean Wrasse, 328.00
Megaprotodon strigangulus, 444.00,
  445.00
Meiacanthus atrodorsalis, 446.00
  atrodorsalis oualanensis, 448.00
  mossambicus, 447.00
Melichthys indicus, 449.00-450.00
  ringens, 449.00-450.00
  vidua, 451.00
Mempachi, 465.00
Merten's Butterfly, 294.00
Mexican Rock Wrasse, 583.00
Meyer's Butterfly, 295.00
Microcanthus strigatus, 452.00
Microspathodon chrysurus, 453.00
Mirolabrichthys tuka, 454.00
Mirrorfish, 172.00
Molly Miller, 237.00
Monacanthidae, 104.00
Monacanthus species, 104.00
Monocentrus japonicus, 455.00
Monodactylus sebae, 456.00
Moonfish, 172.00, 456.00
Moorish Idol, 102.00, 110.00, 398.00,
  591.00
Moray Eel, 385.00
Mottled Blenny, 570.00
Mullidae, 126.00
Mulloidichthys martinicus, 457.00
Mustard Surgeon, 150.00
Mutton Hamlet, 173.00
Mycteroperca interstitialis, 458.00
  rubra, 459.00
  venenosa, 460.00
Myrichthys oculatus, 461.00,
  462.00

Myripristis jacobus, 463.00
  kuntee, 464.00
  murdjan, 465.00
  pralinius, 466.00, 467.00
  violaceus, 467.00
Naso brevirostris, 122.00, 468.00
  lituratus, 469.00, 470.00
Nemateleotris magnificus, 532.00
Neon Goby, 354.00
Neon-banded Butterfly, 303.00
Northern Sea Horse, 407.00
Oceanic Seahorse, 408.00
Ocellate Butterflyfish, 481.00
Ocellate Damselfish, 519.00
Ocyurus chrysurus, 471.00
Odonus niger, 472.00
Old Maid, 172.00
Old Wench, 233.00
Old Wife, 233.00
Olive Surgeon, 154.00
One-spot Butterfly, 312.00, 313.00
Ophioblennius atlanticus, 473.00
Opistognathus aurifrons, 474.00
Orange Devil, 130.00
Orangeback Bass, 561.00
Orange-Finned Anemone Fish, 181.00
Orange-tailed Devil, 142.00
Orbiculate Bat Fish, 495.00, 496.00
Orbiculate Cardinal, 221.00
Oriental Sweetlips, 502.00, 504.00
Ornamented Goby, 588.00
Ostraciidae, 104.00
Ostracion cubicus, 475.00
  meleagris, 476.00
Oxycirrhites typus, 477.00
Oxymonacanthus longirostris, 478.00
Pacific Hog Fish, 243.00
Painted Coral Bass, 587.00
Painted Coral Trout, 587.00
Painted Sweetlips, 569.00
Pakistani Butterflyfish, 286.00
Palani, 149.00
Palau Squirrel, 165.00
Paracanthurus hepatus, 479.00
Paracentropogon longispinis, 480.00
Parachaetodon ocellatus, 481.00
Paracirrhites arcatus, 482.00
  typee, 483.00
Paraglyphidodon nigroris, 142.00
Paraluteres prionurus, 484.00
Parapercis schauinslandi, 485.00
Parrot Fish, 550.00
Parrotfishes, 114.00, 115.00, 194.00,
  548.00, 549.00, 566.00
  Blue, 549.00
  Coral, 552.00

608.00